THE
BICENTENNIAL
GUIDE TO
THE
AMERICAN
REVOLUTION

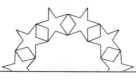

VOLUME THREE

THE BICENTENNIAL GUIDE TO THE AMERICAN REVOLUTION

THE WAR IN THE SOUTH

Sol Stember

NEW YORK · 1974

SATURDAY REVIEW PRESS | E. P. DUTTON & CO., INC.

Library of Congress Cataloging in Publication Data

Stember, Sol.
The bicentennial guide to the American Revolution.

Includes bibliographies.
CONTENTS: v. 1. The war in the North.—v. 2. The middle Colonies.—
v. 3. The war in the South.
1. United States—History—Revolution—Campaigns and battles.
2. United States—History—Revolution—Museums.
3. United States—Description and travel—
1960-   —Guide-books. I. Title.
E230.S74   973.3'3   73-23108

First Edition

10 9 8 7 6 5 4 3 2 1

Published simultaneously in Canada by Clarke, Irwin & Company Limited, Toronto and Vancouver
ISBN: 0-8415-0314-1 (cloth)
ISBN: 0-8415-0316-8 (paper)
Designed by The Etheredges

To my wife, Rosaline,
who packed the bags, made the reservations,
helped with the research,
typed the manuscript, read the maps,
and shared the driving and walking all the way
from Lexington to Yorktown.

PUBLISHER's NOTE: Much of the detailed factual information in this book has been and is subject to change. Visitors to historical sites are urged to check locally on times of opening and closing and on admission charges. They should also remember that highway route numbers may have changed since the book was compiled, especially for county and municipal routes. In addition, speed limits may have been altered in the attempt to conserve fuel. In some cases, continuing restoration on sites may have altered the sites from the way they are described here.

Boldface type has been used to designate major features on the sites—named structures and the like. ***Boldface italics*** point out smaller landmarks, mostly those without particular names.

CONTENTS

LIST OF MAPS

ACKNOWLEDGMENTS

(For all three volumes of the Guide)

No man is an island, particularly when he is trailblazing through territory new to him and most particularly when he attempts to produce a work of this extent. Space does not permit me to acknowledge all the help and advice I received from numerous historical societies and their members who were in touch with me at one time or another during the preparation and writing of this book. A few names, I confess, I either neglected to record or lost along the way. I am thinking particularly of the Francis Marion National Forest ranger who took us to the site of the Wambaw fight and the gentleman at the courthouse in Calhoun County, South Carolina, who finally put us on the right track to Fort Motte. To you and to others whom I may have neglected to mention, my sincere apologies. I am most grateful for your help and for the help of all those persons and organizations listed below by state or agency.

FEDERAL GOVERNMENT: John V. Vosburgh, Chief, Branch of Features, U.S. Department of the Interior, National Park Service. CANADA: David Lee, National Historic Sites Service; Sergeant F. C. Ouellette, College Militaire Royal, Saint-Jean, Quebec; Jacques Seguin, Regional Director, National and Historic Parks, Department of Indian Affairs and Northern Development. CONNECTICUT: Susan C. Finlay, Wethersfield; Preston R. Bassett, Ridgefield; Daniel M. McKeon, Ridgebury; Herbert Barbee, Connecticut Historical Commission. GEORGIA: James G. Bogle, Georgia Historical Commission; William Cox and Josephine Martin, Liberty County Historical Society; Carroll Hart, Director, Department of Arhives and History; Lilla M. Hawes, Director, Georgia Historical Society; Billy Townsend, Georgia Historical Commission; A. Ray Rowland,

Richmond County Historical Society; Dixon Hollingsworth, Sylvania; Mary Gregory Jewett, Director, Georgia Historical Commission; Savannah Chamber of Commerce. MAINE: John W. Briggs, State Park and Recreation Commission; White Nichols, President, Arnold Expedition Historical Society; Ellenore Doudiet, Curator, Wilson Museum, Castine. MASSACHU-SETTS: John P. McMorrow, Boston Redevelopment Authority; Mary V. Darcy, Executive Secretary, Revolutionary War Bicentennial Commission; Bernard Wax, Director, American Jewish Historical Society; Bay State Historic League. NEW HAMPSHIRE: Dr. J. Duane Squires, Chairman, New Hampshire American Revolution Bicentennial Commission; Enzo Serafini, Chairman, New Hampshire Historical Commission; Ralph H. Morse, Department of Resources and Economic Development, Division of Economic Development. NEW JERSEY: Dirk Van Dommlan, Superintendent, Washington Crossing State Park; Frank Ender, Acting Superintendent, Monmouth Battlefield State Park; Milicent Feltus, Monmouth County Historical Association; Margaret M. Toolen, Fort Lee; Mary T. Hewitt, Hancock House, Hancock's Bridge; Isabelle Brooks, Office of Historic Sites, Department of Environmental Protection. NEW YORK: Willa Skinner, Fishkill Town Historian; May M. MacMorris, Argyle; Wallace F. Workmaster, Old Fort Ontario; Dole F. Watts, Thousand Islands State Park Commission; Jean Saunders, Curator and Mrs. Charles Franklin, Historian, Putnam County Historical Society; John H. Mead, Curator, New Windsor Cantonment; Marie C. Preston, County Historian, Livingston County; Raymond Safford, Historian, Staten Island; Virginia Moskowitz, Eastchester; William H. Seeger, Curator, Old Stone Fort, Schoharie; William Meuse, Superintendent, Saratoga National Historical Park; Albert Cerak, Miller House; Leon Dunn, Curator, Oriskany Battlefield; Frank Pabst, Plattsburgh; Dean Sinclair, Cherry Valley; Lieutenant Colonel Merle Sheffield (Ret.), West Point Military Academy; Lieutenant Colonel Patrick H. Dionne, Public Information Officer, West Point Military Academy; Mark Lawton, Director, New York State Historic Trust; Scott Robinson, White Plains; Josephine Gardner, Suffern; John Focht, Garrison; Mrs. Jankovsky, Middleburgh; New-York Historical Society. NORTH CAROLINA: Hugh B. Johnston, Jr., Wilson; Sharon Kuhne, Ruth Little, and Elizabeth Wilborn, Division of Historic Sites and Museums, Department of Archives and History; Edenton Chamber of Commerce; Duke Power Company (Cowan's Ford Hydroelectric Station); Catherine Hoskins, Summerfield; Tryon Palace Commission. PENNSYLVANIA: Mr. and Mrs. O. W. June, Paoli; Wilbur C. Kriebel, Administrative Director, Chester County American Independence Bicentennial Committee; Robert

I. Alotta, President, Schackamaxon Society, Inc.; William A. Hunter, Chief, Division of History, Pennsylvania Historical and Museum Commission; Edward Seladones, Department of Forest and Water, Pennsylvania Historical and Museum Commission. RHODE ISLAND: Albert T. Klyberg, Director, Rhode Island Historical Society; Richard Alan Dow, Rhode Island Development Council; Leonard J. Panaggio, Chief, Tourist Promotion Division of the Development Council. SOUTH CAROLINA: David V. Rosdahl, U.S. Department of Agriculture Forest Service, Columbia; Virginia Richard Sauls, Clarendon County Historical Commission; Dr. Thomas Marion Davis, Manning; Terry W. Libscomb, South Carolina Archives Department; W. Bruce Ezell, Ninety-six; J. Percival Petit, Isle of Palms; John Morall, Beaufort; Thomas Thornhill and Harrington Bissell, The Old Provost, Charleston; Charles Duell, Middleton Gardens; Helen McCormick, Gibbes Art Gallery, Charleston; Jean Ulmer, Calhoun County Library; Dr. and Mrs. P. Jenkins of James Island; Charleston Chamber of Commerce; Georgetown Chamber of Commerce; Camden Chamber of Commerce; Beaufort Chamber of Commerce. VIRGINIA: Howard A. MacCord, Sr., Archaeological Society of Virginia; Elie Weeks, President, Goochland County Historical Society; Charles E. Hatch, Jr., Yorktown Battlefield, Colonial National Historical Park; Mrs. Ashton W. Clark, Yorktown; J. R. Fishburne, Assistant Director and H. Peter Pudner, Virginia Historic Landmarks Commission; Rufus Easter, Executive Director, Charles Long, Program Director, and Mrs. S. Evans, Hampton Association for the Arts and Humanities; Colonel and Mrs. Boris Polanski, Hampton; Alf J. Mapp, Jr., Chairman, Portsmouth Revolutionary Bicentennial Commission; Robert F. Selden, Mathews County Historical Society; Edward A. Wyatt, Petersburg; Mr. and Mrs. John H. Wright, Goochland County; Mr. and Mrs. J. W. Seigfried, Point of Fork; Captain and Mrs. Igor Moravsky, Goochland County; Mabel Bellwood, Red Hill; Mary R. M. Goodwin, Williamsburg; Emily N. Spong, Portsmouth; Park Rouse, Director, Virginia Bicentennial Commission and Jamestown Foundation; Hampton Information Center.

I also wish to express my thanks to my publishers for staying with me all the way and especially to the editors without whose guidance and help I would never have finished: Steve Frimmer who got me started, Stephanie Erickson who pronounced the book acceptable, and Tom Davis who saw it through to the end. I have a particular word of thanks and admiration for Judy Bentley who cast an appraising, critical eye over the finished manuscript and guided me through a polishing process that improved the book immensely. I owe a special debt of gratitude to Joy

PREFACE

(To all three volumes of the Guide)

I fell in love with Clio, the Muse of history, the day I sat in George Washington's chair. At the time I was writing a series of children's educational television programs, and I had been assigned scripts on Washington, Lincoln, Benjamin Franklin, Columbus, Thanksgiving, and the Constitutional Convention of 1789.

The very first of these scripts to go on the air was the one about the Constitutional Convention. This was *live* television and I had obtained permission to use a number of props connected with the actual event, some of them of great historical value, including the chair Washington had sat in while he presided over the convention. It was that chair that stole my heart for the Muse. The chair was the focal point of the set and the script. I had traveled to Philadelphia to get it and had sworn to the authorities in charge that I would protect and defend it with my life, my fortune, and my sacred honor. It had come from Philadelphia by station wagon, carefully crated and heavily insured. It was then placed in my special care for twenty-four hours, no more.

When the show was over, I stood amid the cables and discarded scripts, looking at the chair. It had been left for last while the rest of the props were repacked and sent on their way to their rightful owners. For the moment, it was deserted and forgotten. The bright lights were dimmed now and the cameras were off, but briefly it had regained a measure of its former glory in the eyes of a far larger audience spread out across a nation far greater than anything the man who had made it famous could possibly have imagined or foreseen.

There is a design of the rayed sun carved into it, just above where

Washington's head must have touched when he sat in it, for though he was a tall man, this chair has a very high back. At the end of the convention, after all the wrangling and arguing and bad feelings had been resolved, and old and tired Franklin, who had worked so hard on the side of reason and compromise, rose to remark that all through the weary sessions he had been looking at that sun on the chairman's chair, wondering if it represented a rising or a setting sun. Now he knew, he said, that it was indeed a rising sun.

I too had been looking at the chair during the long hours of rehearsal and repetition and exasperation and frustration over the little but important mistakes and delays that made live television so alive, and then through the final, tension-filled half hour of the performance. What would it feel like, I thought, to sit in the chair that Washington sat in while he was making history? No one was paying any attention, and— what the hell!—it was my life, my fortune, and my sacred honor, right? I crossed the studio, stood in front of the chair for a moment, then turned and sat down.

I cannot pretend that during the few seconds I sat where Washington had sat I was transported back in time to 1789. I cannot say that I felt his eyes staring at me accusingly or felt a well-placed boot on my rear end as I got up and stepped away, which is what I really deserved. The prop men took the chair to its waiting crate, and a few minutes later it was on its way back to Philadelphia; I did not see it again—much less resume my seat—until I visited Philadelphia for this book. I do know that in that moment I felt a sense of continuity of Time and of Man.

I have had in my hands the letter Washington wrote from Valley Forge to Congress asking for money and supplies for his starving, freezing soldiers, the purse he left behind in Jumel Mansion, Lincoln's traveling desk on which he may have written the Gettysburg Address, an astrolabe used by a sixteenth-century Spanish navigator, a hand-illuminated Bible from the twelfth century, Ben Franklin's glass harmonium and a pair of his spectacles, Robert E. Lee's personal copy of Grant's surrender terms, Aaron Burr's dueling pistols, and a set of "running irons" used by rustlers in the 1880s. I have walked on the field where Pickett led his famous charge (in fact, I slept in a motel on that field), stood on Jefferson Rock and looked at much the same view of Harpers Ferry that Jefferson saw long before John Brown made the place famous, touched the stones of the Roman Forum, and felt the pavement of Pompeii under my feet while I listened with my eyes closed for the lost sound of chariot wheels. Still waiting for me are the ruins of Luxor, the fortress on Masada, the climb up the sacred hill to the oracle at Delphi, and the descent into the caves of Lascaux.

This book is for everyone who feels that same sense of continuity, in an American context. This book is an invitation to walk where Washington, Lafayette, Alexander Hamilton, Benedict Arnold, Daniel Morgan, Benjamin Franklin, Thomas Jefferson, Ethan Allen, and Molly Pitcher and all that host of men and women walked who fought and died long before we were born, but who still live in the stones and buildings and hills and fields they touched and held in their eyes. This book is a guide and a passport to a far country in a time past that is in a sense still with us. I have been there myself, visiting all the places I describe in this book. I invite you to follow.

VOLUME THREE

THE
WAR IN THE SOUTH

INTRODUCTION

The war weighed heavily on the South during the last three or four years of hostilities. It was in the South that the British made their final attempts to maintain a military presence south of the Canadian border. Pushed out of most of New England, denied access to the Hudson Valley, unable to maintain lines of communication and supply in New Jersey and Pennsylvania, left with only a New York City toehold, General Sir Henry Clinton (successor to Sir William Howe as commander of British forces in America) invaded the South in an effort to reestablish British authority and destroy the still inferior, underequipped Continental Army and its militia auxiliaries. Three different wars were waged in the South at the same time: a rebellion against British authority, a civil war between rebels and Loyalists, and a frontier war between settlers and Indian tribes who had sided with the British. The result of all this, as far as historical sightseers are concerned, is a scattering of sites throughout New England and an overwhelming number in the Carolinas, Georgia, and Virginia.

At the time of this writing, more than two hundred sites are being authenticated and marked in South Carolina alone. They include just about every exchange of shots between Whigs and Tories, as well as every encounter with British forces, no matter how small, that was ever recorded on paper or held in men's memories. In a war that rarely saw more than a few thousand men engaged on either side at any one time, even a skirmish assumed an importance that would be hardly worth a mention in other contexts. Nevertheless, some of the Revolution's most extensive campaign maneuvering in the classic tradition took place in the Carolinas and Virginia. There were dramatic sieges at Savannah and Charleston and strategic duels, first between Clinton and Lincoln and then between Cornwallis and Greene. Not since the campaign of 1777, which ended with the British snug and warm in Philadelphia and the Americans freezing in Valley Forge, had such a war of movement been fought. It was a huge chess game in which armies marched incredible distances through frontier settlements on wilderness roads, back and forth over a chessboard on which broad, swelling rivers marked off squares filled with inaccessible swamps, wide savannahs, and impenetrable forests, finally culminating in Yorktown.

Be prepared for country roads that take you into distant places where gas stations and rest rooms do not exist. In Georgia most country roads are unpaved, and the same holds true for many roads in South Carolina and Virginia. Follow them wherever they take you, and I promise you will see bits and pieces of America you thought no longer existed.

I.

GEORGIA

Georgia was the only colony not represented in the First Continental Congress. It was the last of the British colonies to be established and when the Revolution began, its settlers still retained strong ties to the mother country. Though it was subjected to the same type of internal dissension that wracked the rest of the South, no serious fighting took place in Georgia until 1778 when the British took Savannah. They had been rebuffed earlier at Charleston, South Carolina, and in Virginia, but with the taking of Savannah the British campaign to reclaim the South for the crown really got underway, and between December, 1778, and June, 1779, Georgia came under British control and stayed there until after Yorktown.

The sequence of events you are about to cover went as follows. On November 27, 1778, Lieutenant Colonel Archibald Campbell sailed from Sandy Hook, New Jersey, for Savannah and came ashore at the mouth of the Savannah River. General Robert Howe, the rebel commander in the area, marched from Sunbury, thirty miles south, to the city's defense. Campbell made an end run around Howe's right, however, and captured the city on December 29. Campbell then took Augusta on January 29, 1779; General Augustine Prevost had arrived in Savannah to take over full command and he moved south and brought Sunbury and Fort Morris under British control.

A new American commander in the South, General Benjamin Lincoln, then confronted Prevost along the Savannah River early in 1779. Emboldened by rebel successes at Beaufort, South Carolina, and Kettle Creek west of Augusta, Lincoln moved to clean up British interior posi-

SOUTH CAROLINA and GEORGIA

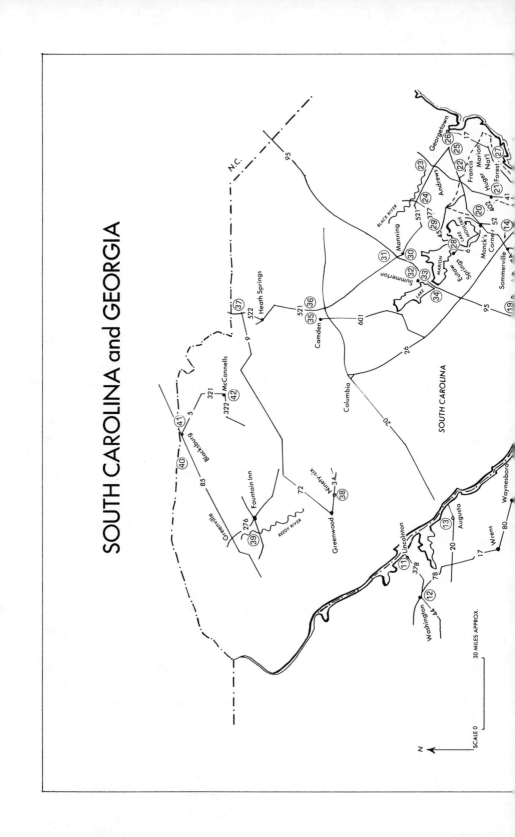

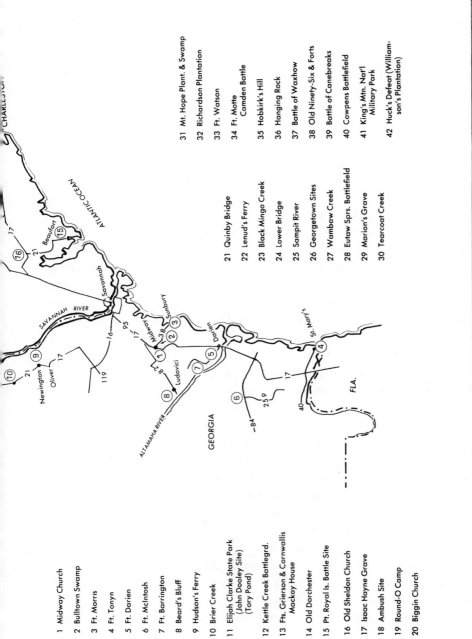

1 Midway Church
2 Bulltown Swamp
3 Ft. Morris
4 Ft. Tonyn
5 Ft. Darien
6 Ft. McIntosh
7 Ft. Barrington
8 Beard's Bluff
9 Hudson's Ferry
10 Brier Creek
11 Elijah Clarke State Park (John Dooley Site) (Tory Pond)
12 Kettle Creek Battlegrd.
13 Fts. Grierson & Cornwallis Mackay House
14 Old Dorchester
15 Pt. Royal Is. Battle Site
16 Old Sheldon Church
17 Isaac Hayne Grave
18 Ambush Site
19 Round-O Camp
20 Biggin Church

21 Quinby Bridge
22 Lenud's Ferry
23 Black Mingo Creek
24 Lower Bridge
25 Sampit River
26 Georgetown Sites
27 Wambaw Creek
28 Eutaw Sprs. Battlefield
29 Marion's Grave
30 Tearcoat Creek

31 Mt. Hope Plant. & Swamp
32 Richardson Plantation
33 Ft. Watson
34 Ft. Motte Camden Battle
35 Hobkirk's Hill
36 Hanging Rock
37 Battle of Waxhow
38 Old Ninety-Six & Forts
39 Battle of Canebreaks
40 Cowpens Battlefield
41 King's Mtn. Nat'l Military Park
42 Huck's Defeat (Williamson's Plantation)

tions. But on March 3, General John Ashe, in charge of the operation, was stopped at Brier Creek by Mark Prevost. In October, 1779, a combined American-French force under Lincoln and a French admiral, the Comte d'Estaing, tried to retake Savannah. Their unsuccessful attempt only served to strengthen the British hold on Georgia.

SAVANNAH

Getting to Savannah may someday take less time than it does now, when Interstates 95 and 16 are finally completed. At present, Interstate 95, the great south-north road which will eventually stretch from the Canadian border in Maine down into Florida, is incomplete. Travelers from the west will pick up 95 south in the Washington, D.C. area. From a point just south of the Virginia–North Carolina border, it is necessary to bounce on and off whatever sections of 95 are completed, using various state and U.S. highways in between. In South Carolina, U.S. 15 is the road that keeps you moving south until it runs into U.S. 17 and 17 alternate, which eventually take you across the state line into Savannah.

To anyone coming from the north, particularly during the winter, Savannah is a pleasant surprise with its palmettos and squares handsome with live oaks and tall, southern magnolias festooned with Spanish moss.

The sites connected with the British capture of Savannah on December 29, 1778, and then the siege by combined American-French forces during September and October, 1779, have both been obliterated by the city's growth. In 1778 the British defeated the American defenders by outflanking them. American defense lines were established southeast of the city in flooded rice fields and swamps. The British found a way through the swamps and took the Americans completely by surprise. Since then, the rice paddies have been drained and built over, as have the swamps. The route the British used, however, to march into the city after the battle, survives as Skidaway Road. Otherwise, suburban developments, new highways, and canals have replaced the plantations, open fields, and marshes that once surrounded the city.

Several sites connected with the French-American siege in 1779 have been identified, including the perimeter of the British defense lines and the locations of the trenches built by the besiegers. At that time Savannah was perhaps a twentieth of the size it is today. The entire city was located on the top of a sand bluff that towered over the mastheads of ships moored in the harbor below. A British visitor told his countrymen to visualize

Savannah by thinking of a city built on the cliffs of Dover. Four major roads going off to the cardinal points of the compass connected it with the rest of the colony. The population in 1779 was several thousand, which included only 751 whites. During the siege this number was augmented by refugees from outlying areas who flocked into the city with their slaves when the British commandeered their homes.

Savannah was laid out in a regular pattern of streets and boulevards running mostly at right angles to each other and series of squares and circular areas breaking up the pattern with delightful patches of green, just as it is today. A British officer remarked that Savannah's buildings were scattered about and were poorly built, mostly of wood, and that the entire city, as far as he was concerned, had a wretched, miserable appearance. The streets were wide and unpaved and were usually composed of white sand that quagmired easily in wet weather. A Hessian soldier likened walking the streets of Savannah to walking through fresh snow a foot deep. On a windy day clouds of sand and dust swept over the streets and houses. During the summer months, inhabitants were tormented by sand flies and mosquitoes, for the town was surrounded by rice plantations that required perpetual flooding. The largest building was the British church on Bull Street, which was eighty feet long and forty to fifty feet wide.

Touring the Revolutionary War sites of Savannah is rather like touring the sites in New York City. We know where the fortifications were and where the important actions took place and they are identified by markers and memorials, but there are no relics to remind us physically, with one exception. The old Jewish burial ground where the French gathered for the final attack is still there and can be reached. Nevertheless, the old part of Savannah is tailor-made for you if you like to walk. It is picturesque and charming with its line of squares going up Bull Street away from the Savannah River and other squares, parks, and old cemeteries in lines that run at right angles to Bull Street. It is also an easy city to find your way around in.

At the Chamber of Commerce just off Bay Street you can pick up an excellent map of the old city with both walking and driving tours outlined on it. With the exception of the Sergeant Jaspar site, however, these tours touch on Revolutionary War sites only incidentally, missing most of them and not giving you a picture of what the British defenses were like, where the French and American positions were, and where the major events of the attack took place.

The Chamber of Commerce building is a good place to begin. You will

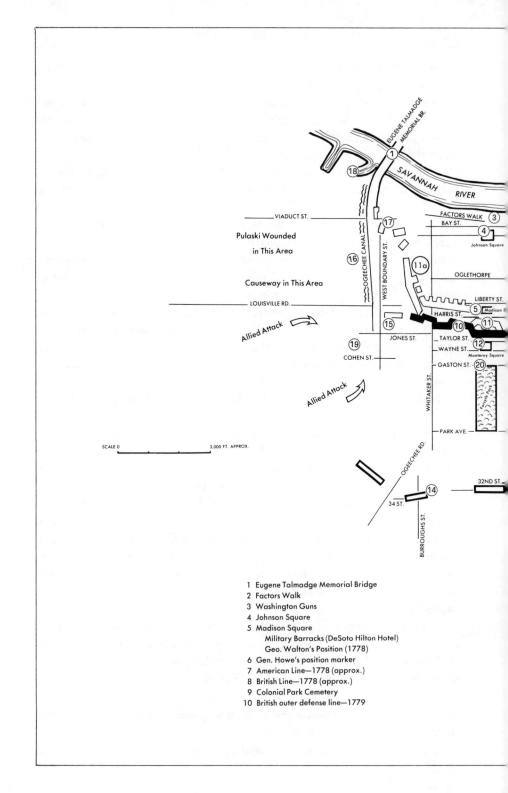

SCALE 0   3,000 FT. APPROX.

1   Eugene Talmadge Memorial Bridge
2   Factors Walk
3   Washington Guns
4   Johnson Square
5   Madison Square
        Military Barracks (DeSoto Hilton Hotel)
        Geo. Walton's Position (1778)
6   Gen. Howe's position marker
7   American Line—1778 (approx.)
8   British Line—1778 (approx.)
9   Colonial Park Cemetery
10   British outer defense line—1779

SAVANNAH, GA.

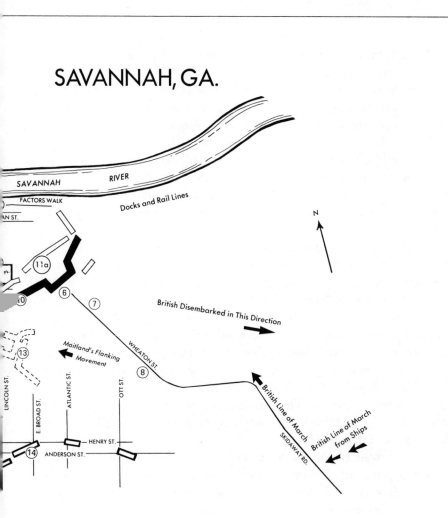

SAVANNAH RIVER

FACTORS WALK

Docks and Rail Lines

N

British Disembarked in This Direction

WHEATON ST.

Maitland's Flanking Movement

British Line of March

SKIDAWAY RD.

British Line of March from Ships

LINCOLN ST.

E. BROAD ST.

ATLANTIC ST.

OTT ST.

HENRY ST.

ANDERSON ST.

11a

6   7

8

13

10

14

11 Central Redoubt—British inner defense line—1779
11a British inner defense line
12 Monterey Square—Pulaski Monument
13 French trenches—1779
14 Allied positions—1779
15 Spring Hill Redoubt—1779 (Jasper killed here)
16 Musgrove Creek (Savannah-Ogeechee Canal)
17 Sailors' Battery (approx.)—1779
18 Yamacraw Swamp (approx.)
19 Jewish Burial Ground—French Camp—1779
20 Georgia Historical Society

probably come into the city on 17A across the Eugene Talmadge Memorial Bridge. As you come off the bridge, the first street available to you is Oglethorpe Avenue, a busy, commercial thoroughfare to your left in the heart of Savannah's hotel, shopping, and business district. Turn left onto it; the first big intersection will be at West Broad Street, which, taken to the left, leads to Bay Street. A right turn on Bay Street takes you along three or four blocks lined with commercial buildings until on your left appears what looks like a park with small lawns, shrubs, and trees, two cannon behind an iron-fence enclosure, a long, red brick building, small parking areas, and a few blocks farther a well-defined park known as Emmet Park.

The Chamber of Commerce at 100 East Bay Street is the building with the clock entrance at the first parking area you come to. It is reached by an iron bridge over, not water to your surprise, but a cobblestone street known as Factors' Walk. The long, red brick building is the old Cotton Exchange; Factors' Walk is where the cotton factors examined bales of cotton as they came off the riverboats tied up at the wharves on River Street. There is a metered parking area in front of the Chamber of Commerce building, with a few free spots reserved for visitors. Metered parking here and on the other side of Bay Street is $.05 an hour or $.10 for two. This quaint, old section extends for about twelve blocks, Emmet Park for four. There is another small, metered parking area in Emmet Park.

You can walk from the chamber to the **Washington Guns,** the two cannon you spotted inside the iron picket enclosure. They are on the left side of Bay Street directly opposite the U.S. Customhouse. The gun with the handles shaped like dolphins is French; the other is British and was captured at Yorktown. Both guns were presented to the Chatham Artillery, Savannah's militia unit, by Washington when he visited the city in 1791, and so are known as the Washington Guns.

In **Emmet Park** is a marker for the old harbor light that stood about where the ornamental beacon lamp is now. This entire side of Bay Street overlooks the Savannah River; this is the old sand bluff overlooking the harbor that made the eighteenth-century, British visitor think of the chalk cliffs of Dover. A promenade along the edge of the bluff in Emmet Park lets you look out over the river where tall-masted ships once tied up at wharves below. It is from a position in the river just beyond this point that the French ships shelled the city during the siege.

A cobblestone drive leads down from the beacon to **Factors' Walk** and River Street along the Savannah. There is a maritime *museum* down there, admission $1.00, and a three-masted vessel which was closed for repairs when we visited. The cobblestones with which these roads are paved were brought here as ballast in the holds of sailing ships.

Drive back along Bay Street toward West Broad Street, looking for Bull Street which comes in from your left. Turn onto Bull Street for some "square-hopping" through old Savannah which will lead you to the site of the central redoubt of the British defenses. As you come to each square, you will find parking at curbside either around the square or on a nearby street. To go from one square up Bull Street to the next, simply follow the one-way arrows, which lead you back onto Bull Street on the opposite side.

You will first come to **Johnson Square** in the middle of a bustling shopping and business section. It is shaded by big, old, live oaks hung with Spanish moss and contains walks, benches, and a *memorial* to General Nathanael Greene, a Rhode Islander. The general and his son were both buried under the monument. Greene died on June 19, 1786, at Mulberry Grove Plantation near Savannah, which had been given to him by the state of Georgia for his service during the Revolution. The cornerstone of this monument was laid by Lafayette in 1825.

From Johnson Square, continue up Bull Street, skipping the next two squares, Wright and Chippewa, until you come to **Madison Square.** You are driving across the width of the area enclosed by the British defenses, which followed the perimeter of the old city itself.

Before you cover the siege of 1779, start here at Madison Square on a tour of the sites connected with the 1778 British capture of the city. Find the DeSoto Hilton Hotel on Harris and Bull streets and the *plaque* identifying the site of a military barracks. To the east of the barracks, in 1778, a Georgia militia company under George Walton (a signer of the Declaration of Independence) were surprised by the British who outflanked the American line. The barracks were dismantled by the British and the remains became part of their line of defense in 1779.

Walton's detachment was stationed to your left as you look up Bull Street in the direction you were going. Return along Bull Street to Liberty Street; make a right turn and follow Liberty Street to the intersection of Randolph Street, which comes in from the left. In the middle of Liberty Street there is a *marker* for the place where, on December 29, 1778, Major General Robert Howe (no relation to the British Howe) drew up his men to face the British advance. The line was about 100 yards east across Sea Island Road, now Wheaton Street, the direction you were traveling along Liberty Street to get here. Liberty Street runs into Wheaton Street directly ahead, going off to the right, as you stand with your back to the marker.

Walton's detachment was positioned to your left front as you face the marker, near what is now Madison Square. As you face up Wheaton Street, you are parallel to the American line 300 feet ahead of you. The British main force faced the American line about 2,400 feet beyond that, engaging Howe's attention. Howe's right flank was to our right and it was off in that direction, over what is now completely built-up, that Sir James Baird's flanking company was guided through a wooded marsh and rice paddies to hit Walton's detachment and take the Americans in the rear.

Drive along Wheaton Street, noting the freight yards on the right and the lumber company on the left where Howe's men awaited the British, then another half mile to where the British were formed in battle order, now an open, grassy area with a power line off the road. You are now driving into the British line of march.

You can get to the approximate site of the *disembarkation* by returning along Wheaton to Randolph Street on your right. Turn onto Randolph Street and take it to an open, grassy area with railroad freight spurs crossing frequently. At the intersection of General McIntosh Boulevard, turn right and make an almost immediate left onto Harbor Street, following it out through a wide savannah with railroad tracks paralleling the road on your left. Eventually you will reach a sign saying "Private Property"; there you are in a freight yard and dockside area with the river to your left. The savannah of grass you drove through, the freight yards and industrial areas around you were once rice fields, part of the plantation where the British landed in 1778. Somewhere in this vicinity was a road that took them to the right to what is now Skidaway Road, along which they proceeded to the point where they stopped to confront Howe's main position.

Retrace your route to Randolph Street and head back toward Wheaton and Liberty streets. You are on your way back to Madison Square to cover the sites and events of the 1779 siege. On the way, however, carry out a small diversionary tactic. Turn right off Randolph Street onto Oglethorpe Avenue, and take it to **Colonial Park Cemetery** on the left which was a burial ground for the city from 1750 to 1853. In it are buried a number of Georgian Patriots, including Major General Lachlan McIntosh of the Continental Army, who fought a duel with Button Gwinnett, a Declaration of Independence signer; John Habersham; General Samuel Elbert; and Archibald Bulloch, great-great-grand-father of Theodore Roosevelt. Here too sleeps Lieutenant Colonel John Maitland, the British military hero who was originally buried in the vault in Johnson Square which Nathanael Greene now occupies. There is also a memorial to Button Gwinnett who died of the effects of his duel with McIntosh. Though the site of his burial is in dispute, this memorial is believed by Savannahans to cover his remains. What did they duel about? Gwinnett and McIntosh represented opposing factions in Georgian politics. There was bad blood between the two men which was not helped when Gwinnett, during his short tenure as governor of the new state, arrested McIntosh's brother on a charge of treason. In 1777 McIntosh denounced Gwinnett in front of the state assembly and Gwinnett challenged him, thus inviting the bullet that cut short his career and made his signature so valuable to autograph collectors.

Continue along Oglethorpe Avenue away from Randolph Street to Bull Street, where you turn left to return to Madison Square and the siege of '79. Madison Square was inside the central redoubt of the British defense line. From here the line extended to right and left in a huge semicircle as you face up Bull Street, all the way around the city's eastern limit down to the Savannah River at the east end of Bay Street and around to a point near the present Eugene Talmadge Memorial Bridge about two blocks south of the river. The diameter of the inner defenses was about 4,300 feet. The outer defenses, which probably consisted of a moat, outer breastwork, and abatises, enclosed an area almost 6,000 feet wide at the widest point. The center of the outer defenses were one block beyond Madison Square up Bull Street.

This is a good spot to review the events leading up to the battle of the siege of Savannah. After his withdrawal from Rhode Island, the French naval commander d'Estaing had his ships refitted and then sailed to the West Indies, an area of conflicting British-French colonial ambitions. In September, 1779, he brought the fleet back to American home waters at the mouth of the Savannah River in response to messages from General Benjamin Lincoln, who was in command of American forces in the southern theater. Lincoln had made an unsuccessful attempt to retake Savannah and capture Augusta in 1779, but had been outgeneraled by the British General Augustine Prevost. D'Estaing responded by showing up with thirty-eight warships and 4,000 French troops. The French fleet blockaded the Georgia coast while Prevost, in command in Savannah, ordered outlying forces back to the city to take part in its defense. The French troops were landed about fourteen miles south of Savannah while

Lincoln marched his army from Charleston to join them. Among the approximately 5,000 Americans and French facing the British was the Pulaski Legion with the Polish count at its head.

On September 16, d'Estaing demanded Prevost's surrender. Prevost had only about 2,400 troops, many of whom were local Loyalist militia, and about ten guns. He was given twenty-four hours to make up his mind. During that time, Lieutenant Colonel John Maitland, who had been sent to Port Royal Island in South Carolina, slipped through the French blockade with 800 men and into the city. These men and other detachments who had made their way in brought Prevost's forces up to 3,200, augmented by a large number of citizens and slaves who were put to work on the defenses. Prevost told d'Estaing he had decided to fight.

As at Newport, French-American relations at Savannah were not of the best, but Lincoln and d'Estaing both agreed that rather that attack the city at once, as some American officers urged, they would first lay siege to it and attempt to destroy the British fortifications. The French fleet then bombarded the town for five days, but though they did a great deal of damage to houses and caused many casualities among the townspeople, the fortifications remained intact.

The main attack against the British came on their right flank, which, as you face up Bull Street on Madison Square, was off to your right and somewhat behind you. Madison Square is noted for its *statue* of Sergeant William Jaspar of the South Carolina militia, which was serving in the Savannah campaign. Sergeant Jaspar was already popular among southern Patriots for his part in the defense of Fort Sullivan in Charleston in 1776, where he kept the flag flying on the parapet despite enemy fire. He repeated his act of heroism here in Savannah, but not with the same results. The statue shows him in a heroic stance with his military hat between his legs. The militia uniform he is wearing, which is also depicted on the bronze plaques around the pedestal of the statue, is authentic. There is a marker here in Madison Square that says the sergeant was mortally wounded a few hundred yards northwest of this spot. According to my calculations that site is farther than a few hundred yards.

The two guns circa 1862 at the southern end of the square point in the direction the British guns pointed when this was a redoubt. The plaques on the guns commemorate the old roads that led out of the city toward Augusta and other towns.

Walk three, short blocks up Bull Street to **Monterey Square**, the next square south from Madison Square. You have now moved out beyond the British defense lines. Two hundred years ago this was open country.

If you had turned and looked back, before the British redoubts blocked your view, you would have seen the roofs and spires of Savannah behind you. In the center of Monterey Square is a *monument* to Pulaski; the plaque states that he fell about a half mile to the northwest, again off to your right rear at the Spring Hill Redoubt. As you face the monument coming up Bull Street, Wayne Street is to your left, coming into the square at its midpoint.

Turn left onto Wayne Street and walk toward the site of the French trenches, passing as you go Congregation Mikvah Israel, founded in 1783, the oldest Reformed Jewish congregation in the country. Two blocks from Monterey Square brings you to Calhoun Square. Walk through Calhoun and beyond it another block to the corner of Wayne and Lincoln streets. This is the point at which the French trenches, dug as an approach to the British fortifications, were closest to those fortifications. You are only a few hundred yards diagonally away from the central redoubt. From here the trenches went off in a somewhat zigzag fashion to the right and left, four or five blocks in both directions.

If you continue south along Bull Street you come to a large rectangular park called Forsyth Park, Park Avenue at its southern edge, and then six blocks beyond, the approximate center of the allied siege lines. The easternmost limit of those lines would be on what is now Waters Avenue, the western limit in the middle of Laurel Grove Cemetery. Two smaller positions were dug just to the east of Forsyth Park on Park Avenue.

Drive to the approximate site of the **Spring Hill Redoubt,** the scene of the final action of the siege, by retracing your route along Bull Street for two blocks north of Madison Square to Liberty Street where you turn left. Liberty Street will take you to an intersection with West Broad Street. On the other side of West Broad is a wide expanse of railroad freight yard. Spot the old Central of Georgia Railroad Depot with its neon sign prominently displayed in front. To one side is a freight-loading area reached from West Broad through a hurricane-fence gate. If the doors of the depot are closed, go into the loading area through this gate and enter the depot through the side door. Inside, at the head of the old passenger platforms, are two historical markers. One commemorates the battle that raged around the Spring Hill Redoubt; the other, the wounding of Pulaski and Jaspar.

If you follow Liberty Street alongside the depot (to the left as you face it on West Broad Street), notice the large, empty field behind a wooden fence on the opposite side. A distance down from the corner is another marker set into a boulder on the left side of Liberty Street. You may not be able to get close enough to read it, for this is a busy, two-way street with no sidewalk along the side on which the marker is located. The marker identifies the site of the Spring Hill Redoubt.

Now walk to the foot of the passenger platforms on the other side of Liberty Street. This brings you out into a large expanse of tracks and switches, none of which are any longer in use. Spring Hill Redoubt was to your left. Beyond and around that broad stretch of ground with tracks going off into the distance and freight yards and industrial waste, was once wooded marsh, field, and swamp. Off to the right was Musgrove Creek now channeled between the sides of a canal. To your right was Yamacraw Swamp, about where the Talmadge Memorial Bridge hits the south bank of the Savannah. This was the weakest part of the British line. Prevost knew it and concentrated as much fire power as he could in this area. Close to the present bridge approach, he placed the Sailors' Battery, two redoubts mounting nine-pound cannon manned by British sailors. Along Musgrove Creek, British ships enfiladed the allies, as they prepared to charge against the Spring Hill Redoubt.

The operation was a smashing defeat for the American-French forces. As Prevost expected, the attack was concentrated against the Spring Hill Redoubt. Had you been on this spot on the morning of Sunday, October 9, 1779, you would have had the panorama of the battle spread out before you. Actions against the Sailors' Battery and other British flank positions failed, as French troops and American militia floundered through the swamps under the fire of British guns. Three French and five American columns were involved in the main attack.

The French left their camp at the old Jewish burial ground, which you will find shortly, joined up with the Americans, and then the two forces marched to the jump-off point, which was off to your left front. Ahead of them lay hundreds of yards of open country before they could reach the British lines which were faced with an abatis and ditch. Led by d'Estaing, they came under fire from the Spring Hill Redoubt immediately and suffered heavy casualties. Eventually they reached the ditch and abatis, which must have extended into what are now the old railroad lines. At this point Jaspar was mortally wounded when he tried to place the American flag on the ramparts of the redoubt. He succeeded, but the flag did not remain long. The British counterattacked and after fierce hand-to-hand fighting cleared the ditch and the area around Spring Hill Redoubt of attackers.

Off to your right, Pulaski and his legion attempted to cut off the Spring Hill Redoubt from the other fortifications to the west by driving a wedge between them. Caught at the abatis, his mounted troops were shot to pieces and he fell with a ball in his thigh, a wound he later died from. All this took place early in the morning before full daylight. By the time the allied forces withdrew, bloodied and beaten, a heavy fog had made British counterattacks impossible. As at Castine in Maine, the attacking forces had delayed the decisive attack too long, allowing the defenders to build up their strength. To all intents and purposes the siege of Savannah was over.

Where the Spring Hill Redoubt stood is that field behind the wooden fence, overgrown with weeds with a factory building just beyond it. The filling in and leveling that preceded the railyard lines has covered over the ground on which the desperate fighting raged. Nothing remains of the breastworks and ditch. The swamps and wooded marshes through which the flanking militia units got entangled is all industrial ground now. A causeway over which the attackers advanced is no longer there; where d'Estaing, in his efforts to rally his men, was wounded, where Pulaski was shot from his horse while his brave legionnaires died around him, is all buried under railroad embankments and heavy steel rails. How many iron horses have passed over the ground on which those earlier horsemen died!

Continue your tour of the British defenses by turning right onto West Broad Street in the direction of the Talmadge Memorial Bridge. At Bryan Street make a left and go as far as you can. The bridge arches above you and a "Do Not Enter" sign faces you. One short block left takes you to the point where the British defense line ended, where **Sailors' Battery** faced the soppy woods of Yamacraw Swamp.

Return to West Broad Street; go back toward the railroad depot, but continue beyond it to Jones Street. Turn right onto Jones, then left onto West Boundary Street at an intersection marked by signs for 17A and 17. Notice the Chatham Metal Company on your right, the highway department building on your left, and just before you come to the building, the street that borders the hurricane fence surrounding the highway department property. Turn onto that street and look on the right, in an open field, for a high, whitewashed brick enclosure, a cemetery. The street closest to it is Cohen Street and runs between rows of old dilapidated buildings interspersed with open lots. A little farther up Cohen Street beyond the cemetery is the family burial ground of Levy Shefftel, dedicated in 1783. The gate to the first and larger *cemetery* is padlocked, but looking through the crack you can see the old tombs engraved with

Hebrew characters. A marker on the wall dates it back to 1773. It was used for a hundred years after that. It attracts our attention because of what occurred around it six years after it was established.

In this area, the French troops formed for the attack on the Spring Hill Redoubt. Standing in front of the cemetery gate, the redoubt would have been to your right front. From here the French marched in column formation on the right flank of the attacking forces over open country. Between here and Spring Hill, their ranks were torn apart by grapeshot until they reached the abatis at the foot of the redoubt where they felt the sting of the defenders' muskets. It was in this area that the French reserves stood fast as the allies fell back from the British counterattack.

Among the interesting sidenotes of this battle, consider the case of Samuel Warren, a former British army officer who had joined the rebel cause. An aunt living in England sent word that she hoped he would have an arm or leg shot off in his first battle. Warren did indeed lose a leg as a result of a wound received here. With great foresight he asked the surgeon to save the bone for him. When the war was over, he had the remains placed in a mahogany box, inscribed with all the pertinent data, and shipped to his aunt, with a note telling her he would rather be a rebel with one leg than a Loyalist with two.

Pulaski's death and burial are shrouded in mystery and controversy. One account says he died leading a foolhardy charge against the British fortifications at Savannah. An eyewitness, however, Captain Paul Benta-lou, stated that Pulaski halted the legion at the edge of a wood to await an opportunity to penetrate the works. Then word reached him that d'Estaing was wounded (the haughty but plucky French admiral rallied his men three times in the face of galling fire), and Pulaski rode toward the scene to see if he could be of assistance. He was hit in the thigh and was carried from the field, bleeding profusely. He is supposed to have been taken on board a French ship for treatment where he lingered for several days before dying. One account has him buried at sea, another at a nearby plantation. To this day, the matter has never been cleared up and though there are many markers in the South and elsewhere to him, there is none that marks his grave.

The musket ball that wounded Pulaski may be seen at the **Georgia Historical Society** at Whitaker and Gaston streets. The society has a number of relics of colonial Savannah and Georgia that it intends to put on display for the bicentennial. Another is an allegorical portrait of Selina, the Countess of Huntingdon, which originally hung in the George Baillie residence in which d'Estaing set up his headquarters before moving into the city. When he entered, d'Estaing saw the portrait and thought it was of the Lady Abbington representing the Spirit of Liberty. It shows a stately woman carrying a wreath of thorns in her hand while trampling on a crown. The Baillies were not exactly warm to the Patriot cause as d'Estaing was soon given to understand by the children of the house, who spoke to him in a most artless manner. In the painting, the crown represents things temporal while the thorns represent things spiritual. The lady who posed for it would have been horrified to learn that her portrait was being mistaken in the colonies as a symbol of freedom.

Conflicting figures describe the casualties suffered by both sides in this battle. The allied army lost between 800 and 1,000 killed and wounded, most of them French. Many of the French wounded were hurt so badly they died. The British lost between 50 and 100 killed and wounded. Lincoln made an effort to continue the siege, but the French withdrew to their ships and he was forced to retire to Charleston. With the British toehold in Georgia secure, Sir Henry Clinton felt free to move against Charleston, which he did for the second time and, as you will see, with greater success.

MIDWAY AND SUNBURY

Follow the signs for U.S. 17 off West Boundary Road out of Savannah. They lead onto Interstate 16 for a short distance; then take Interstate 95 for an even shorter distance to 17 south. A few miles along 17 takes you into Midway. A short distance south of the **Midway Church,** at an intersection with a filling station and a sign for Sunshine Lake, there are at least seven historic markers, all on the same side of the road. If you are an insatiable history buff, you will stop to read them all. One marker is for Sunbury and indicates State Route 38 east. You will take that road by and by to visit the dead town of Sunbury and Fort Morris.

Late in 1778, the British decided to invade Georgia from Florida. At the time Sunbury was an important seaport, second only to Savannah. General Augustine Prevost, who was to command the garrison at Savannah during the 1779 siege, sent one force by sea under the command of Colonel L. V. Fuser and another by land under the command of his young brother, Lieutenant Colonel Mark Prevost. Both detachments were to rendezvous at Sunbury.

Drive south for eleven miles from the Midway Church until you see the marker for the **Bulltown Swamp** skirmish on the right. The swamp is still here on both sides of the road. Since Lieutenant Colonel Prevost had had the foresight to plunder and burn along his line of march, it was only to be expected that the inhabitants of the region would respond accordingly. At Bulltown Swamp he met the first resistance offered by the Georgia militia. A small detachment of mounted militia under Colonel John Baker chose this spot to fight a delaying action against Prevost's mixed force of 400 regulars, Tories, and Indians. From here he proceeded north to an action at Midway.

Turn around, drive back toward Midway for ten miles, and look for a *marker* on your right commemorating the death of General James Screven at a nearby site. As Prevost approached this spot, he came up against about 100 Continental Army regulars and twenty mounted militiamen. The Continentals were under the command of Colonel John White, who also had two pieces of light artillery with him. His mission was to hold Prevost at bay until reinforcements could get there from Savannah. The militiamen were under the command of Screven. There was an engagement here, probably along a line that extended across the road and off to either side. Screven was wounded, captured, and died in captivity shortly after. White fell back on Midway Church and formed a new defense line. He also wrote a letter which he made sure fell into Prevost's hands. When read, it made it seem as though White was leading him into a trap. When Prevost learned that Fuser had not yet reached Sunbury, he chickened out and after burning the church and some other buildings at Midway took his leave.

Now drive a mile back to Midway. The entire action—the skirmish, the retreat, and the burning of buildings—all took place between the Screven marker and the Midway Congregational Church. Near the church is the **Midway Museum,** a reconstruction of a raised cottage, typical of the architecture in this section of Georgia during the eighteenth century. The present church was built in 1792 to replace the one Prevost burned.

Take Route 38 east to Sunbury. After a five- to ten-minute drive through the pleasant, flat farmlands of coastal Georgia, a sign for Sunbury will appear on the right at an intersection indicating a left turn. Several miles after the turn, the road brings you to a dirt road leading off to the right and a marker at that intersection for Fort Morris. A half mile farther, take the left fork in the road and proceed with savannahs showing through the trees and open country up ahead. There are small homes on both sides of the road and then a hurricane fence with an opening through which you drive into the midst of a grove of live oaks. The road leads on through an opening in the old breastworks into the middle of the remains of **Fort Morris.**

This is a beautiful, scenic spot on the banks of the Medway River.

Standing on the old breastworks, you can see the river flowing off to the right into St. Catherine's Sound which empties into the Atlantic Ocean. Colonel Fuser and his 500 men arrived here by boat on Wednesday, November 25, 1778. Unaware that Prevost had already retreated, Fuser demanded the fort's surrender. Lieutenant Colonel John McIntosh, commanding less than 200 men including about 120 Continentals, told Fuser to come and take the fort if he could. When Fuser learned that Prevost was not going to make the rendezvous, he thought better of his bravado and sailed away.

Fort Morris was the scene of a second and more fateful action in January, 1779, after the British had taken Savannah. On the sixth of that month, General Prevost with 2,000 men captured Sunbury and laid siege to the fort. Major Joseph Lane, seven officers, and 195 Continental soldiers held out for three days until on January 9, a Sunday, Prevost brought his artillery into position. After a brief but telling exchange, Lane pulled down his colors. The rebels lost one captain and three privates killed and seven men wounded; the British, one man killed, three wounded.

In *The Dead Town of Sunbury, Georgia* Paul McIlvaine describes the fort as measuring 275 feet in length along the east, or river side; 191 feet on the northern side (to your left as you face the river standing on the breastworks); 240 feet to the west behind you; and 140 feet to the south to your right. Sunbury, the town it was built to protect, was a little more than a quarter of a mile to the south. Marshes surrounded the fort on three sides and the breastworks were ringed by a moat. McIlvaine writes that twenty-five guns of various sizes from four- to twenty-four pounders were mounted on platforms so they could be fired over the walls. C. C. Jones, however, the Georgia historian who visited this site in 1877, wrote in *The Dead Towns of Georgia* that he could distinguish seven embrasures, each about five feet wide, some of which are still evident today and obviously were large enough to admit the muzzles of the big guns. Jones also described the remains of the parapet as being about ten feet wide and rising six feet above the interior of the fort and the moat as ten feet deep and ten feet wide at the bottom and twenty feet wide at the top.

At present, the breastworks and embrasures are still to be seen and so are the remains of the moat. Archaeological work was in progress when we were there and the test diggings had already produced parts of British uniforms and other artifacts. The Georgia Historical Commission hopes to have the fort restored by 1976.

☆

Return to the county road and the marker for the fort and turn right in the direction of Sunbury. About a quarter of a mile along, where the road forks, three markers appear, two referring to Sunbury. One of these roads, the blacktop, leads to the right to what is left of the town.

British rule having been reestablished in Georgia after the fall of Savannah with Mark Prevost as royal governor, life became so harsh for the people of Sunbury, as it did for all Georgians sympathetic to the rebel cause, that many residents of the town left. The American officers captured at Savannah lived in Sunbury on parole, among them Colonel George Walton of the Georgia militia whose detachment had been surprised by Baird.

The paved road takes you to the river and what was Sunbury's wharf area. Occasional roads leading off this road take you through what was a prosperous seaport town that once challenged Savannah as a center of commerce.

McIlvaine drew a map of the town based on his research which shows five wharves along the riverfront, a very large square in the town called King's Square, and two smaller squares marked Church and Meeting squares respectively. The streets were about seventy-five feet wide, the lanes twenty; and according to this map, the town was laid out to include 496 lots. He gives the town's overall dimensions as 3,430 feet long and 1,880 feet wide at the north boundary, and 2,230 feet wide at the south boundary. An aerial photo shows a roughly rectangular light area along the river surrounded on three sides by woods with marshy areas to the south threaded by creeks. Knowing all this seems to be the only way to comprehend what you will see when you visit the site.

The town never fully recovered from the exodus that followed the reimposition of British rule. During the nineteenth century, malarial and yellow fever epidemics, several hurricanes, and the supremacy of Savannah all contributed to its death. By C. C. Jones's visit in 1878, a cornfield covered what were once streets, squares, and homes. Today there is nothing left of the Sunbury Academy, acclaimed in its time as a center of education, nor any of what was once a bustling seaport of several thousand souls. This is only one of a number of "dead towns" to be found not only in Georgia but in other sections of the South and occasionally in the North as well. You will have a chance to explore two other such sites in the South. You can drive and walk over this ground, empty except for the tall grass and clumps of pines here and there, and never suspect the past presence of the town.

There is an old cemetery in this area which is very difficult to find. I could not have found it without the help of members of the Liberty

County Historical Society who led me to it through a maze of dirt roads and tracks. Once we had to turn back because the way was blocked by a fallen tree. If you follow the road around from the wharf area as it curves back from the river, it becomes a dirt county road marked S1134. The Sunbury *cemetery* lies somewhere off that road. You will know it by a historical marker at the old, iron picket fence and the broken burial vaults and stones inside. Some of the stones are mid-nineteenth century. Many of the eighteenth-century tablets, made of wood, have rotted away or been destroyed. General Screven is buried here, and there is a local tradition that Button Gwinnett, who loved the town and owned a Sunbury plantation, sleeps here as well.

GEORGIA'S FRONTIER FORTS

South of Savannah are several sites which were fortified early in Georgia's history or during the Revolution. Late in the seventeenth century, Charles II granted what is now Georgia to the proprietors of the Carolina colony, despite Spanish claims to the entire eastern half of the continent based on the explorations of Hernando de Soto. Firmly established in Florida, the Spaniards had built missions and forts along the Sea Islands in support of their claim. Nevertheless, the British decided that Georgia would make a good buffer between Charleston, South Carolina, and Florida, and declared the area a crown colony. It became a bone of bitter contention between Spain and Great Britain, and at least one major battle, the Battle of Bloody Marsh in 1742, was fought over it. The Spaniards were forced to cede Florida to the British when they were defeated with the French in one of the French and Indian wars.

The leader of the British forces at Bloody Marsh was James Oglethorpe, a philanthropist interested in establishing a refuge for British debtors. As the colony's main citizen and leader, he built a series of forts, usually at the mouths of rivers or at strategic fords and ferries, which you will visit. Though their importance faded once the Spanish threat was removed, they became vital again during the Revolution and some were rebuilt and regarrisoned.

FORT TONYN

The first Georgia fort to claim your attention is an exception to all this. Fort Tonyn was built by the British early in the Revolution to dominate the southern part of Georgia. It stood squarely in the way of Georgia militia forces that, under Colonel Samuel Elbert, tried to invade Florida and capture St. Augustine in 1778.

You can try for this site if you choose, but you may have to give up on it as I did. If you are combining your historical tour with a trip to Florida, however, you might take a stab at it.

Return to Midway and go south on 17 along with the rest of the Florida-bound traffic. If you want to make an overnight stop, take the turnoff to Jekyll Island, one of Georgia's sea islands and a delightful seashore resort with a number of good motels available.

U.S. 17 will take you to Kingsland where, in the heart of town, you will find Route 40. Take it to the left to the town of St. Marys about eleven miles away. As you come into St. Marys, look for Point Peter Road. It intersects 40 from the left just after the sign for Gilman's Hospital. A historical marker at the intersection tells about Fort Tonyn, built by the British in 1776 and captured by an American force in 1778. The site lies at the mouth of Peter Creek where it empties into St. Marys River off to your left front as you face east. Though I used a county map, I was unable to get to the site because of construction and U.S. army roads that were not open to the public. The only possible way to get to the site then was by boat from St. Marys, which did not prove feasible. Perhaps when you make the attempt, the site may have been restored (a War of 1812 fort was built on top of the older fort) and the way opened to the public. The log and sand breastwork built by the British along Borell Creek and referred to on the marker would have been off to the right somewhere in the midst of that marshy estuary.

The description on the marker of the action at Fort Tonyn is far from adequate. Tonyn was named for the royal governor of East Florida. It was probably captured by Colonel Samuel Elbert, a Continental Army officer who in 1778 attempted to invade East Florida. During the attempt, Elbert made a landing on Amelia Island which is immediately south of the mouth of St. Marys River. Since he was in the vicinity, I assume he may also have paid attention to Fort Tonyn. The Elijah Clarke mentioned on the marker as the commander of the American cavalry was a Georgia hero of the Revolution, whom you will meet again before you leave the state.

The area in the vicinity of Point Peter Road is a strange mixture of industry (a large plant belching smoke is clearly visible on the horizon), marshland, farms, airport, and U.S. army lands. Incidentally, keep in mind that Georgia was covered by lumber companies during the early years of our century. They did a very thorough job, cutting down most of the hardwood forests in the state. Gone are the sweet gums and the cherry, the maples and the beech and many of the live oak. In their place grew the so-called southern pine now so prevalent. The forests of the twentieth century, not only in the South but throughout the East, are very different from the forests the armies of the American Revolution marched and fought their way through.

FORTS OF THE REVOLUTION

Assuming you have decided not to try for Fort Tonyn, take U.S. 17 south to Darien. Go through the town to the south end where a bridge carries 17 over the Darien River. Look for a road going off to your left just before the bridge, actually a spur of Route 25.

Though traffic is heavy through Darien, you should have little trouble making the left onto 25. There is a blue and white marker at the intersection for Fort King George and for Fort Darien. The road leads along a bluff overlooking the Darien River on the right and will dead-end after about a mile at a Fort Darien marker which identifies the approximate site somewhere on the bluff. A short distance before the road ends, watch for a little wooden marker indicating a left turn onto another road which leads to the Fort King George site. Take that left and look for another sign directing you to turn right. You will be approaching what looks like a Spanish mission inside an area enclosed by a hurricane fence. Park at the fence and enter the enclosure to visit a delightful little *museum* which explains and interprets the site.

Fort Darien was actually along the bluff the road followed from Darien. The remains are probably on the grounds of one or more of those private homes you passed. This recently built museum explains the history of the bluff from the Spanish occupation to the British settlement. One exhibit demonstrates what Fort Darien looked like, with its long line along the river side of the bluff. According to markers, the fort was built and garrisoned by local Patriots during the Revolution and was the scene of several clashes with British forces.

The town of Darien was settled by Scottish emigrants who first called it New Inverness and had trouble not with Indians but with the Spaniards who claimed this territory. The museum's exhibits were not quite complete when we were there, but what exhibits were open were excellently done, promising a most interesting experience for future visitors.

The area around the museum overlooks the marshes of the Altamaha River. When the original Fort King George was built two hundred years ago, the river and marshes were much farther away. As the river silted up the marshes spread until they now come to the foot of the bluff. A marker behind the museum identifies this as the site of an old sawmill and describes two hundred years of sawmilling that took place here. Beyond that a path leads to the remains of old **Fort King George** which have been excavated by archaeologists. There was a small blockhouse about twenty-six feet square with three floors to it and a lookout in the gables, officers' quarters, and a barracks. The fort was surrounded by a moat and palisades on all sides except along the river. During the six years of its occupation by the English-speaking settlers, over 140 officers and men lost their lives in encounters with Spanish expeditions. You can see gravestones marking some of their graves near the museum.

Return to Darien and get back onto U.S. 17 south. At the intersection with U.S. 84, turn right and go west along 84 to the site of **Fort McIntosh.**

Look for State Route 259 coming in from your left and a marker at that intersection. It describes a small stockade 100 feet square with a bastion at each corner and a blockhouse in the center that stood nearby on the Saltilla River. A force of Tories and Indians attacked the fort and besieged it for twenty-four hours on February 17, 1777. You can proceed a little farther to the river and check out the right-hand side of the road, just as the bridge crosses it, for the actual site of the fort. We followed the road leading off to the right paralleling the river and then tried a succession of dirt roads that went off toward the river, but were stopped each time either by dead ends or high water. The best place to view the fort site is from the bridge at the east end looking northwest or upstream.

If you did not try for Fort Tonyn, the site of Fort McIntosh is as far south as you will travel. Return along U.S. 84 to U.S. 17 and take it back to Darien. In Darien, a short distance north of the bridge, look for the juncture with Route 251. It is in the heart of town on the left and is marked by two historical markers. You will see them as you make the turn. Route 251 is the old **River Road** over which the armies of three wars have marched: Scottish settlers during their struggles with the Spaniards of Florida, armies of the Revolution, and armies of the Civil War. Route 251 will take you through pine woods and farmlands for about twelve miles to a railroad crossing. Cross the tracks and proceed ahead, though 251 ends shortly. About a hundred yards from the crossing, a dirt road goes off to the left. Turn onto it and follow it to a fork in the road. A short distance down the right fork is a private hunting and fishing camp on the east bank of the Altamaha River. The left fork peters out into brush and woods.

This is the site of **Fort Barrington** which controlled the river crossing of a vital road along the southern frontier of Georgia. The British built a fort here in 1751 which was renamed Fort Howe. What might be the remains of breastworks are just off the left fork of the road in the woods, but nothing in the camp area, which may have been the center of the fort, suggests its outlines.

In its time Fort Barrington was an important post and a number of prominent figures of the Revolution, both American and British, served in it. According to the caretaker of the camp, a ferry operated here until sometime during the 1920s.

Return to Route 251 where it ends just beyond the railroad crossing and turn left onto S2387 north in the direction of Townsend. Stay on S2387 through a couple of right-angle turns to where it dead-ends in Townsend at State Route 99. Turn left (west) on 99 into Long County and on to Ludovici. Take U.S. 25 west out of Ludovici (pick it up at a left-hand turn in the center of town), noticing that it is also U.S. 301 and State Route 23. When you reach Route 261, turn left onto 261, a dirt road. There is a marker here directing you to Beard's Bluff five miles along 261 which takes you down to the Altamaha River again, also at a hunting and fishing camp. This is **Beard's Bluff**, the site of an important fortified post on the Georgia frontier during the Revolution. The stockade which once stood at this spot controlling a crossing was the scene of frequent skirmishes between the rebel militia that manned it and local Indian tribes who were encouraged by the British to attack the colonists.

HUDSON'S FERRY AND BRIER CREEK

Retrace your route to Ludovici and take U.S. 82 north to U.S. 17. Continue north along 17 to Interstate 16 just west of Savannah. Interstate 95 was still under construction along this stretch, and though we were able to use it for short sections, we traveled most of the time on 17. If 95 is completed during your tour, take it to 16. Take 16 west to the exit for State Route 119 and take 119 north. Watch the signs carefully along 119; there are several right-angle turns and road junctures that can be confusing, including a fork in 119. Stick with 119 in the direction of Springfield. At State Route 17, turn left and take 17 north for fifteen miles to the town of Oliver where you will come to a juncture with

Route 24 and a sign for Newington. Turn onto 24 and head for Newington. Continue along Route 24 east out of Newington for exactly 4.5 miles from the railroad crossing to a dirt road going off to the right. A stop sign faces down the dirt road. Take that road and count three dirt roads (ignoring the driveways between dirt roads two and three) going off to the left. Turn left onto the third road and follow it downhill. When the road forks, bear left and continue to a little fishing camp on the bank of the river where **Hudson's Ferry** once carried travelers across the Savannah River.

The river flows by swiftly and silently. The clearing you are in now is shaded over by big, old trees. To the left as you face the river is the mouth of a creek. Brush, fallen trees, and thickets conceal whatever may remain of the breastworks that once protected a British camp of 4,000 regulars which General Prevost established here in February, 1779. Six months earlier, in September, 1778, General Lincoln had been appointed commander of the Southern Department. By February, his army was facing General Prevost's men across the Savannah River west of Savannah. A movement by some of Lincoln's forces toward Augusta caused the British garrison there to evacuate the city. General John Ashe with 1,500 militia had been sent to join General Andrew Williamson whose 1,200 men were just across the Savannah River from Augusta preparing to engage the British occupying force commanded by Colonel Archibald Campbell. Campbell left Augusta and dropped down the river to this point before going on to Savannah. Just before Campbell left Augusta, a band of local militia had surprised and routed a large Tory force at Kettle Creek, north of here, an event that hastened his departure.

Ashe followed Campbell and by February 27 was at Brier Creek, fifteen miles northwest of Hudson's Ferry, where he found that Campbell had destroyed the Freeman-Miller Bridge to hold up his pursuit. In the meantime, Prevost decided to do something to check Ashe. He sent his brother, Lieutenant Colonel Mark Prevost, from Hudson's Ferry to swing around the Americans and attack them from the rear while he feinted at them frontally.

For the next act in this little drama, return to Route 24 and drive back into Newington. Pick up Route 21 north and take it to Sylvania. At the traffic circle in the center of Sylvania, turn right onto East Ogeechee Street and out of town first along County Road S720 and then along S1321 bearing left. You will reach an intersection with Route 24 at a stop sign. Continue ahead for a mile or two until you cross three concrete bridges, one right after the other. Coming off the third bridge, make an immediate left into a small park at the side of the road. There are picnic tables, **Brier Creek** flowing under the bridge, and two markers, one very large with a text describing the troop movements and strategy that led to the engagement on Brier Creek.

A map between the markers shows in excellent detail Ashe's position on Brier Creek and Prevost's line of march. As you read the text, keep in mind that the only holds the British had on their colonies at this time were in New York and Savannah; that Campbell had burned the Freeman-Miller Bridge over Brier Creek, cutting a vital link along the main road between Savannah and Augusta. To a certain extent, the control of this crossing would determine the control of Georgia and the British position in the South. After this action Lincoln attempted to retake Savannah, but failed, leaving the British position in the South confirmed.

The Freeman-Miller Bridge was about a quarter of a mile downstream from this spot. Ashe was supposed to hold his position along the creek while the rest of Lincoln's strategy developed. While Ashe was away conferring with Lincoln at Purysburg on the Savannah River, his second in command, General Bryan, moved the American positions from the burned bridge to this area. The camp was along this side of the creek. The picket line extended along the creek in both directions with the left anchored at the burned bridge downstream. Colonel Leonard Marbury was sent upstream fourteen miles to a place now called Millhaven, which you will find shortly, to protect the rear. Marbury was surprised by Prevost who crossed the creek and scattered his men. Before the word of this attack could reach Ashe, who had returned to camp, Prevost was upon him moving toward the creek from his rear.

The British appeared from behind the marker as you face it. Their line stretched from the marker off to your right where the Savannah swamps lie. The marker describes the battle in such vivid detail that you can almost see it happening in front of your eyes. The Americans lost about 200 killed and drowned and 170 captured, while the British lost only five killed and eleven wounded.

Now return along S1321 to Route 24 and turning right, take 24 west. Watch carefully for signs for 24 west when you reach the intersection with U.S. 301–Route 73 and continue along S24. Three miles from that juncture you will come to the town of Hilltonia. Beyond the little town, take the first right-hand turn onto County Road S716. A small sign to the side of the road informs you that you are entering Millhaven Plantation. In about two miles the road turns sharply to the right and then crosses Brier Creek. At the opposite end of the bridge is a historical marker on the left describing the Brier Creek action at this point. You have been following or at least paralleling Prevost's line of march as you followed Route 24. He crossed the creek just as you did and engaged Marbury's men on the other side, the side you are now on. He then followed a route parallel to the creek on this side heading southeast; after a march of fourteen miles, he came up behind Ashe's position at the site you just came from. At present the site of **Prevost's crossing** is occupied by a chemical plant on one side and the entrance to a private school on the marker side.

To round off the story of the Lincoln-Prevost duel for the control of Georgia, go back to Route 24; turn right, and follow 24 north to Waynesboro, which was named in honor of Anthony Wayne. Lincoln moved to occupy Augusta after Brier Creek, but Augustine Prevost feinted toward Charleston, South Carolina, drawing Lincoln off in that direction. Prevost then made his way back to Savannah through the islands off the coast of Georgia and reoccupied it, thus securing the British bridgehead in Georgia.

There is a good *museum* in Waynesboro at 536 Liberty Street (the street 24 leads onto) in which another very good map explains the campaign and shows the important sites connected with it. Notice as you drive into Waynesboro a park and a lake on your left. Somewhere in that vicinity stood the Burke County Jail. Around it a battle was fought between local Whig and Tory militia in which the Tories were defeated.

Take Route 80 out of Waynesboro going west and north to the town of Wrens. Look for the signs for State Route 17 in Wrens and take it north until it joins U.S. 78–State Route 10. Shortly after you will pass the entrance ramps to Interstate 20. Continue for two miles to the turnoff to the right onto State Route 43. Take 43 north to Lincolnton and go through the town picking up U.S. 378 along the way. Continue on 378 east and 43 north. The road will take you to the Georgia–South Carolina line on the Savannah River.

Notice to your left just before the bridge that takes you out of the state the entrance to **Elijah Clarke State Park.** Clarke was a popular hero in Georgia and a leader of the state's militia who fought in a number of battles, including the one at Kettle Creek which you will cover next. The park sites and one a little farther back along 378 are connected with the civil war aspect of the Revolution, which was so prevalent in the South. Conflict between local Whigs and Tories was carried to a violent extreme on more than one occasion as it was here.

The park should perhaps be named for John Dooley whose home

once stood within the park's present limits. As you enter you will see a marker on the right for the *spring* used by the Dooley family. The Dooley cabin was across the road opposite the spring on the hill about where a utility pole has been erected. Dooley, who fought beside Clarke as a colonel of militia, was murdered here in his bed by a band of Tories. The park also contains the grave of Elijah Clarke, a small museum, a reconstructed pioneer's cabin, picnic facilities, and camping sites that draw an estimated 14,000 campers a year. Cabins and mobile home sites are also available. There is a lake for water sports, and all in all it is a wonderful recreation area. The site of Dooley's grave is supposed to be up on the hill near the cabin site.

Now leave the park; turn right, and heading back toward Lincolnton, look for a historical marker on the right side of the road. It stands several hundred feet before a small general store and filling station on the same side of the road. According to this marker, **Tory Pond** was 100 yards to the south. On the shores of the pond some of the Tories who murdered Dooley were hung. We paced off a hundred yards south from the marker by a compass. This took us diagonally across 378 into the woods on the other side, then onto a dirt county road. We found lots of low ground, but the pond has disappeared. The caretaker at the park believes that the pond extended across what is now 378 through the low area between the marker and the general store.

KETTLE CREEK

Go west along 378 past Lincolnton in the direction of Washington in Wilkes County which is advertised on roadside signs as the county that has gone to grass, meaning that it is a cattle-raising district. In Washington take Route 44 south, noticing the sign for Kettle Creek Battleground. Route 44 will cross first Beaverdam Creek, then Little Kettle Creek. After the second bridge take the first right-hand turn onto another of Georgia's bituminous (blacktop or tarred) county roads. A marker at the right side of the intersection indicates the battleground to the right. After 0.65 mile you will cross Kettle Creek over a plank bridge with steel girder supports. Tyrone Road, another bituminous road, will appear to the left. Exactly a half mile along Tyrone Road is a dirt road on the left. Take the dirt road for three-quarters of a mile through the fields and woods up a hill to the Kettle Creek *monument* and a couple of picnic tables. Below you and the monument Kettle Creek runs through a heavily wooded area.

When Campbell pulled off his successful capture of Savannah in

December, 1778, Colonel Boyd organized the Tories of Anson County in North Carolina and marched through South Carolina, picking up adherents among the Loyalists as he went along and living off the country, a euphemism for plundering. Eventually he reached Georgia and came to the banks of Kettle Creek where he camped on February 13, 1779. Most of his 700 men turned their horses out to graze, perhaps in the fields you passed to the left as you followed the dirt road to the monument, and began to slaughter the cattle they had picked up along the way.

While they were thus occupied, a rebel force of about 300 commanded by Colonels John Dooley, Elijah Clarke, and Andrew Pickens crept up on them from the other side of the creek (opposite to the side you are now on) and attacked without warning. Boyd managed to organize his men to put up a fight for about an hour or so before they were routed. Forty Tories were killed and seventy captured and Boyd himself died later that day of wounds he received during the fight. The rebels lost only nine killed and twenty-three wounded. They celebrated by trying the prisoners for treason, found them all guilty, hung five, and turned the rest loose. This action encouraged many Georgia militiamen to join up with Lincoln and encouraged Campbell to get out of Augusta.

The actual fighting raged along the creek below the monument. You can climb down the slope and explore the creek bank in both directions. On a warm, summer day this can be a delightful spot to explore either after or before lunch. When you have tired of climbing along the bank looking for musket balls, drive back to Route 44, take it into Washington, and then take Route 17 north to the little town of Tignall.

At the traffic light in Tignall turn left onto an unmarked road, which is County S902. This will take you first to a bridge that crosses Clark Creek and then 1.9 miles farther to a crossroads with a dirt road to the right and a paved road to the left. There is a general store here and a cluster of small homes and a marker exactly 6.9 miles from where you turned off 17 in Tignall. It informs you that near here on Clark's Creek the Dooley-Pickens-Clarke force camped the night before they attacked Boyd's men on Kettle Creek. You crossed Clark's Creek on that bridge almost two miles back. Clark's Creek runs to your right and left behind you, but the exact site of the Whig *camp* is unknown.

Return to Tignall and turn left onto 17 north to find a site connected with the killing of Colonel Dooley. On the way you cross the Broad River over which some of the Tories escaped after leaving the Dooley cabin. Several miles after crossing the river, at the intersection with County Road S2215, you will see signs for Nancy Hart and Harvey Brown state parks. There is a marker here describing Nancy Hart as being six feet tall, "masculine in strength and courage," a dead shot, and a skilled doctor and good neighbor. Boatner very ungallantly describes her as crosseyed, vulgar, and illiterate. She was also a staunch Patriot, and among the legends that have sprung up around this frontier heroine are several accounts of her exploits as a spy. The Tories who were fleeing from the Whig vengeance after the Dooley killing are supposed to have fallen into her clutches; they were eventually hanged, though not by her.

Drive to the entrance to **Nancy Hart State Park** just a short way along S2215 from 17 and go on in. There is a picnic pavilion under the trees and a marker near it on a boulder for a nearby spring which stood close to the Hart cabin. A path leads off through the park to a restoration of the Nancy Hart cabin, a very good one built on the original site with a chimney on the side made of stones from the original cabin. There are rest rooms in the park, family campsites, fishing and swimming facilities, and picnic areas.

The only Georgia sites left to cover before moving on into South Carolina are in Augusta and have to do with a later period of the Revolution. Take Route 17 back to Washington and pick up U.S. 78–Route 10 which will take you to Interstate 20. Take 20 east to the exit for Route 28 south, which takes you into Augusta.

AUGUSTA

I was unable to find any sites in or around Augusta connected with Campbell's brief occupation of the town early in 1779. The city was the scene of heavy fighting in September, 1780, and again in May and June of 1781, but though the focal point of the 1780 action, Mackay House, remains standing, the forts and positions the 1781 fighting raged around are now only street locations.

The 1781 sites are all contained within a small area close to the Savannah River in what was the oldest part of town, but is now the newest. The renovation of Augusta's downtown area has effectively erased almost all traces of the eighteenth century with the exception of two or three buildings.

Route 28 is Washington Road where it passes under Interstate 20 and then becomes Broad Street which takes you into the heart of downtown Augusta. Turn left off Broad Street onto Eleventh Street and go east two blocks to Reynolds Street. At this intersection stood **Fort Grier-**

son. There is a marker here, but you have to look for it. It is up against the yellow brick wall of the new Fire Department Headquarters.

In June, 1781, General Nathanael Greene moved against Ninety-six, an important British position in South Carolina about fifty miles from Augusta, while Light Horse Harry Lee and his legion, plus a force of North Carolina and Georgia militia, moved against Augusta. There were two forts in Augusta, both in this vicinity, Fort Grierson and Fort Cornwallis to the east. The siege of Augusta by the Georgia militia under Elijah Clarke and General Andrew Pickens had been under way for about a month by then. On Wednesday, May 23, Fort Grierson was attacked from three sides and captured. The garrison of eighty tried to reach Fort Cornwallis a half mile away but were either cut down or captured. The British commander, Colonel Grierson, was taken prisoner and shot. According to the Richmond County Historical Society an unknown Georgian did the killing. According to Benson Lossing, he was killed by Captain Samuel Alexander of the Georgia militia.

The besieging forces now turned their attention to Fort Cornwallis. To subdue its defenders, the attackers had to build a **Maham tower** (first used at Fort Watson, North Carolina) at what is now the corner of Eighth and Reynolds streets, three short blocks along Reynolds Street. The marker for the site is a few feet off Reynolds on Eighth. The tower was made of logs, filled with earth. At the top an embrasure accommodated a six-pounder. The tower's height is unknown, but it was tall enough to dominate the interior of Fort Cornwallis which was just two modern blocks away. At the present time, the site of the tower is occupied by a cotton exchange building which houses a business school and a motel.

Proceed two blocks along Reynolds Street to **St. Paul's Church** at Sixth. When the church was first built in 1750, it stood "under the curtain of the fort," which was then Fort Augusta, built in 1735 to protect a trading post that had been established here. On the same spot the British built Fort Cornwallis, which was captured by the Americans during the action of September, 1780, and then abandoned. The fort was taken down in 1786 and a new church was built which burned in 1916 and was replaced by the present building. At this time there are railroad tracks on the other side of Sixth Street and a skyscraper to the left called the Georgia Building. The fort capitulated on June 4, 1781, after the British had lost about fifty-two officers and men killed. The American forces lost about forty. Of the defenders 334 were made prisoners. There are no apparent remains of Fort Cornwallis.

☆

Turn up Sixth Street in the direction of Broad Street. Cross Broad and go on to the next big intersection which is Greene Street. Turn left on Greene Street, a broad boulevard with a mall down the middle, and look immediately for the **Signers' Monument** a block ahead at Monument Street opposite the courthouse. It commemorates Georgia's signers of the Declaration of Independence. Two of them are buried under it, including George Walton who, as you remember, was captured by the British in Savannah in 1778.

Reverse your direction on Greene Street; proceed to Thirteenth Street, and turn left to Nelson Street. A marker in front of a Uniroyal Tire Center identifies **Meadow Garden,** the home of George Walton, 400 yards west, a white, raised cottage with dormers in front and two brick chimneys.

Make a U-turn on Thirteenth Street and drive back to Broad Street. Turn left onto Broad and look for 1822 Broad Street, the **Mackay House,** Augusta's and one of Georgia's most dramatic sites. It is a big, two-story house with brick chimneys at either end standing on a knoll overlooking the street. A parking lot is available behind the house reached by turning up either one of the two streets that flank the house and lead to its rear. The Mackay House is open to the public Tuesday through Saturday from 10 A.M. to 5 P.M., Sunday from 2 to 5 P.M. It is closed on Monday, Christmas Day, and New Year's Day. There is no admission.

Augusta had been occupied by the British since January, 1779. In September, 1780, at the time of the first rebel attempt to take it, the Mackay House became a British stronghold. Augusta was a hotbed of Toryism and therefore a prime target for Georgia's rebel forces. Colonel Elijah Clarke and 350 men were joined by Lieutenant Colonel James McCall with eighty men and together they advanced on Augusta from Soap Creek, about forty miles away. They captured Forts Grierson and Cornwallis and drove the British under Grierson and Thomas Brown and their Indian allies into the Mackay House. Built by Thomas Red in 1758, the Mackay House, also known as the White House, had become an important trading post. The area it stood in was known as Garden Hill. Its front, which does not face on Broad Street, looked out over a landing on the Savannah River.

The siege lasted from September 15 to September 18 when Colonel John Cruger showed up with a relief column from Ninety-six. The rebels lost about sixty killed and wounded. A Captain Ashby and twelve other wounded rebels were hanged on the outside staircase of the house which can be seen at the rear.

The Mackay House is maintained by the Georgia Historical Commission. A guide takes you through and relates its history. It sits on its original foundations and though it has been restored, the walls, floors, ceilings, and paneling are original. The furnishings are period, but not original to the house. Among the unusual features in this house are its vaulted ceilings.

The outside *staircase* is a reconstruction of the one on which the executions were carried out. Notice that the treads and risers are nailed to the wall at one side just as the originals were.

In a second-floor room you will find a diorama representing the hanging as well as exhibits of relics which have been found around the house. The reason for the hangings seems to have been a letter Lord Cornwallis sent to all commanders of British forts in the South commanding them to punish the rebels with the "utmost vigor" and ordering the hanging of all captured rebel militiamen. Colonel Brown, who had been shot through both thighs during the siege, had himself carried to the ground floor porch to watch the hangings. The bodies were handed over to the Indians who scalped, mutilated, and threw them into the river. Among the hanged were two brothers, aged seventeen and fifteen. The older boy had been wounded in the legs. His brother had refused to leave him and so fell into the hands of the British and shared his brother's fate. Each man was placed on a horse; the rope was attached to a newel post or bannister rail above; the noose was placed around his neck, and the horse was led out from under him. The sixteen prisoners who were not hanged were turned over to the Indians who tortured them to death. Accounts of these events were written in an exultant mood by some of the British officers present and were subsequently printed in newspapers in London and Savannah.

The view of the river from the front of the house is shut off by the buildings in between. Small one-family homes crowd in on the Mackay House and its ground on three sides, while the traffic of Broad Street flows by on the fourth.

II.

SOUTH CAROLINA

There are probably more Revolutionary War sites in South Carolina than in any other state. South Carolinians seem to have fixed in their minds and on their maps every skirmish, every ambush, every firing of a gun that took place in the state during all eight of the Revolutionary War years. There are forty-six counties in South Carolina, and I have been told by state authorities that every single one has sites, more than two hundred all together. Since the last three years of the war were concentrated in the Carolinas and Virginia with British and American armies and Whig and Tory militia marching and fighting all over the place, that is not hard to understand. You cannot hope to cover all two hundred unless you are prepared to stay in South Carolina for several months. What you can do is visit all the sites of events that affected the outcome of the war and visit enough of the locally significant spots to give you some understanding of what the Revolution was like for the people of South Carolina.

Sir Henry Clinton's capture of Charleston in May, 1780, drove the war home to Carolinians with a vengeance. Clinton returned to New York, leaving Earl Cornwallis in command with instructions to make South Carolina safe for the crown before taking on rebel forces in North Carolina and Virginia.

Cornwallis established a series of posts between Charleston and Ninety-six, on the Georgia border, at Camden, Rocky Mount, Hanging Rock, Fort Watson, Fort Motte, and Fort Granby. In response, Congress sent General Horatio Gates to attempt to deny South Carolina to the

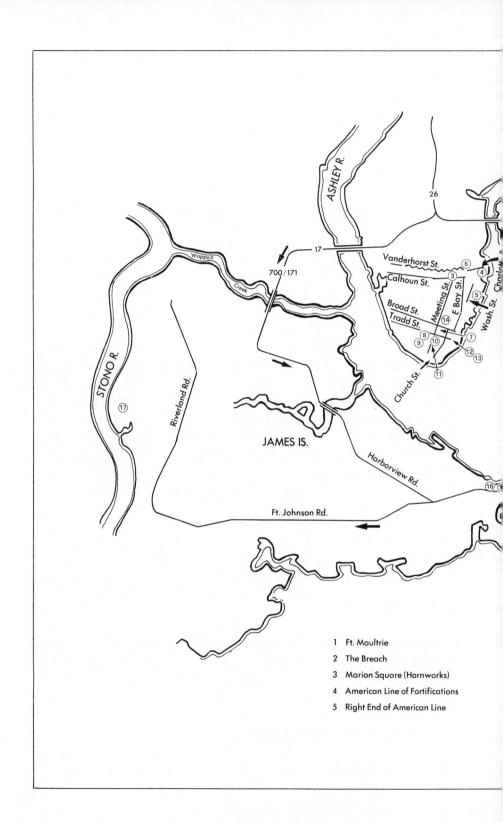

ASHLEY R.

26

STONO R.

Wappoo

Creek

700 / 171

17

Vanderhorst St.

Calhoun St.

Broad St.

Tradd St.

Meeting St.

E Bay St.

Wash. St.

Charl

Church St.

Riverland Rd.

17

JAMES IS.

Harborview Rd.

16

Ft. Johnson Rd.

3

6

4

5

14

8

9

10

11

7

12

13

1   Ft. Moultrie

2   The Breach

3   Marion Square (Hornworks)

4   American Line of Fortifications

5   Right End of American Line

CHARLESTON, S.C.
and VICINITY

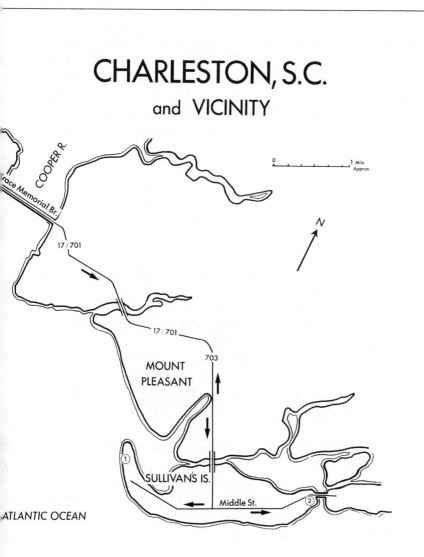

6   Liberty Tree

7   Heyward-Wash. House

8   106 Tradd St.

9   Pringle House (27 King St.)

10 Huger House (34 Meeting St.)

11 William Bull Hse. (35 Meeting St.)

12 Exchange Building

13 Provost Dungeon

14 Old Powder Magazine

15 Ft. Johnson

16 "Marshlands"

17 General Area of "Stono Ferry"

British. The rebel effort began badly. In August, 1780, Gates was roundly defeated by Cornwallis at Camden. Cornwallis was convinced that his commander's instructions were wrong and that the right strategy was to invade North Carolina and head for Virginia while the rebels were weak and disorganized. In this, he had the backing of the front office in London, where his aggressive strategy was preferred over Clinton's more cautious views.

In December, 1780, Nathanael Greene took over command from Gates and divided the army into several smaller groups, forcing Cornwallis to deal with many opposing units. Greene also made sure to keep his commands out of Cornwallis's reach, for he could not risk a general engagement.

The war had been going badly for Cornwallis before Greene came into the picture. His efforts to control the backwoods country were stopped at King's Mountain in October, 1780, by the militia; his forces were again defeated at Cowpens in January by Daniel Morgan. Francis Marion and Thomas Sumter launched guerilla campaigns that tore up British lines of supply and communications.

Morgan and Greene were then chased by Cornwallis across North Carolina and into Virginia, but Greene returned to North Carolina to engage Cornwallis at Guilford Courthouse on March 15. Cornwallis was left in possession of the field, but had to retire to Wilmington to rest his troops.

Greene moved back into South Carolina where he was tactically defeated at Hobkirk's Hill in Camden, but the British were forced to retire to Charleston. Greene then proceeded to close down the British posts between Ninety-six and Charleston. In the meantime, Cornwallis had gone into Virginia. Greene suffered another tactical defeat at Eutaw Springs in September, 1781, but it proved to be one of the last major engagements in the war.

I have arranged South Carolina into four main areas. The first is based in Charleston and includes sites as far south as Beaufort. The second centers on Georgetown and includes many places connected with Francis Marion as far west as and including Clarendon County north of Lakes Marion and Moultrie. The third takes in areas south of the lakes and near Camden. The fourth covers the largest slice of territory, from Ninety-six about fifty miles east of the Georgia state line up through the Spartanburg area, including Cowpens, King's Mountain, other sites connected with those battles, and then Cornwallis's line of march into North Carolina.

CHARLESTON SOUTH TO BEAUFORT

Begin in Charleston, which can be reached from the north on Interstate 95 to Interstate 26, or on U.S. 17. If you are coming from Augusta, the fastest way is to take Interstate 20 east to Interstate 26 just north and west of Columbia, and then take 26 south to Charleston. To go more directly is to follow a succession of connecting roads through a number of cities and towns. You might strike a happy median by taking U.S. 1–78 east from Augusta to Aiken; Routes 215 and 4 to U.S. 301–601 just west of Orangeburg, and then 301 to Interstate 26 to complete the trip.

Charleston was the target of two British expeditions, both masterminded and commanded by Sir Henry Clinton. The first, in 1776, ended in a humiliating defeat; the second, in victory. There are only two sites extant from the first attempt, both built over but recognizable. The sites connected with the second, the 1780 siege, have also fallen victim to the city's growth, but a few have been identified. There are a number of eighteenth-century houses in Charleston, but only a few connected with the Revolution. The old part of the city is a wonderful place to walk through and is probably the most beautiful urban section in any American city. During the spring months the azaleas and cypress gardens attract large numbers of visitors.

Fort Moultrie is the main site connected with Clinton's attempt to establish a British beachhead at Charleston in 1776. To get there, take U.S. 17 north out of Charleston. You can get to the entrance ramp to 17, which is well marked by highway signs, by going north on Meeting Street, away from Broad Street. U.S. 17 takes you over the Cooper River on the Grace Memorial Bridge into Mount Pleasant. As you come off the bridge, stay to your right. Take the exit for Sullivan's Island and Isle of Palms and follow the signs for Sullivan's Island. After you cross another bridge, over Shem Creek, U.S. 17–701 will go off to the left. Bear right onto Route 703.

Another bridge takes you onto Sullivan's Island. Route 703 goes off to the left, but the signs for Fort Moultrie direct you ahead about two blocks where you turn right onto Middle Street. Eventually Middle Street forks at a gun mounted on a white pedestal. Bear right along Middle Street until you see the brick walls of the fort to your left. Park on the street either in front of the fort or on the opposite side in a parking lot marked by two floating mines on pedestals.

The present **Fort Moultrie** is the third to have been built on this site. The fort made of palmetto logs that successfully defied Sir Henry and his ships was somewhere in the area covered by the present fort. You enter through a sally port which takes you to a museum area which contained only a few military artifacts when we were there. Beyond the museum to the left, opposite the information office, is a corridor leading under the walls of the fort. Along this corridor were three palmetto logs to show the original substance of the fort.

From the top of the parapet you get a wonderful view of Charleston Harbor with Fort Sumter in the middle. Beyond is James Island on which Fort Moultrie's sister fort, Fort Johnson, was situated. The beach area beyond the parapet is covered with patches of beach grass and leads to the water. The day we were there a school of dolphins patrolled the beach about fifty feet offshore.

Sir Henry Clinton showed up in these waters on June 1, 1776, almost a year after Bunker Hill. The British Foreign Office had been convinced by the governors of the four southern colonies, who had all been evicted from their palaces, that the South was ripe for conquest. Accordingly, Sir Henry, second-in-command to Sir William Howe, had sailed from Boston on January 20 with about 1,500 men. Along the way, however, he had to stop off at several ports to consult with the royal governors, who now seemed most pessimistic about their chances of regaining their offices, because of a number of rebel victories which seemed to have crushed the southern Loyalists. He also learned that a fleet under the command of Sir Peter Parker, which was supposed to have sailed from the Irish port of Cork to rendezvous with him off the mouth of the Cape Fear River in North Carolina, had been delayed.

By May 31 when the rendezvous was finally completed, Sir Peter had convinced Sir Henry that capturing the unfinished rebel fort in Charleston Harbor would give them a good foothold in South Carolina and a strong base for future operations. And so the combined British fleets sailed for Charleston. On board Sir Peter's ships were troops under the command of General Cornwallis. On board Clinton's ships were the royal governors of the two Carolinas.

Awaiting them in Charleston Harbor was the half-finished Fort Sullivan under the command of Colonel William Moultrie. In the city itself were 6,500 Continental soldiers under the command of General Charles Lee, who had been sent first to New York by Washington, when it was feared that was to be Clinton's target, and then south. He arrived in Charleston a few days after the British had appeared. Lee was more concerned with the city than with the harbor forts, which he did not expect to stand up to the British fleet.

Fort Sullivan had been planned as a four-sided work with bastions at each corner. The breastworks were made of palmetto logs, the only material at hand. Each wall was a double thickness of logs with sand in between. In the **Gibbes Art Gallery,** on Meeting Street a few blocks west of Broad Street, are two very good watercolors painted by Lieutenant Henry Gray, who was in Charleston at the time of the attack on Fort Sullivan and painted these from life. One shows the attack in progress and demonstrates how ships of the line formed to deliver sustained broadsides. The other shows the scene the morning after the fight with two British ships listing heavily and one burning.

Of particular interest is the depiction of the fort showing the walls about eighteen feet high, judging by the height of the figures of the men, with embrasures for guns cut into the top level of logs. Only one wall is shown, a short wall with what looks like a bastion at each end jutting out toward the water. A third bastion is indicated to the rear. Three embrasures show on the wall of each bastion facing the water and three on each side wall. The center wall between the bastions has five embrasures. A few palmetto trees are in evidence, but most of this end of the island resembles a barren sandspit. Three small boats are shown returning from the burning British ship. In one boat someone holds a Union Jack upside down.

When the British appeared, only two bastions and two walls were completed. They mounted twenty-five guns ranging from nine- to twenty-five-pounders. Hastily erected breastworks completed the redoubt to the rear where several twelve-pounders were placed to cover the narrow channel between the island and Mount Pleasant. Lee suggested a floating bridge over which Moultrie's men could retreat, but Moultrie seemed to feel no need to think about retreating.

Clinton put most of his troops ashore on Long Island, now called Isle of Palms, a long spit of land off the north end of Sullivan's Island. A narrow strip of water called the Breach separates the two. Clinton had been told that he would be able to ford the Breach at low tide and so invest Fort Sullivan from the north. When he came ashore on Long Island, he discovered that the Breach was seven feet deep and filled with sand shoals and deep holes, making a ferry operation or fording impossible. To compound his dilemma, facing him on the Sullivan's Island side of the Breach were 700 rebels behind breastworks with a couple of small cannon pointed at him for emphasis.

The entire operation had to be left to Sir Peter Parker and his ships.

On Friday, June 28, Parker's ships opened fire on Fort Sullivan. One line of four ships fired from sprung anchor cables off the harbor mouth, while a second line of three sailed past into the harbor, firing broadsides as they went. The latter three ran afoul of each other and then aground on shoal water. The 413-man garrison in the fort fired back steadily, and the fort itself stood up admirably. The spongy palmetto logs absorbed shot without splintering the way most wood did. Many of the shot that landed inside the fort were buried in sandy, swampy ground and did little damage. Very few of the shells actually burst inside the fort.

At least two of the British ships took heavy punishment from the fort at close range. Parker's flagship suffered particularly and he had his breeches blown off and was wounded. At one point a shot knocked down the flagpole on the fort's parapet and it fell outside the fort. Sergeant William Jaspar, who was later to receive his death wound at Savannah under similar circumstances, leaped to the ground outside the fort, retrieved the flag, and had it flying on another staff before the onlookers (thousands of soldiers and citizens watching from the town) or the British could think the fort was surrendering.

The battle raged from midmorning until late at night when the British ships slipped their cables and left. Two of the three ships that had sailed into trouble in shoal waters managed to get loose, but one remained and was destroyed by her crew the following morning. The British suffered about 225 casualties of which about sixty-four were killed. Lord William Campbell, the governor of South Carolina, was on Parker's ship during the battle and received wounds of which he eventually died. The fort's defenders lost about twelve killed and twenty wounded. Six days later the Continental Congress declared the independence of the thirteen American colonies.

The outer walls of the present fort were built in 1898; most of the interior was built between 1807 and 1811. There was a fort here during the Civil War but most of it was blasted out of existence by Union guns. The three forts were superimposed one on top of the other, and the remains of the palmetto fort may be buried somewhere under the present structure. An attempt will be made by the National Park Service, which administers the site, to locate and reconstruct the original fort if possible by the bicentennial. There will be a program here during the bicentennial commemorating the gallant defense put up by Moultrie and his men.

Notice as you leave the fort the iron-fence enclosure to your left just outside the entrance. It surrounds the grave of Osceola, the Seminole chief who died here in captivity in 1838 after leading an unsuccessful struggle for his homeland.

Take Middle Street back for three miles beyond the turnoff for Route 703. This brings you to the north end of Sullivan's Island and the **Breach** whose treacherous shoals and holes are now crossed by a bridge that carries 703 onto Isle of Palms. Nothing remains of the rebel redoubt that pointed its guns at Clinton as he fretted and fumed on the opposite shore, unable to bring his 2,000 regulars to Parker's aid. Long Island was uninhabited then but today Isle of Palms is a mixed community of private homes and beach resorts.

J. Percival Petit described the American redoubt at the Breach in his book *Freedom's Four Square Miles*. The redoubt's forces were composed of militiamen, mostly from Orangeburg, and several Indians. The commander was Colonel William Thompson of the Third Regiment of Rangers. He mounted two guns here, an eighteen-pounder and a six-pound brass fieldpiece. According to Petit, Clinton did make an attempt to cross the Breach. I found supporting evidence for this in Orangeburg County records. A letter from Richard Hudson written in June, 1776, to Isaac Hayne states that on at least two occasions there were heavy exchanges of fire between the British troops on Long Island and the rebels on the other side of the Breach. Clinton remained in camp on Long Island for about three weeks after the battle, then embarked his troops and sailed back to New York.

We do not know if he said at the time "I shall return!" but return he did three years later to win and stay.

To cover the sites connected with Sir Henry's return, return yourself to Charleston. Clinton came back in February, 1780, in ninety transports and ten ships of the line loaded with almost 14,000 troops, sailors, and marines with horses, supplies, and munitions. The Americans were under General Benjamin Lincoln, then commander of American forces in the South, who had at his disposal by the end of the siege about 5,000 men. Forts Moultrie and Johnson had fallen into disrepair. A line of fortifications stretched across the peninsula on which the city stands from the Ashley River to the Cooper River. Unfortunately Lincoln failed to take full advantage of the two rivers which flank the city on either side and should have been used as lines of defense. Instead, he left them virtually undefended. Clinton took advantage of this by landing south of the city and then crossing the Stono River and the Ashley without opposition. Fort Johnson was taken by surprise, and by April 1 Clinton had cut off the city from the outside world on three sides. From that time on the outcome was inevitable. The only thing surprising about the siege was that Clinton took three months to accomplish what he might have done in half the time. He went through a forty-two-day siege during which the British kept pulling the noose tighter, moving closer and closer to the American lines until finally, with the garrison's supplies running low and no relief in prospect, Lincoln was forced to surrender.

To find the center of the American line of fortifications, take Meeting Street to the intersection with Calhoun Street. If you come to Calhoun from the direction of Broad Street, look for a parklike area on your left (or right from the other direction), Marion Square. Turn left onto Calhoun, find parking wherever you can, and walk to Marion Square. As you face the statue of Calhoun in the park, notice behind it and to your left what looks like a huge, shapeless boulder with a fence around it. A closer look will reveal oyster shells embedded in this odd object. This is what remains of the *hornworks,* the principal feature of the American center, which probably encompassed most of what is now Marion Square. If you place yourself with Meeting Street on your right, you are facing west up the peninsula toward the British lines. The American defense line stretched to your right and left. Behind you was an open area; beyond that were barracks to your left and bivouac sites on both sides. Some distance back from that the outer limits of the city would have appeared.

In front of you, perhaps at about Charlotte Street one block farther, was a continuous line of breastworks and redoubts. In front of that were two lines of abatises and then a canal which connected a line of marshes to form a moat. All of that area is now built up. Urbanization has overtaken the sites of the British lines and the successive parallels they dug as they moved closer to the Americans.

Lincoln's army marched out to lay down their arms on Friday, May 12, 1780, to a spot just beyond the hornworks, probably somewhere along Calhoun Street going away from Meeting Street.

To find the approximate position of the right end of the American line, go back along Calhoun Street toward Meeting Street. Continue past Meeting until you come to East Bay Street, noticing to your right the towers of a radio station. Turn right onto East Bay Street and proceed to an intersection just before the radio towers. Turn right there; drive one block; then turn left and drive slowly along the left curb until you come to an old stucco building with a frame, two-tiered piazza to one side, reached through an iron gate flanked by brick gateposts covered with vines. On the left gatepost is a plaque identifying the site of the Charleston **Liberty Tree**. Here in 1776 the Declaration of Independence was first read to the people of South Carolina. This Liberty Tree shows up on an early nineteenth-century map that was copied from an eighteenth-century French map showing the Lincoln fortifications. The tree then stood behind a redoubt; to one side were other redoubts. They formed the right end of the defense line and were anchored against a marsh with the Cooper River just beyond. If you face the direction you just came from, the redoubt would have been to your front, the right end of the line would have been to your right near the river, and the line of fortifications would have stretched off to your left.

There are a number of old homes east of Broad Street that you should visit. Park your car in the Broad Street area. Walk south on Meeting Street; cross Broad Street, and turn left onto Broad for one block. Turn right onto Church Street and look for 87 Church on the right side of the street. This is the **Heyward-Washington House,** which is open to visitors. It was once the home of Thomas Heyward, Jr., a signer of the Declaration of Independence. During the British occupation of Charleston, Heyward was imprisoned in St. Augustine, Florida. His wife, her sister, and her sister's children kept the home fires burning until a gang of Loyalists broke into the house one day, caused some damage, and abused the ladies and their children. Mrs. Heyward's sister died soon after this ill treatment and Mrs. Heyward left Charleston to stay with a brother in Philadelphia. George Washington paid the Heywards a visit in this house in May, 1791.

Leaving the Heyward House, turn right and walk a block to Tradd Street. Turn right onto Tradd and stroll along this slice of the past. Both sides of **Tradd Street** are lined with old homes, many of them preserved from the eighteenth century. Much of Charleston was destroyed by a series of fires during the 1800s, but Tradd Street is one of the few streets that escaped the holocausts. Notice that many of the old houses are built with their main entrances on one side, not facing out onto the street. The entrance usually faces a square plot of ground planted with trees and shrubs. Above the veranda is a covered porch supported by pillars in the raised cottage style. The two-tiered veranda is called a piazza. During the eighteenth century the streets of Charleston, a seaport town, often swarmed with very unsavory characters, some of them pirates who were not adverse to breaking into private homes and practicing a little freebooting on land. As a result, private homes were built as the Italians of the Renaissance built their palazzos, with no regular means of entry available from the street, presenting a solid wall to the passerby. Lower windows were few and barred or heavily shuttered, and the side entrance was reached through a gate in a high stone or brick wall that turned the side garden into an enclosed courtyard.

Before you leave Tradd Street look for **106 Tradd,** a three-story Georgian building with an open cupola on top and a long, brick wall closing off the garden. Notice the second-floor windows particularly, for through one of them Francis Marion may have leaped and broken his leg. Marion came from a Huguenot family and took part in the defense of Charleston in both 1776 and 1780. One night during the 1780 siege he attended a stag party given by Captain Alexander McQueen who locked the doors so that no one could leave before drinking his share of the wine. Marion, who wasn't much of a drinker to begin with, rebelled and jumped out a second-floor window, breaking his leg as he landed. He was taken to his home on the Santee River some distance from Charleston to recover and while he was there, Charleston fell and Lincoln surrendered his army. Because of the broken leg, Marion escaped captivity and was free to organize South Carolinian resistance to the British occupation. This may have been the party house, though there is some evidence that the actual house was situated somewhat to the west of 106 and was burned.

Continue along Tradd Street to King Street and turn left to visit the **Pringle House** at 27 King Street. This very imposing structure, with a Georgian entranceway, which may have been added on in later years, was originally the home of Miles Brewton. During the Revolution it was the property of Mrs. Rebecca Motte who lived in it while it was used by Sir Henry Clinton as his residence. Rebecca Motte was one of the heroines of the Revolution. You will meet her again in a more remote site of yet another of her residences. Upstairs on a marble mantel was etched (either with a diamond ring or the point of a bayonet) a full-rigged ship and a profile of Clinton. The artist is believed to have been a British officer. Pringle House is now a private residence and is not open to visitors.

Take Ladson Street, just across the street from the Pringle House, to Meeting Street and to the **Huger House** at 34 Meeting. It is directly opposite the intersection of Ladson and Meeting streets, a three-story building in which Lord William Campbell resided, the last royal governor of the colony. Directly opposite it, on the other side of Meeting Street, is the **William Bull House** at 35 Meeting Street, which was built in 1720 and is one of the oldest buildings in the city.

Now walk back to Broad Street, turn right and walk to Exchange Street. Look for the old **Exchange Building** facing onto East Bay Street, an imposing stucco building with broad steps leading up from two sides to its triple-arched entrance. In the old Exchange met the provincial congress that declared South Carolina independent of Great Britain. Before and since then it was used for a variety of purposes, as a meeting-house and as a customs house in which capacity its basements were used for the storage of customs goods. Since it is the basements you are primar-ily interested in, walk around to the little park at the back of the build-ing and find the entrance to what is now called the **Provost Dungeon.**

Part of the Exchange basement had been used as a jail for pirates and felons. When the British occupied Charleston they used the basement as a prison for rebel South Carolinians, including those they falsely accused of breaking their paroles and any who spoke out against the crown or the occupation. Life-size wax figures arranged in tableaux show how the prisoners were chained by their British guards and under what conditions they lived. The figures are very well done and dressed in authentic costume. They stand, sit, and lie where real people sat and lay two hundred years ago in darkness and dampness, suffering cold, fever, and abuse.

You enter into a museum room at the far right end of which is part of one of the most interesting exhibits you are likely to see anywhere. In 1965 a mysterious hump in the floor of the old Provost was investi-gated. What turned up was part of the Charles Towne sea wall of 1701, a circular section called the **Half-moon Battery** because of a battery of guns mounted on it to guard the harbor. At that time the harbor ex-tended right up to where you are now standing. Further digging revealed the full curve of the Half-moon under the basement floor. It was exca-vated to reveal not only the wall but part of the old harbor bottom as well, which yielded up a treasure trove of artifacts of early Charleston history. In a room to the right of the museum room, you can walk out onto a bridge extending from the Half-moon over the old harbor bottom and see artifacts left as they were found. They include several skeletons or human bones, evidence that a gibbet was once situated on the Half-moon. Before the Exchange was built the city council's watchhouse stood in its place, filling the interior of the Half-moon.

Walk to the back of this room and go through the door to your right into another basement room. At the far end is a brick wall with a window. Through the window you can look down into what looks like a storage room containing a number of small wooden barrels and some small arms. They represent 10,000 pounds of gunpowder that General Moultrie hid here when the British occupied the city. To keep the powder from falling into enemy hands, Moultrie bricked it in and left by a window, so as to leave no trace of his work. The British never found the powder. It was recovered when they evacuated the city two years later.

When you leave the dungeon and walk out into the little park behind the Exchange, remember that where you now walk the waves of Charles Towne Harbor once rolled. Turn around and take another good look at the building. The bricked-up windows were originally open. A piazza ran the length of the building just outside the windows, reached by a flight of steps leading up from the ground. Inside public meetings were held, while outside on the piazza townsfolk congregated to listen to the discussions. At night when the building was empty and closed, the homeless and vagrant slept on the piazza huddled against the wall.

Walk back along Broad Street, turn right onto Meeting Street, and walk two blocks to Cumberland Street. Turn right again. A hundred yards or so down the block is the old **powder magazine** in which powder was stored before and during the Revolution. At present it is administered by the South Carolina Society of Colonial Dames of America whose members take visitors on a guided tour. Actually it is now a museum and treasure house of antiques of the colonial period. At one point in the city's history, a city wall was put up on the opposite side of Cumberland Street. The walls of the powder magazine are more than three feet thick, made of a double thickness of brick with sand in between. The two guns in front are British and were brought here before the Revolution.

Walk back to Meeting Street, cross, and continue straight ahead along narrow Horlbeck Alley. At the far end you will come out on King Street. Cross King Street and continue ahead along Clifford Street, a wider thoroughfare. This brings you out onto Archdale Street. To your left, Magazine Street meets Archdale on the opposite side. Walk along **Magazine Street,** a very pretty street with brick garden walls on either side. It was named for a powder magazine that stood somewhere along its two-block length. On the day the American army surrendered, their muskets were brought here from the surrender site and piled inside the magazine. A Hessian officer tried to warn the British soldiers handling the American pieces that some of them might be loaded. His words came too late or fell on deaf ears. One of the muskets went off and exploded 180 barrels of powder. Many of the soldiers standing around were blown to bits. One man was hurled against the side of the tower of a nearby church. About 200 people were killed and six houses in the vicinity were destroyed. It is doubtful if any but two of the buildings presently on or near the site were there at the time. The **Phillip Portia House**, built in

1765, at one corner and the **Unitarian Church** around the corner on Archdale Street qualify. The records of the explosion talk about the "new" church nearby against which the unfortunate victim was blown. This church was built in 1772 and was used by the British as a stable during the occupation.

To locate the site of Fort Johnson, take U.S. 17 south over the Ashley River. On the other side, take Routes 700–71 to the left. After two and a half miles, you will reach Harbor View Road after seeing a sign on the right for the College of Charleston Marine Science Station. Turn left onto Harbor View Road and drive through a Charleston suburb called Dogwood Park. To the left you will get a magnificent view of Charleston and its waterfront along the Ashley River. After 3.7 miles Harbor View Road dead-ends at a stop sign. Another sign for the marine science station directs you along a road lined with live oaks and suburban ranch homes, then with homes on the right and woodlands on the left. Finally the road runs into a hurricane-fence gate. A sign announces the Marine Resources Center—South Carolina Wildlife Resources Department. The road beyond the gate was marked Private–No Trespassing, but the Charleston guidebooks gave directions for getting right to the fort site, so I assumed the sign did not pertain.

The road becomes a dirt road which leads to the fort. At the time we were there, construction of new buildings for the center was in progress and much of the site had been obliterated. To one side were old frame buildings that were still in use. You are on the east end of the harbor with the city across the water to the left, Fort Sumter off to your right, and Mount Pleasant ahead. Sullivan's Island and Fort Moultrie are to your right beyond Fort Sumter.

Behind the old buildings to the right, as you face the water on a stretch of lawn close to the beach, is an old brick building with a peaked roof. A plaque on it identifies this as the site of **Fort Johnson.** According to the plaque, General William Moultrie raised the "first flag of liberty" on this spot long before the Battle of Sullivan's Island. A fortification had been built here in 1765 from which Moultrie fired on a British sloop and drove it out of the harbor, another act of resistance to the Stamp and Tea acts. There is also a Civil War monument; the first shot of that war was fired from here against Fort Sumter.

A wooded area beyond the monument with sections of chicken-wire fence contains interesting humps of earth that might be the remains of breastworks. On the beach, which we reached through a fringe of trees at the edge of the lawn, we found the brick and stone footings of other structures. A bulldozer was happily working away, putting in a road so that construction machinery could be brought in.

Whether you will find what we found when you visit is problematical. The new labs may be operating, but whether they will completely overshadow the historical significance of the ground they stand on had not been determined. Yet it was here that Clinton's men took the fort's garrison by surprise early in 1780 and thus eliminated one of the two positions dominating the entrance to the harbor, allowing their ships to enter unhindered, except for a few shots from Fort Moultrie across the water.

On your way out, after you have gone back through the hurricane fence, notice a big, white, raised cottage on your right. This is **Marshlands,** a prerevolutionary rice planter's house which originally stood on the other side of the harbor. When it was recently threatened by the construction of a new naval base, it was lifted off its original foundations, placed on a barge, and with most of the city's residents watching, towed across the harbor to its present site. It was a private residence when we passed by and was not open to the public.

Continue along Fort Johnson Road past Harbor View Road (which takes you back to Charleston), across Route 171, and shortly after the 171 intersection onto Riverland Drive to the right. You are on James Island with the Stono River to your left and Johns Island beyond that. Clinton landed his troops at North Edisto Inlet and came across the Stono River at Stono Ferry where he met his first, if slight, resistance, a redoubt or line of redoubts manned by militia. You are driving through what was once plantation country where Eliza Lucas Pinckney introduced the growing of indigo in the eighteenth century. Rice was grown here, too. In the fields off to the left you may notice the remains of what were once flooded rice paddies and flood-control gates. This is the beautiful South Carolina low country, flat and green with broad savannahs off to either side dotted with clumps of live oaks. Old farmhouses and suburban homes appear from time to time and small subdevelopments occasionally sprout up just off the road to the right.

When you see golf links on your right, you are just west of Wappoo Creek along which Clinton hid the boats that eventually carried his men across the Ashley River. Riverland Road ends close to where the creek meets the Stono River. Somewhere in this area is the site of Stono Ferry, unmarked at the time I tried to find it. Somewhere off to the left across the broad, winding Stono the British troops were ferried to march across the road you are now traveling on to camp in nearby areas, where they lived for several weeks before moving onto the Charleston peninsula. This is Civil War country, too. Union and Confederate redoubts and breastworks are visible in many places off in the woods. Here Southern guns dueled with Union ships and batteries along the Stono, and live shells that have to be defused are turned up during plowing with some frequency by the farmers in this region.

If your history buffness extends to the Civil War, then take in Fort Sumter while you are in Charleston. There is also a historical park marking the site of Charles Towne, the original settlement, which features reconstructed sites, gardens, a theater, and a reproduction of a seventeenth-century sailing ship. You can reach it off U.S. 17 by following the signs for Charles Towne Landing.

There are several other sites of particular interest in the Charleston area, including some of the South's and the country's most famous gardens. Among them are the Middleton Gardens, fourteen miles northwest of the city. You reach them by taking U.S. 17 south to Route 61, then 61 to the entrance. The drive is a delightful one once you get away from Charleston's outlying districts. In some wooded areas you will notice Civil War breastworks just off the road. Middleton was the home of Arthur Middleton, a signer of the Declaration of Independence. Most of the original house was burned, but during the Revolution it played host to many of the illustrious Patriots of the era. If you want to get a firsthand idea of what early Southern plantation life was like, see Middleton Gardens. It's on the way to the next site which means you won't be going out of your way.

FORT DORCHESTER

Take Route 61 (west of Charleston) to Route 165 and turn onto 165 in the direction of Summerville. When you come to Route 642, turn right. A sign for Old Dorchester State Park will appear on the right in about two miles. Shortly after you enter the park, you will see the brick remains of the parish **Church of St. George** on the right which was burned by the British, then partially restored before it fell into disuse. The road curves around and leads to a parking area. The remains of the *fort* just beyond are made of tabby wall, a building material made with oyster shells as a binder.

This is the site of the dead town of **Dorchester.** It was laid out in 1697 as a market town by Congregationalists from Dorchester, Massachusetts. Originally it contained 116 quarter-acre lots, a town square, and a commons. It grew during the first half of the eighteenth century, until by 1781 it was a trade center with about forty houses. For some unexplained reason, it declined after the Revolution, until by 1788 it was abandoned. The fort was built during the French and Indian wars.

In 1775 the fort was expanded under the command of Francis Marion. During the Revolution both town and fort changed hands a number of times. The last change occurred in December, 1781, during the final months of the war. The British had surrendered at Yorktown in October less than two months before, but a Tory uprising brought General Nathanael Greene (in command in the South) back into the field. He had already fought the Battle of Eutaw Springs in South Carolina in September, which had so weakened the British regular army that British domination of the South was virtually at an end. As Greene moved against the Tories, he decided to take Dorchester, which was garrisoned by almost 900 men. He and Colonel Wade Hampton approached with about 400 men while the rest of the army was sent on to Round O, to encamp. The Dorchester commander learned that Greene was among the officers leading the approaching enemy column, concluded that the entire army must be with him, and after some skirmishing ordered the stores destroyed and the guns thrown into the river and withdrew toward Charleston.

Tabby walls are interesting because they are studded with recognizable pieces of oyster shell. The shells and the lime made from them make for a very tough substance which stands up to the weathering of the years remarkably well to judge by the remains of Fort Dorchester. The fort's remains consist of a squarish, empty enclosure. You can walk into it to explore a bastion that goes off to the right and one to the left. Trees have grown up inside the fort and there is a back exit, or old sally port, directly opposite the main entrance. The ground falls away in back and as you walk out you discover a curtain wall to the left protruding from the enclosure. At the foot of the slope runs the Ashley River where there was probably a landing to receive supplies. To the left of the fort as you face it from the parking area, you will notice rest rooms. Close to the rest rooms on the brow of the hill we found a picket fence enclosing what was obviously an archaeological dig. You can explore the empty shell of the old church as well. There are picnic facilities here and a chance to do some fishing in the river.

BATTLE OF PORT ROYAL ISLAND

Retrace your route to Route 165 and take it south. Instead of going back onto Route 61, continue south to U.S. 17 and go farther south on it. After forty miles, when you reach Gardens Corners, make a left onto Route 21 south. You are now heading for the town of **Beaufort** (pronounced Boford), which is near the marine corps base on Parris Island. It is also the site of an engagement that took place in February, 1779, while Generals Lincoln and Prevost were facing each other across the Savannah River after the British had taken Savannah.

Prevost set up a naval landing operation by which Major Gardiner was to occupy Port Royal Island in an attempt to come up behind Lincoln's rear about thirty miles away. General Moultrie was waiting for him in Beaufort with a force of militia and a couple of cannon. In about five miles from the turnoff onto 21, you will cross the Whale Branch of the Coosaw River. In 1779 a ferry was in operation where that bridge is now. Moultrie came over the ferry and waited at Halfway House, a tavern at Gray's Hill, for the Beaufort militia to respond to his summons. The tavern was so named because it was midway between the ferry and Beaufort. About 3.4 miles farther you will see a half-mile warning sign for a historical marker and then the marker for the tavern on the right side of the road. To follow the course of the action in sequence, however, drive into Beaufort, a pretty, busy town on **Port Royal Island** tucked into a bend of the Beaufort River.

There has been a settlement on this spot for 400 years since the first Scottish emigrants arrived in the sixteenth century. They were followed by the Spanish, then the French, and finally the English, who established the town that was here during the Revolution and is here today. John Morall, the town's unofficial historian who probably knows more of the history of the town and county than anyone else, traced the course of the Battle of Port Royal Island for us and explained the site.

On Wednesday, February 3, 1779, the Beaufort militia gathered at the arsenal, now the **Beaufort Museum** on Craven Street between Scott and Carteret streets. From there they marched north on what is now Route 21. Follow their line of march back to the marker you noticed on your way to Beaufort. It will now appear on your left. The site of the battle, which took place across the road, is marked by a small roadside *park* with picnic tables and the Beaufort water tower close by. Hopefully the marker and park will still be there when you cover the site. Road construction was adding two lanes to Route 21 when we visited.

The British probably approached from the Broad River to the west of this site. The militia were lined up across the road in the open; the British had the advantage of wooded terrain. Ammunition ran out for both sides and both started to withdraw. Moultrie realized what was happening and ordered his few mounted troops to pursue Gardiner, but the British returned to their boats safely and got away to Savannah.

American losses were eight killed and twenty-two wounded. Every British officer involved in the action is supposed to have been wounded and British casualties in general were said to have been heavy. There is little here to remind you of the battle, though there is the low, swampy ground in the area which may correspond to the swamp area Moultrie mentions in his account of the battle. Moultrie wrote that he tried to reach that area before the British, probably to get his men under cover, but Gardiner beat him to it.

SHELDON CHURCH

Take Route 21 north, retracing your route to U.S. 17. Where 17 goes right and 17–21 goes left, follow 17–21 0.5 mile to a road, S721, leading off to the right. A sign at the intersection reads "Old Sheldon Church—Two Miles." Turn onto S721 for 1.6 miles to the ruins of Sheldon Church on the right side of the road. The lovely, haunting remains are surrounded by live oaks, some of them very old, and a number of old graves and tombstones. This is what is left of a church that was destroyed during the Civil War. It stands on the site of a former church that was burned by the British in 1779. The brick shell with its four brick columns and the tall, arched windows forming a ghostly colonnade, are well worth seeing if only for the beauty and romance of the spot. There are picnic tables under the oaks. Memorial services are held here every year on the second Sunday after Easter.

Take S721 back to U.S. 17–21 and continue back to where 21 branches off to the left toward Beaufort. Stay on 17 heading north; you are on your way to Parker's Ferry.

BATTLE OF PARKER'S FERRY

U.S. 17 will take you clear across Colleton County to a juncture with Route 64. Turn left onto 64 and proceed northwest until you see a dirt road to the right and a historical marker for the **grave** of Colonel Isaac Hayne. Drive down the dirt road for a mile to a small graveyard enclosed by a hurricane fence with two stone gateposts surmounted by mourning urns. Isaac Hayne was a South Carolina militia officer who was captured at Charleston in 1780 and paroled. When the British tried to force him to join the British army, he decided that his captors had violated the parole and therefore he was free to resume his former activities.

Back in service again with the militia, he took part in the recapture of General Andrew Williamson. Williamson had been the Whig commander in the first Revolutionary War action at Ninety-six. He had submitted to the British when they took Ninety-six, however, and had remained inactive. Williamson was rescued and Hayne was recaptured at the same time, charged with treason, imprisoned in the old Provost in Charleston, and hanged on August 4, 1781. The British were accused of hanging him improperly for violating his parole, which they themselves had violated. They insisted they had hanged Hayne for his subsequent activities during which, they said, he had played the role of a spy.

The British thus created a martyr and a controversy that is not exactly dead in South Carolina. Hayne's grave is now a shrine and there are other memorials to him in other parts of the state. The grave site took on additional significance in August, 1781, when Francis Marion joined forces with a local body of militia to ambush a column of British dragoons who had been sent here to support the Tory uprising Greene was trying to suppress.

To find the site of the ambush return to Route 64, turn right, and in a half mile you will see a road on the right marked by a sign for Round O. Take that road a short distance to a dirt road going off to the right, marked by a sign reading "Battleground, Seven Miles." Turn right for a seven-mile drive along a dirt road that leads through nowhere, with woodlands on both sides, other dirt roads leading off to left and right, sometimes with gates blocking them, and not a house or sign of a human being anywhere. At the end of about 6.2 miles, the road turns sharply to the left. As it turns you will see a sign for "Revolutionary Breastworks" and the **breastworks** themselves to the right off the road.

You can climb to the top of the breastworks and walk their length to where they are split by a road that leads to the Edisto River a few hundred feet away. At the time we were there that road was flooded and it was impossible to reach the riverbank. The breastworks continue beyond on the other side of the road for a short distance. Signs along the breastworks identify them as "hallowed ground." Since no American casualties were suffered in the ambush, I thought the signs were unwarranted and unnecessary on an otherwise well-preserved historic site.

After the fall of Charleston to Clinton in 1780, effective rebel resistance to British rule was broken and disorganized until several rebel leaders managed to collect enough men and supplies to carry on the struggle. One of these was Francis Marion, who developed a strategy of guerilla warfare that is studied to this day. Living off the land, he moved his men from place to place, striking the enemy wherever he could. His attacks were so effective and became such a source of worry to the British that in October, 1780, Cornwallis finally sent Banastre Tarleton to track him down and destroy him. The Tarleton-Marion duel of wits and strategy is one of the legendary and epic stories of the Revolution.

By 1781 Marion and his guerillas were playing a coordinated role in

Greene's campaigns in the South. When he was dispatched by Greene to assist Colonel William Harden in his attempt to stop Major Thomas Fraser's 200 dragoons, he made a forced march of 100 miles with 200 men and set up an ambush on this spot along the causeway leading to Parker's Ferry. On Monday, August 13, 1781, he lured Fraser into the trap and shot the British command to pieces from behind these breastworks without losing a man. Fraser charged the position three times and each time was hit by a volley at short range that emptied saddles and sent him in retreat. British casualties may have been as high as 100, or 50 percent of his troops in this one, small action.

The character of the area is probably as it was in 1781, though I could find no sign of the causeway other than the road to the river. Thick, tangled woods surround the breastworks on three sides, but they are in full view from the river side. This is a wild, lonely place. The signs leading to and on the breastworks were recently made, showing there is local interest in preserving the site and attracting visitors.

Continue along the dirt road in the direction you were following for another 5.5 miles to a hard surface road. Turn left onto this road (17A) toward Cottageville. Take 17A through Cottageville and beyond for a little over two miles. A half-mile warning sign for a historical marker will alert you (the South Carolina Highway Department provides half-mile warning signs for roadside parks and historical markers) to **Round O.** At the half-mile point, you come to the intersection with Route 45. The marker, which is a little beyond the intersection on the left, identifies the area as a campground for Greene's army and his headquarters in December, 1781. According to the marker, he was here to offer his protection to the state assembly which was meeting in Jacksonboro to the southeast. Round O is open farm country and a few houses and stores at a crossroads. There does not seem to be any evidence remaining of the encampment or of Greene's headquarters.

The road from here leads north to Monck's Corner, the Francis Marion National Forest sites, and a tour of other sites connected with the Swamp Fox.

WEST OF CHARLESTON

MONCK'S CORNER

Turn around and head east along 17A back through Cottageville and beyond and into Berkeley County. Where 17A meets U.S. 52 there are two small triangles of grass. One of them is next to the Berkeley Motel close to a stop sign. Here on April 14, 1780, as part of Sir Henry Clinton's siege of Charleston, a British force under Tarleton cut the American line of communications to Charleston only thirty miles away and captured an important supply depot. According to the marker, Colonel William Washington, cousin to the commander in chief and a popular southern war hero, was surprised by a superior force and routed. Actually General Isaac Huger was in command of the force that was guarding both the Monck's Corner depot and Biggin's Bridge, a short distance from this spot.

You can reach the present *bridge* by going north along U.S. 52 until it crosses the Tail Race Canal connecting the west branch of the Cooper River with Lake Moultrie. (Lake Moultrie is an artificial lake created by damming the Cooper River.) Huger posted mounted troops under Washington near the bridge and militia on the bridge itself. Tarleton took advantage of Washington's lack of security, routed his men in an attack that almost cost Washington his life, and sent the militia flying. The Americans lost about twenty killed and wounded, and sixty-seven men fell into British hands as prisoners. According to Tarleton, he also captured about 400 American cavalry horses and suffered only three wounded. The British subsequently built redoubts here and remained in control until July, 1781.

Cross the bridge, continue north for a short distance along 52 until you come to the intersection with Route 402. Take 402 to the right (east) and head for Huger and Quinby Bridge twenty miles away. A short distance along 402 takes you to the ruins of **Biggin Church** which was burned by Lieutenant Colonel John Coates of the British army in 1781. At the time Coates was in command at the British outpost at Monck's Corner. General Thomas Sumter was a partisan leader and guerilla fighter like Marion, but unlike Marion he sometimes balked when he was asked to cooperate with Continental Army forces, as Greene discovered. Sumter, who was called the Gamecock, preferred to fight the war in his own way. He moved in July, 1781, against Coates who dropped back to a strong position around the church which had been fortified. Finally Coates decided to withdraw, put the torch to the church, and moved down the Cooper River to Quinby Bridge. The remains of the brick colonnaded walls of Biggin Church will remind you of Sheldon Church. There isn't as much of the building left, but the spot is just as attractive.

As you approach Huger, you will be driving past the Santee Experimental Forest on your left and then Francis Marion National Forest on your right. In Huger 402 meets Routes 41 and 98 going off to the right. Go right and notice the warning sign for a historical marker as soon as you make the turn. Drive to the marker (on the right), a hundred or so feet before a bridge which crosses a creek. The marker for **Quinby Bridge** stands in an open parking area off the shoulder of the road, a favorite spot for local fishermen who can launch their boats from here.

When Coates arrived, he loosened the planks of the bridge preparatory to removing them once his rear guard arrived. Henry Lee, whom, with Marion, Greene had lent temporarily to Sumter, had caught up with the British rear guard, however, and forced it to surrender. By this time, Coates's men were strung out along a causeway which led from the south end of the bridge and also down a lane leading off the causeway. When the American dragoons appeared, Coates got the column organized into a defensive position and placed a howitzer at his end of the bridge. Marion's dragoons under Armstrong charged, followed by supporting units, right into the howitzer. As they came over the bridge, they knocked the planks into the water, leaving the men behind them to cross on the stringers. Somehow they got over and fell upon Coates's command. Coates himself was attacked by Armstrong but managed to get away. Most of his men broke and ran across the fields to find shelter in some buildings attached to the Quemby Plantation which stood nearby.

Coates formed his men into a square using the buildings as part of his defense. Later that day Sumter arrived on the scene, organized an attack, and placed his men in the center where they were able to get some protection from the plantation buildings. The other units, including Marion's brigade, spearheaded the attack which at one end of the line had to be carried across open fields. As a result the flank units suffered heavy casualties, which was also due to Sumter's failure to bring up his artillery to support the action. The next day both Marion and Lee led their men out from under Sumter's command. By that time a British relief column was approaching and Sumter had to withdraw.

The **Quinby Bridge Road** along which Coates's men and the pursuing American cavalry moved ran from the Quemby Plantation (named for Quemby Hall in England), which stood near the junction in Huger of Charity Church Road and Green Bay Road, across Quinby Creek to a point close to Huger Bridge. According to a local legend about Quinby Bridge, many of the Americans killed in the fighting were buried along this road. Two of them had been found holding hands and lying in such a way that their bodies blocked the road. Sometime after rural free delivery was introduced, the mailman was uncommonly late one day delivering the mail. When he was asked what had delayed him, he said that his passage over Quinby Bridge had been blocked by two men in uniform who stood in front of him holding hands, refusing to allow him to pass.

I have some doubts concerning this site. MacReady in his *History of South Carolina in the Revolution* writes that Sumter was in a great hurry to get to Quinby Bridge, hoping to keep Coates from destroying it since it was the only crossing over the east branch of the Cooper River for miles. The bridge near the marker crosses Quinby Creek, however, not the river which is a half mile or so to the west.

If you cross the bridge and go up the road a little way, you will see a dirt road leading off to the right to Quemby Plantation. The day we were there a padlocked gate blocked that road as effectively as any two men, alive or dead, so that it was impossible to investigate the site of the fighting there. If you have no better luck, turn around and go back to where 98 turned off from Route 41. Take 41 north, being careful to follow the jog 41 leads you through before it straightens itself out and heads for Jamestown, fifteen miles away, and Lenud's Ferry.

LENUD'S FERRY

Route 41 takes you through part of Francis Marion National Forest. The swampy area on your right is known as Hell Hole Bay which requires some explanation since this is a far remove from the ocean. South Carolina seen from the air is pockmarked with strange, rather circular, low-lying areas, usually sandy and covered with marsh vegetation, that so resemble the "seas" on the surface of the moon they are called "bays." The forest is home for a number of animals, including deer, bear, alligators, and campers. Since you will be in the forest on foot to find two sites, and to find one you will follow a foot trail, let me assure you concerning the question of the gators. The park rangers say that most of the stories one hears or has heard concerning alligators are simply not true. Alligators are very timid of man and with good cause, considering the value he has placed on their skins. In Francis Marion National Forest they spend their time wallowing in mudholes that are remote from the scent and sight of humankind. Rarely are gators seen by the forest's human visitors unless a deliberate effort is made to seek them out. You may see deer, however, and pheasant and quail as well.

At Jamestown U.S. 17A joins Route 41. A half mile from the juncture is a marker for the Battle of Lenud's Ferry which actually took place between the marker and the concrete *bridge* a half mile beyond that replaced the ferry that once crossed the Santee River there.

After the action at Monck's Corner on April 14, 1780, Lenud's

Ferry became one of several places along the Santee River where the rebel survivors gathered to re-form. Among the men gathered here was a force of about 350 under the command of Colonel Abraham Buford, who had been trying to get through to Charleston to assist Lincoln in its defense. The news of Lincoln's surrender stopped him cold.

In the meantime, Tarleton was continuing his sweep through the Cooper and Santee river country. When he learned of the American forces at Lenud's Ferry, he attacked on the afternoon of Saturday, May 6. The Americans were caught entirely by surprise, including a cavalry detachment that had just captured some of Tarleton's men at a nearby plantation and were preparing to take them across the Santee into captivity. Tarleton's men killed and wounded about forty-one of the rebels, made sixty-seven officers and men prisoners, and freed their own men. Many of the Americans at the ferry escaped by swimming the river.

Cross the Santee River and head north along U.S. 17A–Route 41 to the next site, one of four connected with a campaign that was directed specifically against Marion.

THE SWAMP FOX AT WORK

Look for Route 21 going off U.S. 17A to the left and take it to County Road 16 which again goes to the left. Follow 16 to an intersection with County Road 219. Turn right onto 219 and take it to State Road 377. Turn right onto 377. Shortly after it intersects U.S. 521, it crosses the Black River. It was here at **Lower Bridge** that Marion fought the second of a series of engagements against a British force under Lieutenant Colonel John W. T. Watson. Watson's mission was to disperse Marion and his men. All through March, 1781, he followed Marion along a line that eventually led from Wyboo Swamp to the west in Clarendon County to near Georgetown on the coast.

The action was fought in the immediate vicinity of the present highway bridge where it crosses the Black River. The piles that were put down for the bridge have undoubtedly destroyed the original bridge site and left nothing but the general area and the river.

Return to U.S. 521 and turn left to take it southeast back to Route 21 in Andrews. Turn left onto 21 and take it north. Eventually Route 41 will join 21 at a stop sign. Bear left or north along 41 toward the Battle of Black Mingo Swamp.

Continue north along 41, but stay alert for an intersection at which County 24 comes in from the left and State Road 51 comes in from the right. About two miles beyond, you will come to a bridge that crosses **Black Mingo Creek.** It was near here on Thursday, September 14, 1780, that a band of about forty-six Tories under Colonel John Coming Ball were attacked by Marion and his men. At the time, the crossing was served by Shepherd's Ferry. The ferry passengers were served by Dollard's Tavern which stood nearby. Colonel Ball and his men were stationed here as an outpost for the British in Georgetown. Marion had been at one of his camps north of the creek on the Peedee River when he heard about Ball and his men and decided to attack. Though the Americans approached the ferry quietly, a British sentry heard them as they crossed a bridge a mile upstream, to your left as you face the bridge from the south. Though Ball was alerted, Marion continued to move into position for attack, swinging around the ferry and coming up from the south.

Drive back for a half mile to the actual site of the battle. Ball deployed his men in a field. Marion moved north along what is now Route 41. The fight lasted for fifteen minutes and ended when Marion turned the enemy's right. The Tories fled into the *swamp* which is still there, off to your left as you face north. Marion lost two dead and eight wounded, the Tories three dead and thirteen wounded and captured.

Now return along 41 to Andrews as you travel toward the site of the final engagement between Marion and Watson at Sampit Bridge.

Take U.S. 521 east out of Andrews staying alert for U.S. 17A which will come in at an angle from your right. At the juncture of 521 and 17A, turn right onto 17A which, in half a mile, will take you to a small bridge over a branch of the **Sampit River.** There was no bridge on March 20, 1781, when Watson arrived early in the evening on his way back to Georgetown after chasing Marion unsuccessfully and decided to ford the stream. As his men splashed across, there was a sudden volley of shots from the woods. Marion's men attacked, catching Watson's detachment in midstream and in no position to form and answer. Within a few minutes, Watson lost twenty killed and an even larger number wounded. His losses forced him to abandon his mission, which made this the last of the Watson-Marion encounters. Marion is supposed to have lost only one man.

Return north on 17A to the juncture with 521 and follow the combined road east to Georgetown to a site associated with the Sampit site. As you come into Georgetown, you will reach the usual city fringe, small-home developments, stores, and automobile showrooms. Soon after you pass the Georgetown city limits sign, look for White's Bridge Drive on your left, and turn left onto it. There is a historical marker at the intersection to guide you. The *marker* commemorates the site of Gabriel Marion's execution.

Turn right onto White's Bridge Drive. It will take you north for a short distance before it swings left and becomes a dirt road. This is a residential neighborhood bisected by at least two small creeks, one of which was spanned by White's Bridge. According to the marker Gabriel Marion, the Swamp Fox's nephew, was part of a reconnaissance force sent to patrol the area in January, 1781. The patrol ran into a band of Tories; shots were exchanged, and Gabriel Marion was captured. The Tories discovered his identity and killed him. The bridge is no longer in evidence. White's Bridge Road dead-ends in front of a private home with low ground beyond, which may or may not mark the creek.

According to Bass's biography of Marion and Boatner's account, however, the incident occurred on or about November 15, 1780. Marion made an attempt to capture Georgetown, but met stiff resistance at White's Plantation. (The plantation would account for the name given to the bridge; obviously it was on the road leading to the plantation. The plantation might have been on the other side of present 521, however, on the Sampit River.) One of his patrols met Captain Jesse Barefield's Tories in a swamp near another plantation. In the ensuing melee, Gabriel Marion was unhorsed and captured and then killed sometime after near this spot. According to this account, the action was more extensive than a mere reconnaissance. The greatest discrepancy between the two accounts is in the dates.

Unfortunately it proved impossible to check out the facts by consulting local records because most of Georgetown's official documents, records, and files were destroyed during the Civil War. Since the town was vulnerable to Union attack because of its position on the coast, all of its records were sent to Atlanta for safekeeping. Fate twisted the screw. Atlanta was burned; Georgetown was damaged but spared.

GEORGETOWN

Return to 521, turn left and drive into Georgetown to cover its few Revolutionary War sites. Two of the sites are connected with the British occupation, which began when Cornwallis established a British post here in the summer of 1780. **British headquarters** were in a building that stood on the corner of Front Street (the town's main avenue running parallel to the Sampit River a half block away) and Broad Street. At present the site is occupied by an old bank building which was empty at the time of our visit. The marker is on the Broad Street side of the building.

A block and a half from Front Street, on the same side of Broad Street as the headquarters site, is the **Bolen-Bellume House** at 222 Broad. A two-story, frame house with a louvered attic, this was the residence of the British commanding officer. The question I tried to answer without success was, "Which commanding officer?" On January 24, 1781, Marion and Lee raided Georgetown and captured the commander, Colonel Campbell. I was not able to find any record of where Campbell lived while he was in Georgetown other than a reference to the parade ground which is supposed to have been close to his quarters. There has been some research by the local historical society to determine the site of the parade ground, but whether 222 Broad Street is where Marion and his men grabbed Colonel Campbell remains a mystery.

Continue up Broad Street in the same direction to Highmarket Street which meets Broad at right angles. Cross Highmarket and park in front of the **Prince George Winyah Church** at the corner on your right. This church was put to the same use the British reserved for other churches whenever they occupied a rebel town: it became a stable for their horses, which are supposed to have left their hoof marks on the floor. We examined the old stone floor wherever we could find a part of it not covered by the rug, but were unable to find anything that looked like a hoofprint.

The most interesting building in Georgetown is the **Rice Museum** which was built in 1825. Turn the car around, return down Broad Street to Front Street, turn left and drive one block to the foot of Screven Street. To your right, facing Screven, is a brick building with a clock tower in front and a flight of steps leading up to a second-floor entrance. The Rice Museum looks like the market buildings you have seen in Philadelphia and Boston, but on a smaller scale. It was a market building for the rice planters of the area. A marker on the museum commemorates the first landing of Lafayette in America at Georgetown on June 13, 1777. Actually the marquis landed on a nearby island called North Island. From here he and his friends, all French adventurers, traveled to Philadelphia to offer their services to the Continental Congress. The Rice Museum's exhibits have to do with the history of rice and jute cultivation in the area. They are very well done and explain what this South Carolina lowland country was like at the time of the Revolution.

Return along Front Street four blocks to Wood Street; turn right onto Wood, and take it four blocks to Church Street, which is also U.S. 17. Turn left and almost immediately notice a road going off diagonally to the right. Take it and follow it onto U.S. 701.

Continue north on 701 until you see the Georgetown Country Club on your right and a short distance farther on, the Georgetown Shopping Plaza to your left. Somewhere in this area a local Revolutionary War hero, Sergeant McDonald, caught up with and bayoneted Major Gainly after his Tory command had been routed in a skirmish that took place, according to a marker that once stood here, in January, 1781. If this is the same action in which Gabriel Marion lost his life, however, the same discrepancy in dates may exist here as well. This site gives us some geographical perspective on the White's Bridge road site about two miles southwest. In fact, it might give us an approximate site for the plantation on which the action took place. However, the entire area has been built over with small homes, larger private residences, shopping centers, filling stations, and other characteristicly urban features.

WAMBAW CREEK

Turn back on 701 and pick up U.S. 17 south in Georgetown. You are now en route to the Francis Marion National Forest to cover the battle at Wambaw Creek and to visit the site of a plantation that may have played a role in the action. The old rice plantations, or the land they once occupied, stretch off to the horizon on all sides, flat marshlands bisected by old irrigation and drainage ditches, with clumps of trees and distant woods standing out like islands and headlands in a lake of level green. You will pass over the north and south branches of the Santee River and then enter Charleston County. A little more than a mile beyond the Santee look for County Road S857 which crosses 17. A furniture store, Bonnie Barnes, occupies a white frame building at the intersection. A sign reading "Big Game Check Station" appears to one side of the road as you turn right onto S857.

After a while, the road becomes a dirt road which will curve to the left and eventually take you through a gate onto a road marked 211, Mill Branch Road. Shortly before that point, you will reach an intersection with signs announcing Elmwood Wildlife Station to the right and Still Landing Boat Ramp to the left. Turn right toward the wildlife station and go through a camping area with picnic tables and a camp building showing off to the left. This is the Waterhorn or Watchorn recreation area. The road dead-ends into another road. A sign indicates the wildlife station to the left, but this time turn right. You are still driving on dirt roads with beautiful forest lands around you. At one point the road swings left as another road goes to the right. You go onto 204, Echaw Road which leads through low, boggy land on both sides. When you come to a bridge crossing a creek, you have reached **Wambaw Bridge** the site of one of Marion's last military engagements.

In January, 1782, Marion was attending a meeting of the general assembly at Jacksonboro to which he had been elected a member. Yorktown was over and though there were no more large-scale battles or campaigns shaping up, the British were still in the South in some force and some skirmishing and fighting was still going on. A feud had broken out between two of Marion's dragoon commanders, Colonels Peter Horry and Hezekiah Maham. Colonel Benjamin Thompson in Charleston, which was still in British hands, heard that Marion's brigades were disorganized and decided the opportunity was too good to pass up. He crossed the Cooper River was 200 mounted troops, 500 infantry, and two cannon and moved east across what is now the national forest, advancing on this site.

Marion's men under Colonel Horry were encamped on the north side of Wambaw Creek. If you cross the bridge, you will be on the American side of the creek. At that time, two roads met here; one went to Lenud's Ferry, the other to a plantation belonging to a relative of Horry's whose own plantation was on the other side of the Santee River. On February 24, Horry decided to visit his home and crossed the river, leaving the brigade under the command of Colonel McDonald. Maham's brigade was elsewhere and Maham, also a legislator, was in Jacksonboro with Marion. Thompson's force approached the Americans from the west by forced marches and by mounting the infantry behind the cavalrymen for part of the way.

If you face in the direction from which you came, the British attack would have been coming at you from your right and left front. The American forces were disposed from Wambaw Creek to Echaw Creek to your right. Most of the American officers were sitting down to dinner and at first did not believe reports of the enemy's proximity. Then firing broke out and they believed. Major Benison advanced Horry's dragoons over the bridge and formed about 100 yards down the road you came up. Thompson's mounted militia faced Benison. The rest of the British force came up and suddenly charged. Most of Benison's men were recruits and they broke, falling back across the bridge while the pursuing British shot and cut them down. Luckily the bridge broke under the weight of men and horses and the British advance was checked. The rest of the American force fell back, leaving forty dead behind and four of their men prisoners.

When the news reached Marion, he and Maham hurried back to the Wambaw, which was about forty miles from Jacksonboro. They did not stop until they had reached the Tydiman Plantation at a point about five miles from the British. Thompson, who was driving off a herd of captured cattle he had gathered along his line of march, discovered two American pickets near the Tydiman home. Realizing Marion's men were again in the vicinity, Thompson formed his line quickly and advanced. The Americans rushed into position with the infantry along a rail fence and the dragoons in column; Marion ordered the dragoons to charge. As they did, they inclined to the left to avoid a pond, breaking ranks. Thompson took advantage, charged, and routed them. Many had to escape by swimming the Santee, which is about a half mile from Wambaw Bridge.

As the rest of the British command advanced, a party of Americans managed to get to the bridge and raised it, stopping the British reserves. The Americans had had enough warning this time to form. Nevertheless, the British claimed to have killed twenty and taken twelve prisoners, which is probably close to the truth. The Swamp Fox had only one more opportunity to get his licks in at the British at Fair Lawn the following summer before the peace was signed. Thompson, who later became Count Rumford, is well known even today for his contributions to physics.

The area around Wambaw Creek probably closely resembles the same area two hundred years ago. The creek remains and there is still a bridge, woodlands, and even the remains of a plantation not far away. The forest is almost all pine now, however, and one of the logging roads that were laid out at the beginning of this century probably destroyed the rise of ground on which the Americans formed to meet the British advance.

To find the plantation site, drive a little farther on from the bridge to the first road going off to the right. It is closed to vehicular traffic by a gate. Park on the side of the road or pull off, walk around the gate, and follow the trail in for a half mile or so. Eventually you will come across rubble heaps to the left of the path covered with brambles and vines in a grove of beautiful, old, live oaks. Poke around the vines and find bricks and bits of mortar, the remains of what may have been the **Elias Horry Plantation**. The Santee River is close by. If you walk on a little way, you will see the land slope down toward the stream, which is blocked from your view by the forest.

The walk through the woods to reach the plantation site will be a treat if you appreciate forest lands. The site itself at the end of the walk, with its great, old trees which were there when the plantation house was whole and the vine-covered ruins is a haunted spot.

Retrace your route through the forest to S857; take it back to U.S. 17–701; turn right, and head south on 17 to County 45. Turn right onto 45 and follow it through the forest to Jamestown where you pick up U.S. 17A. Take 17A back to Monck's Corner where it intersects State

Route 6, which will take you west to Eutaw Springs, the site of the last major battle fought during the Revolution in South Carolina.

EUTAW SPRINGS

As you come into the town of Eutaw Springs, look for the battle-field site on the right side of the road. The site is a *park* set off by an iron picket fence pierced by a gate with brick gateposts. Inside are several markers and memorials and beyond an inlet of Lake Marion. Private homes and the usual roadside buildings border the park. A good portion of the scene has been under water since the Santee River was dammed to form Lake Marion. At the time of the battle most of the water you now see beyond the trees, including the little cove where local fishermen launch their boats, was dry land. The road was there, the same one that passes the site today. At that time it was a part of the main Charleston Road. It forked just about where it forks now, beyond the park where Routes 6 and 45 go off to the right and 137 continues on to skirt the lake.

There is a map plaque here that shows the disposition of the armies and their movements. Note also the grave of Major John Marjoribanks, a British officer. In reconstructing the scene, remember that the park was the site of an encampment of approximately 2,000 British and Tory troops under the command of Lieutenant Colonel Alexander Stewart. Nelson's Ferry on the Santee River was nearby. Face the plaque and you are generally facing into Greene's advance. Behind you and to your right was Eutaw Creek which led to the springs for which the place was famous. The creek and springs have since been covered by Lake Marion. In that general area was a brick building, probably part of the Roche Plantation that Stewart had fortified as a precaution. Marjoribanks and his men were stationed in a thicket immediately to your right.

In March, 1781, Cornwallis won a victory at Guilford Courthouse in North Carolina, but was forced to retreat to Wilmington. This left Greene free to enter South Carolina and operate against the chain of interior posts the British had established. Beginning in April, 1781, Greene moved against Camden, Fort Watson, and Ninety-six, fighting losing battles, winning occasional victories, but always weakening the British and forcing them through attrition to give up their outposts and fall back toward Charleston. By the time Greene moved down out of the Santee Hills, where he had been resting his men after failing to take Ninety-six, Cornwallis was in Virginia. This left British fortunes in the Carolinas in the hands of capable subordinates like Francis Rawdon and Alexander Stewart who were forced to operate with little or no support.

By now all that was still under British control in the South was Savannah and Charleston.

This was the general strategic situation as Greene began his approach to Eutaw Springs from a position seven miles to the west early on a Saturday morning, September 8, 1781. Warned of his approach, Stewart formed his line some distance beyond this immediate area in front of you as you face the plaque, while an advance unit met the Americans four miles away and did their best to delay them. The British reserves were to your left rear. As the engagement became general up and down the line, Greene attempted to turn the British left flank (to your left). Though some of the American militia units broke under British attack, the British left flank and center also broke and their camp was overrun. Marjoribanks, however, was able to hold fast in his position and so were the defenders of the brick house, despite the guns that were brought to bear on them.

While this was going on the militia and Continentals entered the British camp, forgot the battle, and raided the tents instead. The food and drink they found spurred them on to further looting and the American center fell into disorganization. Taking advantage of this, Marjoribanks led a spirited counterattack, captured the guns, and swept the Americans from the field. He received a death wound in the process, but his action turned what should have been an American victory into a defeat.

Greene's army suffered 500 casualties, but the British lost 693, which Boatner distinguishes as the highest percentage of men involved lost by any army or other unit during the Revolution. As a result, Stewart was no longer able to hold his position at Nelson's Ferry and had to withdraw to Charleston. This was the fourth battle Greene had lost, but he was, nevertheless, the victor. The losses he managed to inflict on the British in these engagements, combined with the number of interior posts he managed to capture, loosened the British hold on the South and forced them back into their beachheads in Charleston and Savannah. A month later Cornwallis, forced back into Yorktown with the French fleet cutting off help from his own navy, surrendered and the war was lost for the crown.

MARION'S TOMB

Turn back along Routes 6 and 45 in the direction from which you came. When you get to where 45 goes off to the left and 6 goes straight ahead, follow 45. Four or five miles farther on, you will cross the Diversion Canal which connects Lakes Marion and Moultrie. Five miles beyond the canal, a warning sign for a historical marker will alert you to the turnoff for Marion's tomb. On your left will appear an iron picket fence with brick gateposts and a marker announcing Francis Marion's grave. Turn onto the long approach road that takes you to the tomb. The road dead-ends at a fence. The *burial plot* is to the left surrounded by a hurricane fence. A smaller enclosure within an iron picket fence contains the last resting place of one of the first practitioners of modern guerilla warfare.

Marion was born in 1732. The location of his early home is unknown. In his memoirs, Henry Lee describes him "as about forty-eight years of age, small of stature, hard of visage, healthy, abstemious, and taciturn." Lee relates how his first meeting with Marion came about only after a long and difficult search. By luck Lee came across a band of foragers from Marion's camp who undertook to guide him to the place. Marion, however, had changed his position since the foragers had left camp and his own men had to search diligently before they could locate him. Lee further describes him as "a rigid disciplinarian. . . . Columbia itself never charged him with violating the rights of person, property or of humanity. The country from Camden to the seacoast between the Peedee and Santee rivers was the theater of his exertions."

The general rests in a raised sarcophagus, his wife in a smaller tomb beside him. The other graves are those of members of the Marion families and their descendants, some by marriage. Marion's original tomb was like his wife's, but a falling tree crushed it, and it was replaced by the general assembly of South Carolina in 1893.

It was impossible to determine if Belle Isle Plantation, the family plantation, still exists or if any remains are visible. The area around the tomb is fenced off and the plantation roads in evidence are gated and padlocked. The site of Francis Marion's own plantation is now under the water of Lake Marion.

For a tour of other sites in this part of the state connected with Marion, continue along Route 45 to U.S. 52. Take 52 north to U.S. 521, turn left onto 521, and take it for three miles to the town of Greeleyville. Watch the signs carefully and follow 521 on into Manning fifteen miles away.

THE SWAMP FOX AT BAY

This is a tour within a tour which we were fortunate to take under the expert guidance of a local resident and officer of the county historical society whose family has lived in the state since prerevolutionary times. He has not only lived here for most of his adult life, but has made the researching and finding of the sites you will now visit a second vocation.

Take U.S. 301 north out of Manning to an intersection with County Road S14–50. This is Wilson's Crossroads, distinguished when we were there by a '76 filling station. Turn left onto 50 and continue west with the Black River and its swamps to the right. Within a mile and a half, the road crosses **Tearcoat Creek** over a concrete *bridge* and continues on with swamp on both sides. Continue over the overpass that crosses Interstate 95 and look to the right across open field and ahead to a line of trees (a windbreak) going off to the right from the road. The road dips down into a swampy area. This was part of the old Durant Plantation. Somewhere along the line of trees is located the old Durant family cemetery. The windbreak divides two fields, the farther of which is believed to be the old militia **Muster Ground.**

In the fall of 1780, Marion was doing what he could to harass the enemy. When he learned that the Salem Tory militia were gathering for an uprising near what is now Tearcoat Swamp after General Gates and the Continental Army had suffered a disastrous defeat at Camden, he left his camp at Port's Ferry on the Peedee and with 150 men marched to the Black River, crossed, and divided his men into three units. On Thursday, October 26, he attacked in the early morning hours. According to Robert Bass, his biographer, he moved in on the Tories on three sides from the direction of the bridge you just crossed and routed them, causing many to flee into the *swamp* that lies on the far side of the field. The Tory uprising was nipped in the bud, and some of the erstwhile Loyalists "turned coat" (tearcoat) and joined Marion.

The site is very much as it was at the time of the attack. The open fields were open then; the Muster Ground is here; so is the swamp which has never been drained, and so is Tearcoat Creek, the swamp branch that flows into the Black River a quarter to a half mile from the bridge. Except for Interstate 95, the general character of the surrounding countryside is as it was two hundred years ago. There was probably not as much open farmland at the time because of a lower population density in the county.

As you retrace your route to Wilson's Crossroads, look to your left as you go over I–95. If you slow down or even stop for a moment, you will be able to make out tombstones in the Durant *cemetery* among the distant trees. In 1780 the Durant home stood at the north end of the Muster Ground. The cemetery began with the burial of the Durants' first child who died in infancy. The plantation house was eventually abandoned and burned and the exact site disappeared.

At Wilson's Crossroads, turn south onto U.S. 301 and return to Manning. Before you reach the center of town, turn left onto U.S. 521

which will curve left after a signal light taking you over **Ox Swamp** on a highway bridge. According to tradition, this is the site where Marion earned his nom de guerre in October, 1780. Tarleton had been chasing him for seven hours, from Richardson's Plantation, past Richberg milldam (sites we will visit), and along Pocotaligo Swamp for twenty-three miles before Marion turned into Ox Swamp. Here Tarleton finally reined in his horse and said to his officers, according to Bass, "Come, my boys! Let us go back and we will find the Gamecock [Sumter]. But as for this damned old fox, the devil himself could not catch him!" The name caught on and made Marion a legend in his own time.

Continue along 521, turn right on S14–48, and head for the old *river road.* When the road forks, bear right and stay on 48 until it seems to T-end in a road that meets it at right angles. To the right is County Road S14–351 but to the left 48 continues. Turn left and you are now traveling along the old Camden-Charleston highway, the river road Marion patrolled along the Santee River from Murray's Ferry to Nelson's Ferry (Eutaw Springs) to Fort Watson and to the high hills of Santee. Except for the paving, this is the old river road. The swamps off to the right border the Santee River about two miles away, just as they did when Marion fought a hundred skirmishes up and down the route.

Watch for a dirt road marked by a sign for a hunting club on Black Oak Island. A little farther, where the road begins to curve to the left, another dirt road goes off at a tangent to the right through the fields. About a quarter of a mile farther on 48 is a clump of trees and a little cemetery, all that remains of Candy Plantation which was known as the **Mount Hope Plantation.** Marion was resting at the plantation when, according to tradition, the news came of Cornwallis's surrender at Yorktown. A ball was given in his honor and he announced that the war was over and American independence was won. Behind the clump of trees is **Mount Hope Swamp**, a favorite rendezvous for Marion's brigades.

Continue for a short distance to where the right side of the road rises in an embankment. On the opposite side notice what seems to be a ditch. That ditch is part of the original river road. At this point, a curve was straightened out, leaving the bed of the old road off to the side without the blacktop paving.

Now drive on into Williamsburg County until you come to a point where 48 curves sharply to the left and a dirt road continues ahead. The dirt road is the river road (it is marked by a stop sign). Continue on the dirt road toward the site of the Battle of Mount Hope Swamp, the first of the series of battles fought between Watson and Marion.

Eventually you will be driving along what is really a causeway with swamp on both sides. When you reach a small *bridge* over a creek (the swamp branch) you are at the scene of the action. Watson and his Tory band had been pursuing Marion down the river road. When Marion arrived here, he had his men take up the bridge planks and left a detachment of riflemen to hold up the Tory advance. The road goes up a rise of ground on the other side of the bridge, the rise on which Marion posted his rear guard under Hugh Horry (Peter's brother) and McKuttry. Watson's force was halted here for several hours until a howitzer was brought up and cleared the road with a charge of grape. From here Marion went on to make his stand at Lower Bridge.

Turn around (you can find a place to make a U-turn a little beyond the bridge) and head back down the river road to the site of the fight at **Wyboo Swamp.** When you get to a juncture where 48 goes back to Manning, however, continue ahead along 351 until the road seems to turn sharply to the left and a mileage sign slows you down. The old road goes ahead for a short piece and then disappears under an arm of Lake Marion where the flooded Santee has filled in low ground. Follow the road to the left onto County 323 until you see water to the right. A dirt road comes to the right while the paved road goes left to the Santee River Dam. The road over the dam is closed off. Turn right onto the dirt road which becomes paved road shortly. Make a right onto a piece of State Route 260 which leads you back to the old river road. To the right it is still 351, but to the left it has become County Road 410. Directly ahead on the other side of the intersection is County Road 292.

The intersection of 260 and 351 is still called the Signpost by local people because there used to be a signpost standing here for Camden and Charleston. There was also a tavern here called the Signpost. Turn left onto 410 and follow the old river road until it swings sharply left. Instead of following it, continue ahead onto a dirt road. The water of the lake will show up ahead of you and you will come to a hurricane fence at a point where another dirt road goes off to right and left. To the left is a cedar-shake house. Beyond the fence is the lake and in the middle distance an *island.*

During the Revolution there were seven bridges here that crossed seven branches of what was then Wyboo Creek. The river road crossed those bridges and continued on the other side. Colonel Watson left Fort Watson and came up the river road. Marion, who was at Murray's Ferry, advanced to meet him. They made contact here at Wyboo on Tuesday, March 6, 1781, exactly midway between the two ferries. At the time the bridges and the road formed a causeway. The battle was fought on that causeway approximately on that island out in what is now Lake Marion. It involved Marion's 250 men and Watson's 500 and ended in a draw.

Return to the Signpost; turn left onto County 292, and take it to the little town of Jordan. At Jordan turn left onto County S14-25 in the direction of Summerton. In Summerton at a stop sign make a right turn onto County 56, which will take you to U.S. 301, Summerton's main street. Turn left onto 301 and take it out of Summerton to the little settlement of St. Paul where you turn right onto S14-373. At the top of a rise in the road you will see Spring Hill Church, a brick church with a square, crenellated tower. Just beyond the church look for a road, S14-76, going off to the left. Turn onto it and drive for a long stretch with flat farmlands on either side punctuated by occasional orchards. This was all part of the **Richardson Plantation**. The road will swing sharply to the right and as you follow around you will see to the left and ahead the tall monuments of the **Richardson Cemetery**. A long dirt road leads to the cemetery which sits out in the middle of a big, open field. It is marked by a historical marker at the dirt road entrance.

Brigadier General Richard Richardson of the South Carolina militia is buried here as are other members of his family, including two governors of the state of South Carolina. This is the site of one of the many outrages committed by Tarleton that made his name a household word.

Richardson was famous for leading the Snow campaign against the Tories in the backcountry in the winter of 1775. The general had died and been buried about six weeks when Tarleton showed up looking for Marion. Under the pretext that he wanted to look into the face of a brave man, Tarleton had the body dug up. What he was actually after was the family silver which he was convinced had been buried with the general. There was no silver in the grave, of course, and after some pleading on the part of other members of the family, Tarleton had his men rebury the body. The house stood just to the right of the cemetery, possibly where three magnolia trees stand by themselves. Richardson's grave is marked by the third monument from the left, a round column with a figure on top.

Continue along 76 until it curves to the right and goes over a bridge with a cypress swamp to the right and an old frame building to the left. This is the site of Flood's Mill, now called Elliot's Mill. Tarleton paid a visit here, too, to wreck the mill and throw the millstones into the stream. Going on you will cross railroad tracks and enter Sumter County, on your way to the site of **Halfway Swamp**. Look for a number of private homes on the road, including a contemporary brick house on the left set off from the road. A little way beyond is an open field to your left. Look across the field and notice the roof of an old house, showing above a modern brick home, with a high, peaked roof with a brick chimney at either end. It is at just about this spot on the *road* that Marion fought his famous duel with McLeroth.

Major Robert McLeroth and his regiment were marching with 200 recruits along the road from Charleston to Winnsboro where Cornwallis was headquartered. Marion heard of the movement, mounted up 700 men, and rode to intercept them. On Tuesday, December 12, 1780, contact was made and McLeroth's pickets were driven in. McLeroth took up a position along the road. Finding his way to Winnsboro blocked, he sent a flag to Marion accusing him of shooting pickets and challenging him to a duel. Marion answered that he would shoot pickets until the British stopped burning American homes and accepted the challenge. He offered to pit twenty of his men against twenty of McLeroth's. McLeroth ostensibly agreed and the duel was arranged to take place along this stretch of road.

Marion picked his team and was ready to take the field when the British team marched away. A relief column of 140 men under Captain James Coffin, who was later to command Stewart's reserve at Eutaw Springs, was on the way. McLeroth had been stalling for time. That night under cover of darkness with his campfires burning, McLeroth sneaked away. A detachment sent to intercept him again prepared an ambush on a hill on the Singleton's Plantation. When McLeroth's men reached the spot, however, the Americans fired one volley and then took off. They had just learned that the Singleton family was suffering from smallpox. Marion withdrew his force and the British continued on their way.

If you go on a little farther to Manchester State Forest, you will find a crossroads with a dirt road going off to the right and a pine woods on either side. This is known as the **Sand Hills** where a summer colony of some fifty homes was established during the eighteenth century as a retreat for the Richardsons and other plantation families in the area. It was a place where they could escape the hot summer's weather and malaria of the lowlands along the Santee. They came on April 1 and stayed until the first black frost, which usually occurs in October. The summer homes eventually burned down. A little way farther on is a marker for St. John's Church in which the Richardsons worshiped. The present church was built in 1854.

Retrace your route into Clarendon County; go back along 76 to U.S. 301 and head for Summerton. Before you get to Summerton, 301 intersects County S14–373. Turn left onto 373 going north; take it to an intersection with County 26, and turn left. A short way down 26 takes you to the bridge which crosses Jack's Creek. Several hundred yards to the left is supposed to be the remains of the **Richberg Milldam.**

Marion was camped near the dam while Tarleton was looking for him just before the chase to Ox Swamp. Tarleton was camped near the Richardson Plantation. His men lit such enormous fires that Marion, seeing them, thought the plantation was being burned. He sent out a patrol that returned with the news of Tarleton's proximity. A slave on the plantation is supposed to have tipped Tarleton off to Marion's hiding place and, so the story goes, one of the Richardson's sons overheard and rode hell for leather to warn Marion. He and his men are said to have gone in such a hurry they left all their supplies behind. Local tradition has it that as they rode off one end of the milldam, Tarleton's dragoons rode onto the other end. From here the chase led along Pocotiligo Swamp until Tarleton abandoned it.

THE INTERIOR LINE

Since you have just about run out of Marion sites in Clarendon County, it is time to get involved with the capture of two British forts and the battles for the control of the South Carolina interior that took place in and around Camden.

FORT WATSON

Return to U.S. 301 and take it south for about four miles until you see the blue and white sign for Fort Watson.

The Fort Watson sign will appear at the intersection of County Road 803 which meets 301 from the right. There will also be a sign for the Santee National Wildlife Refuge. Both signs indicate a right turn onto 803. You will pass the wildlife refuge on your left as you follow the road along the shore of Lake Marion. A one-mile drive brings you to a dead end against a hurricane fence and a wide, sandy parking area at the edge of a wooded area. Walk in through the gate on a path that leads to an ancient Indian mound. Several flights of wooden steps take you to the grass-covered top of the mound where you can sit on benches or walk around what was the interior of Fort Watson.

At the present time, Fort Watson overlooks Lake Marion. In April, 1781, when the fort was besieged by the combined forces of Marion and Lee, the Santee River had not been dammed. The river was close by and so was a small pond or lake called Scott's Lake, but the mound was then surrounded by land on all sides. Fort Watson was one of the line of British forts that stretched from Charleston to Ninety-six. It was named after that Colonel John Watson who unsuccessfully attempted to break up Marion's guerilla command. As Greene advanced on Camden, he dispatched Marion and Lee to Fort Watson with orders to capture it. The fort was actually built on the top of this Indian mound which is about forty to fifty feet high. It consisted of a stockade with three rings of abatises around it, and it was garrisoned by eighty British soldiers and forty Tories under the command of Lieutenant McKay of the British army.

The siege lasted from April 15 to April 23. During that time, the British had to dig a new well and a trench from the lake to fill it, while the attackers dug a series of trenches around the mound in their efforts to get close enough to undermine it. With the danger of a relief column hovering over them, some way had to be thought of to quickly force the surrender of the fort. Colonel Hezekiah Maham suggested building the tower that thereafter bore his name, the Maham Tower. We came across a Maham tower in Augusta, Georgia, where it proved to be just as effective against Fort Grierson two months later. After some days spent cutting down trees and trimming and notching the logs, the tower was finally built in sections and erected under cover of darkness. The next day, the fort's defenders found themselves under fire from a detachment of riflemen stationed above them who were firing down into the fort. At the same time, strong attacks were launched against the abatises which the defenders were unable to respond to without exposing themselves to fire from the tower. Before the day ended, McKay struck his colors and the fort fell to the Americans.

Much of the ground that originally lay to the east of the fort is now under water, including, I assume, the site of the well the defenders dug and the trench. Poking around in the woods on the opposite side of the mound uncovered a number of long depressions in the ground which may be the remains of the American trenches. There is nothing to mark the position of the Maham Tower or any of the other events that occurred during the siege. Beyond the area around the mound, there is a grove of pine woods threaded by paths with split-log benches to sit on here and there. A considerable amount of construction was going on outside the hurricane fence when we visited, suggesting that a paved, parking field was being prepared and possibly other facilities.

This was the first of the British line of fortified positions to fall to Greene's strategy. Greene himself was marching to Camden where he would fight the Battle of Hobkirk's Hill.

FORT MOTTE

Go back to U.S. 301 and turning right when you reach it, take it across Lake Marion. On the other side of the lake, in the town of Santee, turn right onto Route 6 and take it northwest to the town of Elloree. Beyond Elloree, pick up Route 267 which goes to the town of Fort Motte, which is near the fort site. Before you reach the town, however, turn off 267 onto Route 419 and take it north to Route 601. Turn right onto 601 and shortly after, look for a bituminous road going off at a diagonal to the left. It is marked by a stop sign with its back to you and its designation is County Road 151.

Follow it for 3.1 miles at first through open fields on both sides and then downgrade through woodlands to a dead end. At the dead end, a dirt road goes off to right and left. Directly ahead you will see a path through the trees. Park your car and walk up the path as it crosses railroad tracks and leads up a heavily wooded hill. A fifteen-minute walk at a brisk pace up the hill takes you through thick forest on either side to the Fort Motte site. The path follows the contours of the hill, winding around it gradually, so that by the time you reach the site you are on the opposite side of the hill from where you left your car.

Toward the end of the fifteen-minute period, keep an eye out for a big block of granite off to the left. It will look like an irregularly shaped rock or boulder. There is an inscription cut into it on the opposite side which you cannot see from the path. Actually it is a memorial tablet set up here by the Rebecca Motte Chapter of the D.A.R. and it marks the site of Fort Motte.

This was a highly strategic location during the Revolution, overlooking the juncture of the Congaree and Wateree rivers where they join to form the Santee River. Up the Santee from Charleston came supplies to Fort Motte where they were stored and sorted out and then sent on along the Congaree and Wateree to British posts farther west, like Fort Granby and Ninety-six. The capture of Fort Motte was another Lee-Marion operation. In April, 1781, Greene fought and lost the Battle of Hobkirk's Hill. Nevertheless, he persisted in his strategy of capturing

British interior forts. On May 8 Lee and Marion reached this site and invested the fort. Its principal feature was a large mansion belonging to Mrs. Rebecca Motte whose name became familiar to you in Charleston where you visited a home that belonged to the family.

The Mottes owned a number of plantations and this was one of them. Rebecca Motte was the widow of Jacob Motte who had been an ardent Patriot up to the time of his death. When the British fortified this Motte home, they forced the widow to move into an old farmhouse on a hill to the north where Lee made his headquarters. The reconstructed drawings I have seen show a two-story building of the raised cottage type with large chimneys at either end and a piazza in the front. Around the house and the immediate area, the British dug a deep trench surrounded by what Lee in his memoirs describes as a "large and lofty parapet," probably a stockade, and an abatis. The garrison ordinarily consisted of 150 soldiers under the command of a Lieutenant McPherson. At the time of the siege, however, a small party of dragoons carrying dispatches to Camden had stopped off and were impressed into service.

Lee and Marion brought their men into position around the fort from the hill to the north by marching them through a ravine between the two hills. At first they dug trenches and tried to inch their way close enough to launch an assault. They had with them a six-pounder which was mounted to rake the north end of the house. On May 10 they learned that Lieutenant Colonel Francis Rawdon, who had been victorious at Hobkirk's Hill but was retreating to Charleston because he was in danger of being isolated, was approaching Fort Motte. Realizing they would have to act quickly, the Americans decided to burn the garrison out by shooting fire arrows onto the dry shingles of the roof and so setting it afire. Since Mrs. Motte had gone out of her way to make things comfortable for them at the farmhouse and had attended to their sick and wounded, the American commanders felt obliged to inform her of their plans. The widow responded by handing them the very instruments with which they could practice arson on her home, a quiverful of African arrows.

According to a Mrs. Ravenal writing in Scribners' *Women of Colonial and Revolutionary Times,* the arrows had been given to Mrs. Motte's brother, Miles Brewton, many years before by the captain of an East Indiaman. African arrows were inflammable projectiles that ignited upon impact. Boatner says they were called African arrows because the bow used at Fort Motte came from the West Indies and was of African design. One source says that the arrows were fired from muskets, however, while another insists that African arrows were not used at Fort

Motte but rather a ball of rosin and brimstone which was hurled onto
the roof by a private in Marion's brigade.

By May 12 Rawdon was just across the river from the fort and
the garrison was looking forward to being rescued. A trench dug by the
attackers to get them into range, however, had just been completed.
From it the African arrows were shot onto the roof. The first one did
not ignite but the second did and the roof caught fire. McPherson sent
a party of men up to the attic to pull down the burning shingles, but
the six-pounder sent them scurrying back to shelter. Shortly after, a white
flag showed at a window and though his relief was only across the river,
McPherson surrendered. All hands then fell to and extinguished the
blaze thus saving Rebecca Motte's home. That night she feasted the officers of both commands at her own table. Only two men, both in Marion's command, had been killed. All prisoners were paroled. The house
eventually reverted to its owner, but ironically it did finally succumb to
flames early in the 1800s. The name of Rebecca Motte, however, has
been preserved through the years and today you will find few people in
Calhoun County who do not know her and her story.

"Oh, yes," they will say when you stop to ask directions. "Rebecca's
house. Up on the hill yonder."

Though I searched the woods around the site, I cannot say that
I found anything that might definitely have been a trench or breastwork. The woods on that hill are filled with hummocks and depressions of all kinds. Only careful, selective test digging will determine
which, if any, are the remains of trenches or fortifications. If you walk
on a little way beyond the monument, you can see where the ground
falls way toward the river, now hidden from your sight by trees. Two
hundred years ago that was probably cleared land all the way down
to the river landing. The area around the house site that is now so heavily
wooded must have been cleared, too, to deny cover to any enemy. If
you stand on the path with your back to the monument and walk ahead
into the woods, you will find the ravine along which Lee and Marion
led their men to their positions around the house.

The land on which the Fort Motte memorial stands is private property and is posted, but from talking with local people who are concerned with the site and the observance of the bicentennial, I received
the impression that arrangements will be made for the public to visit.

From Fort Motte, Henry Lee was sent to take Fort Granby. Urbanization has destroyed the site, though at one time it had been marked
somewhere on the outskirts of the city of Columbia. From Fort Motte,

return to Route 601 and take it north into Camden to cover the Battle of Hobkirk's Hill and the terrible defeat General Horatio Gates suffered at the hands of Cornwallis in the Battle of Camden.

CAMDEN

Camden and its environs to the north were the scene of two battles fought for the control of the town. To cover them in chronological order, take 601 into Camden where it becomes Dekalb Street. Camden has grown along two main axes: an east-west axis that runs along Dekalb and a north-south axis that runs along Broad Street. The two streets meet in the center of town at the intersection of Dekalb and Broad, marked by traffic lights. Turn left onto Broad Street, which is also U.S. 521, and take it up Hobkirk's Hill and out of town.

About five miles from the Dekalb-Broad streets intersection, look for State Route 58 going off to the left. It is also called Flatrock Road. Turn onto it and in 2.1 miles look for a big, **granite block** standing upright off the road in a wooded area to the right. When I was there a short piece of dirt road leading off 58 permitted me to pull in and park. The marker is on the site where Baron de Kalb was mortally wounded during the Battle of Camden, the first battle at Camden. As far as I could determine, this is the only marker or monument on the site of the battle, which was actually fought over a wide area of woods and fields.

To follow the development of the battle, clock 4.2 miles from this marker along Flatrock Road to a creek running under the road. About a half mile upstream, out of sight, are the remains of the milldam of *Rugeley's Mill* which was owned by a local Tory. Since it is on private property, it is not accessible to the public, but the owner has assured me the site has been verified.

Horatio Gates, the victor of Saratoga, had been placed in command of the Southern Department by Congress in July, 1780, following the surrender of Lincoln's army and the fall of Charleston. Gates found what was left of the Continental forces at Coxe's Mill in North Carolina where they had gathered under the command of General Johann de Kalb, a German volunteer who had had a great deal of military experience in Europe before coming to America with Lafayette to seek his fortune as a professional soldier. Gates gathered together as many militia units as he could, including the survivors of Monck's Corner and Lenud's Ferry, and expecting more to join him along the way headed south for

Camden. Most of the men were in no condition to march and supplies were low, but Gates ordered them out to campaign against the advice of de Kalb and other officers.

The British were then actually in control of all of Georgia and South Carolina but Cornwallis, who was in command, had far from enough troops to garrison the area effectively. He was preparing to invade North Carolina using Camden as an advanced base when Gates began his advance south. Lord Rawdon, who was in command at Camden, reported to Cornwallis that some 7,000 Americans were approaching. Actually by August 15, 1780, the day before the battle, Gates had only about 3,000 men fit for duty. Cornwallis, however, was convinced the odds were three to one against him and came to Camden to take command. The British had a large number of sick on their hands who could not be moved and would have to be abandoned if Cornwallis decided to withdraw to Charleston. Instead he chose to stay and fight, counting on his regulars to defeat the American militia.

By Tuesday, August 15, Cornwallis decided not to wait for the American attack, but to attack himself and he marched out of Camden north along the Waxhaw Road. At the same time Gates advanced from the mill, spearheaded by what was left of Pulaski's Legion now under the command of a French volunteer, the Marquis de la Rouerie, Armand Charles Tuffin, who had been Pulaski's second-in-command. British advance patrols met Armand head on and the two armies became aware of each other. The rest of the night was spent getting the armies into position.

This was a particularly bad experience for many of the Americans. According to eyewitness accounts, Gates made up for the lack of food from which they suffered by doling out a mixture of cornmeal mush and molasses strengthened with chunks of badly cooked meat and bread. The mush and molasses had an electrifying effect on the digestive tracts of men who had been existing for days on makeshift rations. All night long, men were going off into the woods to relieve themselves. By morning, half of Gates's men, most of them militiamen, were in no condition to stand up against an army of well-trained British regulars, but Gates no longer had any choice. He was committed to battle.

On Wednesday, August 16, the armies faced each other across what is now Flatrock Road. At the time it was the road to Camden and Charlotte and was known as the Waxhaw Road because it went to the Waxhaw River. Turn around and head back toward the de Kalb marker. Today this is an area of open farmlands with some small, private homes along the road. Topographically it is much the same as it was two hundred years ago. Notice that as you drive south, you are traveling down a gradual slope. The land also falls away from the road on either side so that you are traveling along a narrow plateau which widens out the farther south you go. There are still swamps off to left and right where the British anchored their flanks. The American right was far off the road to your right facing the British left. The centers of both lines were located just about at the road.

The battle opened with a cannonade and then a general British advance in columns. An attempt was made to attack the British right before it could deploy, but the militia units on the American left did not get there fast enough. Instead they were confronted by the British already in formation advancing on them, cheering and shouting as they came. They broke and ran followed by most of the other militia units. Since the militia made up about two-thirds of Gates's army, this left few American fighting men on the field. The Continentals held fast to their position, particularly on the right which now came under furious attack. All attempts to relieve that pressure were thwarted. De Kalb, who was wounded several times, refused to leave the field until ordered to do so by Gates, but Gates had been swept away by the militia rout and was no longer there to command. De Kalb led a counterattack that checked the British, but he was wounded again, this time fatally, and the American line collapsed completely.

Gates's army was so utterly defeated that to this day we do not have an accurate breakdown of his losses. Out of the almost 4,000 men in his command at the beginning of the battle, only 700 reached Hillsboro, North Carolina. Gates himself rode sixty miles to Charlotte that day and then went on to Hillsboro, ostensibly to reform his army as quickly as possible. It has been estimated that about 1,000 Americans were killed and 1,000 captured; several hundred more were killed or captured during the days that followed the battle as Tarleton's cavalry followed through with mopping up operations at Rugeley's Mill and Hanging Rock. The British lost more than 300 officers and men killed and wounded.

Return to Camden along U.S. 521 and when back in town, continue along Broad Street across Dekalb Street for about a mile to the site of **Historic Camden.** This is a reconstructed area that is open every day but Monday. There is a museum and a number of restored buildings which represent the town of Camden as it was, 1780–81. A trail, along which visitors may walk or ride electric carts, leads to restored British fortifications and the excavated remains of the house in which Cornwallis made his headquarters. Following the Battle of Camden, Cornwallis ordered the town fortified. It was surrounded by a stockade and breastworks with six redoubts spaced around the perimeter. According to a diagram of the fortifications drawn by Thaddeus Kosciuszko after the British withdrew, the inner log wall was over 1,200 feet square and the outer ring of redoubts was over one and a half miles in circumference. More than 25,000 logs had been built into the breastworks, palisades, and parapets through the efforts of the townspeople and slaves the British impressed into labor gangs.

Two of the redoubts have been located, as well as the site of a powder magazine that was built by the people of Camden in 1777 as part of their defenses against the British. The British redoubts and part of the stockade have been restored. These were the fortifications General Greene moved to attack after the capture of Fort Motte. Cornwallis was on his way to Virginia having recovered from the Battle of Guilford Courthouse in North Carolina, another British victory the crown could not afford. Lord Rawdon in command at Camden had to face Greene without Cornwallis's help. In addition, he had been left in command of all British forces in South Carolina. As it turned out, he did very well in Camden but in the long run, he lost.

Old Camden was about a third the size of the modern town. A mile and a half to the north was **Hobkirk's Hill.** As you look up Broad Street from the restoration area, you can see the hill on the other side of Dekalb, now built over and part of the town. It is actually a ridge about eighty feet high, running from east to west. In 1781 it was covered with pine woods. At its foot to the west (your left as you look up the hill) was the Wateree River, while to the east (your right) Pine Tree Creek wound around its foot through a low, swampy area. Between the town of Camden and the foot of Hobkirk's Hill was Logtown, a settlement of log huts just outside the town limits.

Greene took up positions on Hobkirk Hill overlooking the town on April 20, 1781, after reconnoitering and deciding that Rawdon was in too strong a position for him to attack at once. At about this time, Watson, having tired of chasing Marion, was on his way back to join Rawdon. Greene moved across Pine Tree Creek to intercept him, but Marion and Lee kept Watson occupied and he moved back to the hill. His 1,100-odd men took up their old positions. Early on the morning of Wednesday, April 25, Rawdon, who had about 900 men in his garrison, left his fortified position with about 800 and advanced up Hobkirk's Hill against the American left, to your right as you face the hill. His route approximated the present Southern Railway tracks which pass close to the restored area from the south, go north to Dekalb Street, and then skirt the foot of Hobkirk's Hill to the east. Greene first learned of the approaching British when they drove in his pickets. Seeing that Rawdon was advancing in a narrow column formation, he tried to overlap both British flanks. Rawdon responded by extending his front line and moving up his reserve to overlap the American line. However, what Rawdon didn't know was that the Americans had three six-pounders which now made their presence known and felt. They checked him and the American line advanced down upon him.

There then occurred one of those freak happenings that seemed to plague American armies throughout the war. At Germantown the fog had caused one American unit to fire on another, disrupting the advance. At Wambaw a pond had caused an advancing American unit to deflect its course, thus laying it open to British attack. On Hobkirk's Hill a crack Maryland regiment advancing down the hill became disorganized for a moment. Its commander ordered it to halt and fall back to reorganize, causing some confusion in the ranks. Before the unit could be reorganized, the British were at them and the damage was done. First one unit and then another broke and ran until only one regiment was left holding its position. The British pressed their advantage and almost captured the three six-pounders. A heated battle raged around the guns until men could be brought up to drag them out of British reach.

By this time the entire American line had fallen back and Greene had to withdraw to a position near the site of the first Camden battle. The next day he moved north to Rugeley's Mill. American losses were about 260 casualties, including eighteen killed. Rawdon lost 258, thirty-eight of them killed. Despite his victory Rawdon was now cut off from his supply base to the east and had to retire to Charleston, leaving Camden to the rebels. He left on May 10 after first destroying the fortifications and most of the town. The next day Greene moved in and had Sumter destroy what was left of the British redoubts.

All that is left of the American positions are several markers identifying the sites. As you drive up Broad Street to Dekalb you will pass over the site of **Logtown** before you start mounting the hill proper on the other side of Dekalb. Just beyond Kirkwood Terrace to the left, a marker on the right identifies the hill. You are now surrounded by one-family homes and side streets going off to left and right at odd intervals. A little way farther up the hill, another marker on the right locates Greene's *headquarters,* 150 feet due east or to the right. At Greene Street, make a right (there was another Greene Street or maybe it's the same one some distance back going to the left but not across Broad Street) and proceed to Lyttleton Street. Turn right again and look on the left for Holly Hedge, a house set back in a large plot of landscaped ground with a lake behind it. Continue down to the corner of Greene Street and turn left.

It was here the American troops stationed on the left of Greene's line were having breakfast and attending to their personal wants on the morning of the battle just before Rawdon attacked. The site where the three American guns were placed has not been marked, but it might have been anywhere between this point and the area around the markers on Broad Street at the top of the hill. If you return to Broad Street and go uphill past the second marker, you will find a third one for the Battle of Camden. Somewhere in this area is where Greene's reserves were camped before the battle.

Drive north again along U.S. 521, go off once more onto Flatrock Road (the old Waxhaw Road), and continue beyond the de Kalb marker, over the Camden battlefield, and beyond the site of Rugeley's Mill to Hanging Rock.

HANGING ROCK

After approximately twelve miles you will come to County Road 467 going off to the right. A further identifying feature is a historical marker near the intersection for the James Ingraham home. Turn east onto 467 and go down a steep incline to Hanging Rock Creek. On the other side of the creek, a dirt road climbs to the right and curves out of sight. Beyond it there is a little parking space on the right equipped with a single picnic table. Pull in there and walk up the dirt road as it leads along the rising east bank of the creek which eventually runs into a box canyon.

Across the creek to the west is a ridge you drove parallel to as you came along Flatrock Road to 467. As you approach the *rock* that gives the battle site its name, you will pass a number of other large boulders but none as big as the one that awaits you on the left. It is perched in such a way on a supporting rock ledge that it forms an overhang at its foot. Naturally it has been decorated with graffiti over the years, but none dating to the Revolution. The creek is about a hundred feet below you. Along its bed you will see a number of other huge rocks deposited there probably either by glacier or stream action.

This is not the site of the battle. The fighting took place between the ridge on the other side of the creek and the road. In August, 1780, a British force of Tories under Major John Carden were camped above the west bank of the creek up on the ridge. They were one of the outposts detailed to protect the British in Camden. While Sumter was attacking Rocky Mount, a British post north of Camden, Major William Richardson Davie led another force against the Hanging Rock garrison. On the night of August 5, 1780, he was joined by Sumter who was operating in support of Gates's action developing against Camden. The next morning the two forces attacked the Tory position and a fierce battle developed that seesawed back and forth for about four hours. The Loyalists lost almost 200 men to the rebels' fifty-odd killed and wounded. Two of the Loyalist units were virtually annihilated and their camp was plundered.

Looking over the site from Flatrock Road at the intersection with 467, you can see the *ridge* on which the Loyalists were camped. A cottonfield now intrudes between the road and the ridge. Whether the British position was as wooded as it is now is debatable, though part of the action was fought out in wooded areas close to the camp.

BUFORD'S MASSACRE

Continue north along Flatrock Road into the town of Heath Springs where you pick up U.S. 521 north. A mile or two on, in the little town of Pleasant Hills, turn right onto State Route 522 and head for Monroe. About nine miles farther, just before the intersection of 522 and State Route 9, you will see two *monuments* on the left in what looks like a small roadside park. A half-circle driveway leads into the area. This is the scene of a notorious Tarleton victory, often called the Battle of Waxhaw.

In May, 1780, Colonel Abraham Buford and his Virginians were on their way to Charleston when the city fell. After the rebel defeats at Monck's Corner and Lenud's Ferry what was left of Buford's command from the latter encounter was the last organized body of rebels left in South Carolina. As the British fanned out to take control of South Carolina, he was ordered to march to Hillsboro, North Carolina. Cornwallis tried to catch up with him, but when he realized Buford had too great a lead, he dispatched Banastre Tarleton with 170 cavalry and 100 infantry. By mounting his foot soldiers behind the cavalrymen, Tarleton rode 105 miles in fifty-four hours and caught up with Buford on Monday, May 29, 1780.

Buford had just marched north from Rugeley's Mill; therefore we may assume he followed the route we used to get here, the Waxhaw Road, part of which we know as Flatrock Road. Tarleton knew that Buford had been at Rugeley's Mill and probably followed the same route. Though he was outnumbered by Buford, he demanded his surrender and was defied. He then formed his men on a nearby hill only 300 yards away in full view of Buford who formed a line facing him. Buford had several artillery pieces with him, but they were up front with the baggage and somehow were never brought into the action. The British charged the American center while Tarleton with a unit of cavalry circled around the American position.

The American line held its fire too long. By the time the men were ordered to fire, the troopers were so close they broke the American line despite the volley. The infantry followed the cavalry with the bayonet and the American center became a shambles. At the same time Tarleton swooped down on their rear and cut down an officer who was raising a white flag. In the same moment his horse was killed and Tarleton went down. Seeing him fall and thinking he had been killed, the British infantry went to work with vengeful bayonets, killing men who were trying to surrender and bayoneting the wounded. The Virginians lost 113 killed; 150 were so badly wounded they could not be moved, and altogether 203 were captured. Tarleton lost nineteen men killed and wounded and gained a reputation as a bloody butcher who gave no quarter. The story of "Tarleton's quarter" spread throughout the rebellious colonies and he became a symbol of British brutality.

The granite memorials mark the common grave in which the American dead were buried. One is the original marker, which is no longer legible; the other replaced it recently. There is another grave here, that of an infant who died in 1895, but there is no explanation of why she shares the site with the victims of the massacre. There are picnic tables, a grove of trees behind the grave which were undoubtedly not here at the time of the battle, and beyond the trees a pond. The site is surrounded by open farmland. Close to the road juncture are a number of contemporary, one-family homes. Otherwise, there is nothing to mark the positions of the opposing forces. There are a number of small hillocks or rises of grounds in the vicinity, but not one is identifiable as the one on which Tarleton formed for his attack.

FISH DAM FORD

Leaving the scene of the massacre behind, proceed the short distance to the intersection of Route 522 and State Route 9, turn left on 9 and drive west into Chester County. As you approach the town of Chester, take the Route 9–72 bypass to save yourself from becoming entangled in Chester traffic. Continue on 72 south about fourteen miles until you reach an intersection with Route 215. Continue on 72, but keep your eyes open for a granite marker which should show up just before you reach the bridge across the Broad River.

Sumter with 300 men was camped on the *ridge* to the right of the marker on Thursday night, November 9, 1780. Seeing an opportunity to catch the Gamecock off guard, Cornwallis, then in Winnsboro, ordered Major James Wemyss to make the attempt. Wemyss and 140 men, including some of Tarleton's horsemen, crossed the river on an old Indian fish dam and surprised him during the early morning hours. Wemyss was wounded almost immediately, and many of the British who charged into the camp were sitting ducks against the light of the campfires. The rest of the British command fought on foot. During the fighting a small detachment of dragoons found their way to Sumter's tent under orders to take him alive or dead. Sumter went out the back before they could grab him and hid under a bank of the river.

If the river is low enough, you can see the old *dam* as you cross the river when you look to your right. It should show up a hundred feet or so upstream of the bridge just under the surface. You might be able to reach it by walking down the bank of the river. At the time we visited, the river was swollen after two days of heavy rain and the riverbanks were overrun.

Continue west along 72 through the town of Whitmire, then on to Clinton and from Clinton southwest to Greenwood. You are on your way to one of the most exciting sites in the South.

GAINS AND LOSSES IN THE BACKCOUNTRY

NINETY-SIX—THE FORTS AND THE TOWN

At the eastern edge of Greenwood, 72 meets a bypass marked U.S. 221. Take it south to a juncture with Route 34. If you miss 221, continue ahead into the center of town and pick up U.S. 25 south which, a short distance south of Greenwood, also meets 34. Take 34 east into the modern town of Ninety-six.

At the traffic light in town, turn right and drive 1.9 miles along a road to the site of **Old Ninety-six.** Look for a two-story reconstruction of a *log cabin* on the left. At the time we visited the site, the cabin, which will probably be doing business as the Visitor's Center when you get here, was being constructed. A short distance beyond you will see on the left a fence with a gate, a large granite marker, a numbered sign, a small enclosed paved area with two old tombstones cemented into a low brick wall, and beyond all that, in an open field, a very definite breastwork.

Ninety-six is a fascinating and somewhat complicated site which requires some explanation before you plunge in. It is a multiple site. It began as a trading post in the 1730s where English traders did business with the Cherokee. It was given its odd name because it was supposed to be ninety-six miles from Keowee, an important Cherokee Indian town in the foothills of South Carolina. The trading post, the farthest from the coast, became a settlement along the Charleston Path which led into the Cherokee territory. In 1769 it became the courthouse town for the Ninety-six district, which included about twelve of the modern counties in the state.

Its importance grew as the colony developed, for it stood at the crossroads of just about every road that led through the region to any other point of the compass traders and travelers wished to reach, including the cities on the coast. In 1775 it was the scene of the first land battle fought during the Revolution in the South, became the western anchor of the line of fortified posts Cornwallis established across the state from Charleston as he prepared to invade North Carolina, and was besieged by General Greene in 1781.

Ninety-six contains the site of the settlement (the third dead town on your tour of southern sites), the site of the 1775 breastwork and engagement, the remains of the fortifications built by the British, and the remains of the works connected with Greene's siege. Extensive archaeological work has begun to restore and interpret this complexity of sites. You will probably be able to see some of the work in progress if you visit Ninety-six before 1975. At the time of my visit, there was a tour map available. The sites were numbered on the map and correspondingly numbered markers had been placed at the sites. Eventually a museum at the Visitor's Center will offer interpretative exhibits and relics and some programs will probably be conducted at the actual sites.

Ninety-six is one of the most satisfying of any of the Revolutionary War sites because of its complexity and the physical remains themselves which authenticate the story right before your eyes. Begin at the enclosed *tombstones,* the first site on the walking tour. They mark the remains of James Mayson and his third wife, Henrietta. They were originally buried near the Saluda River but were moved here in 1939 when Lake Greenwood was created because Mayson took part in the first Battle of Ninety-six in 1775. He was among the first South Carolinians to act for the Patriot cause. In June, 1775, he and Captain Moses Kirkland and a Captain Caldwell with two companies of rangers took over Fort Charlotte on the Savannah River west of Ninety-six and carried off to Ninety-six a supply of powder and lead. In July a force of 200 Tory militia, invited in by Captain Kirkland who had decided to defect, took the powder away and threw Mayson into the Ninety-six jail.

As the news of Lexington and Concord, Bunker Hill, and the siege of Boston reached the South, rebels and Loyalists began to declare themselves and prepare for action. The South Carolina Committee of Safety sent a deputation through the interior to organize the rebel effort. The Tories under Thomas Brown, Patrick Cunningham, and others moved quickly to counteract the effort. A wagon train filled with 1,000 pounds of powder was sent by the Committee of Safety to the Cherokees to insure their neutrality. The Tories intercepted the train and made off with the munitions.

The committee of safety, through one of its most vigorous members, William H. Drayton, had been actively arming its followers and taking over British posts, including Fort Charlotte. Major Andrew Williamson, in charge of Fort Charlotte, heard that about 1,500 Tories were planning to cross the Saluda River near Ninety-six and decided to intercept this force. On Sunday, November 19, Williamson and 500 men (including Mayson) marched to Ninety-six and prepared to do battle by erecting in two hours breastworks in a field near the town.

Walk from Mayson's grave site into the field where Williamson and his men prepared to make their stand. This also happens to be the site of Fort Holmes which was built by the British in 1781 and intersects the breastworks of Fort Williamson. We found the partial outlines of both **breastworks** marked by colored wooden stakes, the white representing Fort Holmes, the blue representing Fort Williamson. The Fort Holmes breastworks were ditched and surrounded by an abatis. Excavations have revealed the ditch and the charred remains of the abatis or of a stockade. Fort Williamson was a breastwork made of old fence rails joined to a barn (the field was part of the Savage Plantation) and covered with straw, hides and anything else the defenders could get their hands on. It was built roughly in the shape of a square, according to Mayson's account, enclosing an area of about 185 yards. The exact dimensions and other details were blurred by the town of Cambridge, another settlement that developed on the site between the 1780s and the 1850s, further complicating the archaeologists' attempt to interpret the site exactly. (Fort

Holmes, built with redoubts at its four corners, successfully resisted the efforts of Harry Lee to take it during Greene's siege in 1781. Marker 15 on the tour map identifies the spot where Lee dug his parallels as he tried to get close enough to land an assault.)

On November 19, 1775, the Tories appeared in Ninety-six, about 1,800 or 2,000 of them, took over the town, converted the jailhouse into a fortified position, and invested Fort Williamson. The rebels had enough supplies to withstand a siege of several days, but no water. The nearest water was a spring located in the ravine that lay between the town and the fort. The remains of the ravine are still there; you will cross it over a footbridge on your way to visit the town site. The Tories demanded that the Patriots disperse and some parleying went on between the two forces. The commitment to armed conflict was made when the Tories seized two of Williamson's men outside the fort. The Patriots sallied forth to the rescue and the battle was on.

It lasted for two days during which the two swivel guns the fort mounted were instrumental in keeping the attackers at bay. The Tories tried to burn the rebels out by firing the grass and fences around the fort, but the ground was too wet and the flames went out. Then they tried some sort of "rolling battery," behind which they attempted to approach the barn and set it afire, but the machine caught fire instead. The thirsty defenders overcame their lack of water by digging a forty-foot well which produced the right results. They suffered one man killed and twelve wounded, but the Tory losses, which the Patriots claimed were considerable, are unknown.

Finally on Tuesday, November 21, both sides agreed to call off the fight, just in time for the garrison, which had only forty pounds of powder left. The Tories withdrew across the Saluda and Fort Williamson's breastworks were leveled. The swivel guns were surrendered but only as a gesture. They were later returned to the rebels who mounted them in Fort Charlotte.

During the excavations on the site, an attempt was made to find the well the defenders had dug. Instead the digging turned up a skeleton believed to be the remains of James Birmingham, the one Whig killed. The evidence consists of the place where the skeleton was found, the remains of the clothing, the height and race of the dead man, and the bullet in the skull pan (revealed by X-ray) proving that he died as Birmingham died, shot in the head. All of this indicates that the remains may be of the first South Carolinian to die in the Revolution and, in fact, the first southerner to have that honor.

☆

Follow the trail from the double fort site across the *ravine*, which may not be as deep today as it was in colonial times. Somewhere in this area a covered trench led from the town stockade to Fort Holmes. From here on you will follow the trail of markers through what are now fields of high grass and wooded sections where once stood the town of Ninety-six and an intricate series of fortifications and siege works that surrounded it. After passing through one open field, then by a marker for the old Cherokee trail, you will come into a second, very large, rectangular, open area bordered by trees. This is the site of the *town* proper which the British surrounded by a stockade in 1780. Through this field, about two-thirds of the way across it, was where the Charleston-Augusta Road ran. The sites of the various buildings are marked by numbered signs. The jailhouse site is just to your right as you enter the field. It was a two-story, brick building whose basement has been uncovered. On the left side of the trail opposite is the site of one of the blockhouses the British built.

When we went over the field, we found that the archaeologists had partially uncovered several other building sites. By the time you visit, the work should have uncovered many more and you may be able to walk along the Main Street of this dead town visualizing the homes and public buildings that once bordered it on either side. A partial description of the town of Ninety-six in 1780 has been left by a Loyalist officer, Lieutenant Anthony Allaire of the American Volunteers, who wrote that it contained "twelve dwelling houses, a courthouse, and a jail in which are confined about forty rebels brought in by the friends to Government . . . Ninety-six is situated on an eminence, the land cleared for a mile around it, in a flourishing part of the country, supplied with very good water, enjoys a free, open air, and is esteemed a healthy place."

Some distance off outside the Ninety-six town stockade area is the site of the Robert Goudy House, built in 1751. Goudy was a merchant whose home was a trading post. It was surrounded by a stockade in 1759 as a protection for the settlers during the Cherokee War that broke out the following year. It became a base for punitive expeditions against the Cherokee and in March, 1760, was attacked by the Indians.

The trail takes you beyond the town stockade area to the site of the **Star Redoubt** or Star Fort, the principal British position during the siege of May–June, 1781. Ninety-six and the area around it was returned to British control in the spring and summer of 1780 after the fall of Charleston. Under the command of Lieutenant Colonel John Harris

Cruger, an extensive fortification system was built which included the Star Redoubt, the stockade, a number of blockhouses around the town, and Fort Holmes on the site of Fort Williamson. Bruce Ezell of Ninety-six, who has been largely responsible for getting the restoration and archaeological work started, believes the fortifications grew or evolved as the need for them arose.

The 1781 siege of Ninety-six by General Nathanael Greene and his Continental regulars and southern militia was part of the same strategy aimed at reducing or weakening Cornwallis's line of fortified posts that had been successful at Forts Watson and Motte. Greene was out to make the interior areas unhabitable for the British and confine them to their coastal positions, thus keeping them from extending their control of the South into North Carolina and Virginia.

The siege began on Tuesday, May 22, 1781. Inside the forts were 550 Tories. Among them were Loyalist militia units from New York and New Jersey. Greene opened the siege with something less than 1,000 Continentals (eventually he was joined by Lee's legion) and only light artillery. Trenches were dug around the Star Fort under the direction of Kosciuszko who had built the West Point defenses. A number of devices were tried by the Americans including a Maham tower and a mine in an attempt to blow it up. When Lee joined the siege, he concentrated his efforts around Fort Holmes which guarded the Ninety-six water supply in the ravine. After digging a series of trenches, he succeeded in reaching a position from which he could keep the spring under fire. The enemy was forced to send black slaves out at night into the ravine to get water.

The inhabitants of the town suffered many of the effects of the siege along with the garrisons. Trenches had to be dug to protect them from artillery missiles; the water supply ran low during a very warm May and June; and all contact with the outside world was cut off, except for an occasional messenger who managed to get through the siege lines. On June 17 it was learned that a relief column of 2,000 men was on the way from Charleston under the command of Lord Rawdon. A final assault was tried against Fort Holmes and the Star Redoubt. There was a brief, bloody encounter in the ditch around the Star Redoubt and the Americans were driven off with heavy losses. A cease-fire was arranged to exchange prisoners and bury the dead and on the nineteenth, Greene lifted the siege and withdrew.

The Americans lost fifty-eight killed, seventy-six wounded and twenty missing. The British lost twenty-seven killed and fifty-eight wounded. Rawdon reached Ninety-six on June 21. Realizing that he could not hold the position, he left Cruger with orders to destroy the fort and escort to Charleston those who wished to remain under British protection.

Today you can walk inside the Star Fort and along the top of its earthworks that were once covered with sandbags. The markers continue in and around the redoubt. The American trenches are discernible and so is Kosciuszko's tunnel by which he hoped to blow up the fort. It has been left just as it was on June 19, 1781, with the exception of some brickwork inside that was added by subsequent owners to keep it from collapsing. The ditch around the foot of the redoubt is evident. During the final desperate assault, Americans raced into the ditch armed with long poles with hooks at the end and tried to pull down the sandbags on the top of the parapet. The British counterattacked and engaged them in hand-to-hand fighting which left forty Americans dead and forced the rest to withdraw.

You can also walk along a bit of the old **Charleston Road** that leads around part of the Star Redoubt showing how well the fort guarded and dominated the road. The area around the fortifications and siege positions is now wooded. As the tour trail takes you from site to site, you will notice what must be recent farm roads and part of the old Charleston Road leading in and out. At the time we were there, it was still possible to poke around in the woods and walk almost anywhere. As the restoration work progresses that much freedom may no longer be possible.

Drive back to modern Ninety-six, pick up Route 34 east, and take it to a meeting with Route 121, which in turn will take you to Interstate 26. Take 26 north in the direction of Greenville and the Reedy River battle site.

Leave Interstate 26 for U.S. 276 and take it as far as the exit for Fountain Inn. In Fountain Inn, take State Route 418 west toward the Reedy River. Follow the signs for 418 carefully, for it twists and turns. In exactly six miles, you will reach a bridge crossing the **Reedy River.** This is the second bridge since 418 left 276. If you want to make sure you are at the Reedy River, continue on across the bridge. If shortly after you reach an intersection with County Road 146, you have just crossed the Reedy River.

The Battle of the Canebrakes took place on the east bank of the Reedy, the bank you first came to along 418. It was soon after the truce of Ninety-six between the Whigs and Tories on November 19, 1775. Three days later on Wednesday, November 22, a force of some 4,000 rebel militia and regulars broke up a gathering of Loyalists and captured one of their leaders. There is another date given for this battle in some accounts, December 22, but despite the discrepancy, it is the same action.

Take 418 back to 276 and head north on 276 for the sites of two major battles, one on a mountaintop, the other in a cow pasture.

KING'S MOUNTAIN

Travel on 276 north toward Greenville and leave it for Interstate 85 north. Leave 85 at the Blacksburg exit and take Route 5 toward Blacksburg. In Blacksburg, at the big intersection in the center of town, turn left onto Route 29 and take it seven miles to the turnoff for **King's Mountain National Military Park.** The King's Mountain Highway is a county road that leads you through a hilly area. After several miles of steady climbing, you begin to see ahead of you a range of hills called the King's Mountain Hills. At a stop sign, South Carolina 216 comes in from the left. A sign for the park and an arrow point the way down a hill then across a bridge and then up a steep incline. Another sign alerts you to the Visitor's Center one mile ahead; a third informs you that you are following the British line of march of October 6, 1780. Actually both forces, American and British, used the same road to get to their battle positions on King's Mountain.

At the Visitor's Center is a two-story fieldstone building to the right with a flagpole and parking area to the left. Both a path and a car road take you up the hill from this parking lot to the top where the battle trail actually begins. The road leads into an upper parking lot, saving you the trouble of walking the last two hundred yards or so to the summit.

King's Mountain National Military Park is open daily from 8:30 A.M. to 5 P.M., Sundays and holidays from 9:30 A.M. to 5 P.M. The little *museum* in the Visitor's Center building has two interesting maps: one shows routes of the British invasion of the South; the other, the various locations throughout the South from which the mountainmen came to fight at King's Mountain. There is also an excellent diorama of the battle showing the terrain and giving some idea of the kind of fighting that raged over the mountain. There is an excellent exhibit on Major Patrick Ferguson who commanded the British forces, the same Ferguson who invented the first breech-loading rifle and had Washington in his sights at Chadd's Ford, but did not shoot for honor's sake. Part of this exhibit is a Ferguson rifle, one of the few still extant. Another exhibit displays the sword carried at King's Mountain by Lieutenant Colonel Frederic Hambright, one of the American militia leaders.

☆

Drive or walk up to the summit of King's Mountain where Ferguson was surrounded by the mountainmen who defeated him. During the summer of 1780, Cornwallis was in Camden preparing to invade North Carolina in September. At the time Major Ferguson was in command of a Loyalist force operating out of Ninety-six, organizing local Tory forces, and doing his best to subdue local rebels. Until then the mountainmen living in the Appalachian Mountains along the western frontier had not been involved in the war. With Ferguson operating close to their homes and settlements, however, and with Tory activity on the increase everywhere, some became involved and fought several engagements with Tory forces in which they were victorious. Alarmed at this prospective threat to his rear, Cornwallis ordered Ferguson out on an expedition through the backcountry aimed at crushing any possible rebel moves from that direction and organizing effective Tory rear guards.

Early in September Ferguson was at Gilbert Town in North Carolina (present-day Rutherfordton). In an attempt to frighten the leaders of the mountainmen, he sent a paroled prisoner through the mountains with a message for them, threatening to lay waste their country with fire and sword and hang their leaders should they actively espouse the rebel cause. The message had exactly the opposite effect. Instead of frightening the men, it unified them in a campaign aimed at wiping Ferguson out before he could make good on his threat.

On September 25 about 1,000 of them gathered at Sycamore Shoals on the Watauga River, in what is now Tennessee near modern Elizabethton. Among them were a number of "over the mountain men," North Carolinians who had migrated to Tennessee, over the mountains. They were eventually joined by other mountaineers and militia units, among them a body of Virginia militia. At the time of the battle there were about 1,800 representing Virginia, what is now Tennessee, and both Carolinas.

On September 26 they left Sycamore Shoals to pick up Ferguson's trail. On the twenty-seventh Ferguson withdrew to the south from Gilbert Town. He had heard of the force coming against him and had decided to avoid a direct confrontation in favor of picking off small groups of rebel militia as they marched to join the main force. He sent messages to Ninety-six and Cornwallis asking for reinforcements, but there were none to spare. By October 6 he had reached King's Mountain where he decided to wait out the enemy in what he considered an impregnable position.

After chasing after Ferguson for eleven days, losing the trail once or twice, and picking it up again, the rebels located him on King's Mountain and sent a picked body of about 900 mounted men ahead of the main force to make sure the quarry stayed in place. On Saturday, October 7, 1780, the 900 slipped into positions around the sixty-foot high mountain according to a prearranged plan. Ferguson's command, which consisted of a little over a thousand Loyalists—he was the only man in the battle on both sides who was not an American—occupied the top of the mountain you are now on.

Actually King's Mountain is a ridge about 600 yards long running in a northeastern direction and from 60 to 120 feet wide. You are at the narrow or southwest end. An old Indian trail, now blazed with white paint, leads from here to a public camping area a mile or two away. The tall monument here was erected in 1880 on the centennial of the battle. The Tory camp was at the northeast end at the widest point on the ridge. No field fortifications of any kind were built. Ferguson believed the wooded, rock-strewn slopes around him would do more to protect his men than any breastwork or redoubt. Despite his previous experiences in this country, he had not yet learned that trees and rocks were perfect cover for the frontiersman who had learned his fighting techniques from the Indians during years of frontier warfare.

The battle began at about three in the afternoon as Ferguson's pickets discovered the mountainmen advancing up the slopes at them. The opening shots were fired about where the Visitor's Center stands. The Tories were firing downhill and probably too high; though they fired steadily, they did little to stop the steady advance of the rebels. Ferguson ordered a bayonet charge down the slope. The attackers simply gave way before the pointed blades—none of the rebels were equipped with bayonets nor would they have known how to use them if they had been—thinning out the ranks of the Tories with well-aimed shots as they fell back. Once the attack was spent, the long rifles of the frontiersmen forced the Tories back up the slope to their mountaintop.

Three times the Tories charged and three times they were driven back. The third time, as they regained the summit, they were pushed off the narrow end of the ridge back to their camp area despite Ferguson's effort to rally them. He rode from end to end of the ridge on his horse blowing a silver whistle and waving his sword with his one good arm. (The other had been shattered at Brandywine and was practically useless.) As he attempted to break through the encircling attackers, eight or nine marksmen among the mountainmen got his range. He was shot out of his saddle and died a few minutes later. Captain Abraham de Peyster of New York took command. He tried to rally the survivors but was forced to surrender. It took a while for the firing to stop, however.

As fresh groups of mountainmen reached the summit, they fired into the prisoners, some of them unaware of the cease-fire, others in revenge for Tarleton's quarter at Waxhaw.

When it was finally over, after an hour of fierce fighting, the tally of dead and wounded included twenty-eight mountainmen killed and sixty-four wounded, 157 Tories killed, 163 too badly wounded to be moved, and 698 who were prisoners. The next day the prisoners were marched away. A week later, near Gilbert Town, a court-martial was held and thirty of the Tories were condemned to death. Nine were actually hung. Most of the others eventually escaped, as the mountainmen drifted back to their homes, leaving them unguarded.

A foot trail leads along the length of the British position on the ridge before winding down around the mountain from site to site where the individual rebel units were stationed. At each point markers tell the story of the action there or identify units or individuals by name. The very tall monument at the campsite was erected by the federal government in 1909.

The markers and monuments along the ridge cover the climactic moments of the battle right up to the last charge, the death of Ferguson, and the surrender of the survivors. The view is wide and beautiful with the Blue Ridge Mountains off in the distance and closer hilltops and ridges in every direction. There are benches along the ridge; the trail leads you back here after touring the entire battle area.

The trees now on the mountain are very different from the thick-trunked forest giants that covered the slopes. The terrain, however, is unchanged. The same spring-fed brook that wound its way over the lower slopes is still there, though deeper in its bed after two hundred years of digging its way down through the forest floor. If you like, you can try a charge or two up the hill just to see the kind of climb the rebels faced, always remembering, of course, that they did it carrying long rifles and muskets and in the face of enemy fire.

The trail leads down from the Tory encampment end of the ridge winding around the hill as it descends. The marker for Ferguson marks the traditional spot of his death. It lies just below the summit because he is believed to have been attempting to cut his way out through the encircling rebel line. A little farther down is a *cairn* of stones marking his burial place. It stands near the original grave marker and a newer one which was dedicated by President Herbert Hoover. The cairn represents an old Scottish custom according to which visitors to the grave leave a calling card in the form of a stone.

Here and there you may use stepping stones over the brook as the trail leads from bank to bank, particularly if there have been rains immediately prior to your visit. Mark the sign for Hambright's North Carolinians. Up the hill about a hundred feet behind this sign, you will find a marker for the spot on which Major William Chronicle fell as he turned to encourage his men. A short distance farther along the trail you will come to the Chronicle marker, at the **burial place** of Chronicle and three others, the only rebels to be buried on the battleground. According to the park literature, this is one of the oldest battlefield markers in the country. It was dedicated on July 4, 1815, by a friend of Major Chronicle. A comparison of the area now around the marker with the engraving of the same spot in Benson Lossing's *Field Book of the American Revolution* reveals many similarities, despite the passage of time since 1849 when he was here. The same brook flows over the ground; the same granite marker is there, though now it has been joined by a newer marker; and the trees have been replaced several times.

There is also a marker for Colonel William Lacey who tried to ride his horse up the hill, but was forced to continue on foot after the animal was killed. Look for a huge **poplar** on the bank of the brook with a widespread system of thick, ground roots. This tree predates the battle; it has been bored to determine its age and it is estimated that it was about eight to fourteen inches in diameter in October, 1780. There are a number of other trees along the brook, white oaks and other poplars, that were here two hundred years ago. Somehow these few giants managed to survive the several logging operations that cut over the entire mountain. Between 1780 and 1878 when the park service took over the site, the area was logged at least three times and burned over more than once.

Note the marker to Colonel James Williams who received his mortal wound near that spot. Shortly after, the trail makes a hairpin turn to the right. Ahead on the left you will find one of the two **springs** the Tories used for drinking water. It is off the trail to your left and has been ringed with stones to keep the soil from filling it in. The other spring is to the right somewhere. As the trail now winds up the slope, you come to the position of Colonel Isaac Shelby's men who were forced down the slope by a Tory bayonet charge. When they reached the ravine at the bottom of the hill, they turned, fired a volley, and using their tomahawks and knives fought their way back up to the top of the ridge. From these positions at the foot of the hill, it must have been like play for the marksmen among the mountainmen to pick off the Loyalists on the top of the hill as they showed themselves against the sky.

It has been claimed of many battles of the Revolution that each was a turning point in the war. In the case of King's Mountain, it is undoubtedly true. This battle marked the beginning of the end of British occupation of the South. Aroused by the news of the victory, fresh militia forces flocked to join Greene when he assumed command of the Southern Department. It forced Cornwallis to delay his invasion of North Carolina and set him marching back to Winnsboro, lest his rear be left open to attack. The second major defeat the British were to suffer in the South took place less than four months later a few miles west of King's Mountain when Cornwallis tried again.

COWPENS

Return to Interstate 85, take it south, and leave it at the exit marked Chesnee–Gaffney–Cowpens Battlefield. Do not turn off the exit ramp onto State Route 11 south to Gaffney, but continue straight ahead to the stop sign. A sign for the battlefield with an arrow points Route 11 north, straight ahead of you. As you drive toward Cowpens you will see the Blue Ridge Mountains in the distance. The entire range is spread out before you along the horizon, growing larger with every passing mile.

After nine miles you will see to the left a tall, granite *monument* and an American flag flying from a flagpole. A dirt road leads to a small parking area in front of the monument. The one and a quarter acres which constitute **Cowpens National Battlefield Site** at the time of this writing do not encompass the entire battlefield. It does, however, take in Morgan's central position. There is a diagram of the battle and an audio tape to go with it, though the tape was not operating at the time of our visit. Actually this memorial forms a triangle with converging roads on two sides forming the apex to the north and the entrance road forming the base. It was here Morgan stopped running and turned to face his pursuers.

In 1780 Brigadier General Daniel Morgan had been ordered to employ his command of 600 infantry and dragoons in the harassment of the enemy in the South Carolina backcountry. Forced momentarily to give up his plans for the invasion of North Carolina after King's Mountain, Cornwallis had decided to try again by the end of the year. He was uncomfortable, however, with Morgan operating behind him, particularly as he seemed to be making threatening moves toward Ninety-six. Tarleton proposed that he eliminate Morgan either by drawing him into battle and defeating him outright, or by forcing him to retreat toward Cornwallis who would come out of Winnsboro at the right moment to deal the veteran of Saratoga and Quebec the coup de grace.

Morgan, first cousin to Daniel Boone, was a veteran of the French and Indian wars. He had been a wagon driver with Braddock when he went down to defeat at the hands of a French and Indian force. A six-foot giant of a man, Morgan had once been lashed 500 times for striking a British officer who had hit him with the flat of his sword. He carried the scars all his life. He had joined the American siege lines around Boston with his own company, led Arnold's march through Maine to Quebec, taken over command of the attack after Arnold was wounded, and had been captured. After his exchange, he and his riflemen had done excellent work at Saratoga and had endured the rigors of Valley Forge.

Realizing that most of his command consisted of militiamen who could not be counted on to stand up to Tarleton's regulars, Morgan beat a hasty retreat when he learned Tarleton was after him. When Tarleton got so close that he was faced with the choice of fighting a running battle and making a stand, he decided on the latter. He selected a wide, grassy area near Hannah's Cowpens, a well-known local spot where farmers wintered their cattle. The field was bordered by low ridges just high enough to conceal small bodies of men. He had been joined by an additional 500 militia, but Tarleton was coming against him with 1,100 infantry and mounted men. Approximately 520 of Morgan's men were veteran Continentals who could be expected to hold firm. Colonel William Washington was also with him with a force of eighty dragoons augmented by a number of mounted troops from Georgia.

As you stand at the monument facing south, the direction from which you came, you are seeing the field of battle as Morgan saw it from his command post. The same roads were here at the time, though Route 11 was then called Mill Gap Road. The ground fell away then, too, to the south in a gradual slope. There was a fork in the road as there is now behind you where Routes 11 and 10, the other road to the right, meet. What is different is the contemporary farm homes, one of them directly opposite the monument, the others along Route 10 to the right.

Morgan's command post was probably close to the apex of the triangle. He arranged his infantry in three lines, planning to use the militia, but relying on his Continentals to form the spine of his position. The first line consisted of 150 picked militiamen. They were drawn up somewhere out in front of where you are now standing at the foot of the slope. Their line stretched across both roads and they were partially concealed in high grass and behind trees. Their job was to fire two volleys and then retreat to the second line, firing as they fell back. The second line was made up of Colonel Andrew Pickens's militia, 300 men in a line drawn across the roads farther up the hill. They were to fire until the enemy came close enough for a bayonet charge. The entire line was then to fall back behind the third line, the Continentals, who were drawn up near the top of the rise under the command of Colonel John Eager Howard. Behind this third line was a depression and then the slope continued to rise to the north. The reserve, which included all the mounted troops under Colonel Washington, was stationed behind that low ridge, now behind you.

After some preliminary reconnoitering, Tarleton's men marched onto the field early in the morning of Wednesday, January 17, 1781, and formed an extended line 1,100 strong about 300 yards from the first American line. A company of dragoons was stationed at each end of the line and a battalion of infantry and 200 mounted men formed his reserve to the rear. In the center of the line were two three-pound cannon called grasshoppers.

Tarleton began by sending a company of dragoons forward to feel out the American position. The hidden riflemen sent them back with fifteen empty saddles, then fell back on Pickens's command, firing as they went. Tarleton ordered the entire line to advance. They moved forward to meet the fire from the second line, sustaining heavy casualties but steadily advancing. When they came too close for comfort, Pickens's men hightailed it for the protection of the third line. According to Kenneth Roberts who wrote a good little book on the battle, the second line was in a real panic when they ran, despite the destruction they had wrought on the British who had lost about half of their officers. Once they were behind the Continentals, however, they reformed and prepared for another go at the enemy.

The British dragoons, seeing what they thought was their chance, charged into the militiamen running to get around the left flank of the third line (to your left), but Colonel Washington's men dashing out from behind the ridge that concealed them, slashed into the dragoons, and sent them reeling back.

Thinking the Americans were in retreat, the rest of the British line pressed forward only to be stopped cold by that third line of Continentals. Volley for volley, the two lines had at each other until Tarleton committed his reserves to turn the American right flank. Seeing the movement, Howard ordered his flank company to wheel to meet the threat. As the men obeyed, turning their backs on the enemy for a moment, the company next in line thought they were retreating and followed suit. The entire American right was in seeming retreat with the British now charging after them when, with about thirty yards between the two forces, Morgan commanded them to turn. Turn they did to deliver a volley into the ranks of the British that tore the attack apart. They followed through with a bayonet charge that sent the redcoats stumbling back, while the reformed militia came back onto the field to join the attack on the British right. At the same time, Washington's mounted troops coming from behind the line hit the British left.

Tarleton tried to rally his dragoons, but for the first time in the unit's history, he was unable to make them obey. They fled instead with the rest of the army after them. Rallying what men he could, Tarleton retreated with Washington in pursuit. Then occurred the duel between Washington and Tarleton that has been recorded in William Ranney's famous painting of Cowpens. Accompanied by two officers, Tarleton turned back and attacked Washington hand to hand. Washington's sword broke off at the hilt during the melee and a British officer was about to bring his saber down on him when a black (according to the painting) bugler hit the threatening sword arm with a pistol shot. Tarleton again rode at Washington, who deflected his saber with his broken sword; Tarleton pulled out his pistol and fired, hitting Washington's horse, and then galloped away. Morgan lost twelve men killed and sixty wounded. Only 200 British cavalrymen rejoined Tarleton the next day. The British left on Cowpens battlefield 110 men killed, 200 wounded, and 550 captured.

Despite Morgan's victory, Greene was in a dangerous position and moved to save his army by retreating with Morgan into North Carolina, at the same time luring Cornwallis out of South Carolina. Cornwallis, who was under instructions from Clinton not to attempt an invasion of North Carolina or Virginia without first making Georgia and South Carolina secure British bases, took the bait and followed.

WILLIAMSON'S PLANTATION

With one more site to cover in South Carolina before we follow Cornwallis into North Carolina, return to Interstate 85 and take it north to the Blacksburg exit. Off the exit ramp, take Route 5 south toward Blacksburg. In Blacksburg at the traffic light where you made the turn for King's Mountain, turn right on 5 and take it south into York County. Just beyond the York County sign you will come to a junction with Route 321. Turn right and take 321 into the town of McConnell's where you make a left onto Route 322. In 2.3 miles you will come to County Road 165, a macadam road going off to the right. Take it for 1.6 miles to a marker on the left side of the road at the site of Huck's Defeat.

On Wednesday, July 11, 1780, Captain Christian Huck, a Loyalist officer who served with Tarleton, brought 500 Tories and British here, including some of Tarleton's legion from Rocky Mount to wipe out a band of rebels who were preparing to join Sumter. Sumter was marshalling his militia for his role in the Camden campaign. He found two Whigs melting lead into bullets, imprisoned them, threatened to hang them, and then looted the home of Colonel William Bratton. At the time we visited, **Bratton's home,** an old cottage a short distance back up the road on the same side as the marker, was in the process of being restored.

There are several other old, frame buildings here at a crossroads forming a settlement known as Brattonville. A marker on the other side of the road on an old, but imposing frame building with end chimneys and a porticoed porch identifies the site of the fight that occurred the next day, July 12, on Williamson's Plantation a half mile east. At the intersection we turned left to go east for a half mile that brought us to a wooded area on the right opposite an open field on the left and farmlands farther along the road. There was a local garbage dump in the field and evidences of yearly plowing, but nothing to suggest the site of a plantation home.

The wife of one of the men threatened with hanging rode off to Sumter's bivouac with news of the raid. Colonel Bratton and Captain Edward Lacey, Jr., with several other officers and about 500 men, left at once, but by the time they reached the vicinity of Huck's camp, their 500 had somehow melted away to 90. Captain Lacey, who lived nearby, had to have his own father, a Tory through and through, tied into bed to prevent him from warning Huck. At dawn on the twelfth, the Whigs attacked, catching the Tories where they were camped between plantation rail fences. Huck was killed and so were thirty to forty of his men; only twelve of Tarleton's men escaped. The Whigs lost one man killed, and the two men who were awaiting Huck's justice were freed.

Return to Route 322, turn right onto it and follow it into Rock Hill where you turn right onto Route 5. Coming out of Rock Hill you will be on 5 and 21 until 5 goes off by itself. Stay with Route 5 and take it in the direction of Lancaster. Shortly after you reach the city limits, go off onto Route 200 east toward Monroe. On the way you will cross the state line into North Carolina at the very point where Cornwallis led his army into North Carolina in September, 1780, on the way to Charlotte.

III.

NORTH CAROLINA

The first years of the Revolution in North Carolina were marked by the attempts of the royal governor to first assert then reassert his authority. In May, 1775, hard on the news of Lexington and Concord, the Mecklenburg Resolutions were passed in Charlotte declaring that royal officials no longer had any authority in the state. Before the year was out, Governor Josiah Martin was living on a British man-of-war off the coast of his province, working for the return of British control. In 1776 the governor's Tory supporters attempted to rally support for Clinton's first try at capturing Charleston, but were squelched by Patriot forces at Moore's Creek before Clinton's expedition got anywhere near Charleston. Three years of comparative peace followed as the Loyalists lay low while the rebels established a state government.

In 1779 the British returned to the South in force. As they began a campaign to reestablish their hold over Georgia and South Carolina, the Tories of North Carolina began to reorganize in anticipation.

Cornwallis invaded North Carolina in 1780 and 1781, and Whig-Tory fighting was renewed, particularly in the coastal areas and the Cape Fear River region. Once Cornwallis crossed the state line to stay, North Carolina became the arena for another round with General Nathanael Greene. As in South Carolina the two armies marched and countermarched, while Tarleton raided and partisan leaders and their followers played hare and hounds. Out of all this activity, however, only one major battle was fought on North Carolina soil between the two major opponents at Guilford Courthouse in March, 1781. Two months later Cornwallis moved into Virginia where he was finally defeated.

☆

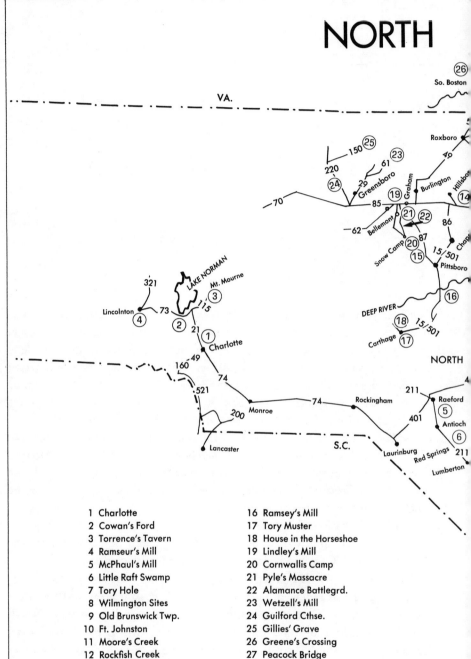

NORTH

㉖
So. Boston

VA.

Roxboro

150 ㉕
220 61 ㉓
㉔ 29 Greensboro 49
70 85 ⑲ Graham Burlington Hillsbor
62 Bellemont ㉑ ㉒ 86 ⑭
Snow Camp ⑳ 87 Chap
15 ㉕ 15/501
Pittsboro

LAKE NORMAN
321 Mt. Mourne DEEP RIVER
③ ⑯
Lincolnton 73 ⑮ 15
④ ② 21 ① Charlotte 15/501 ⑱
Carthage ⑰ NORTH

49
160 74
521 74 Rockingham 211 Raeford
200 Monroe ⑤
401 Antioch
⑥
Lancaster S.C. Laurinburg Red Springs 211
Lumberton

1 Charlotte	16 Ramsey's Mill
2 Cowan's Ford	17 Tory Muster
3 Torrence's Tavern	18 House in the Horseshoe
4 Ramseur's Mill	19 Lindley's Mill
5 McPhaul's Mill	20 Cornwallis Camp
6 Little Raft Swamp	21 Pyle's Massacre
7 Tory Hole	22 Alamance Battlegrd.
8 Wilmington Sites	23 Wetzell's Mill
9 Old Brunswick Twp.	24 Guilford Cthse.
10 Ft. Johnston	25 Gillies' Grave
11 Moore's Creek	26 Greene's Crossing
12 Rockfish Creek	27 Peacock Bridge
13 Tryon Palace	28 Swift Creek
14 Hillsborough Sites	29 Fishing Creek
15 Chatham Cthse.	30 Historic Halifax

CAROLINA

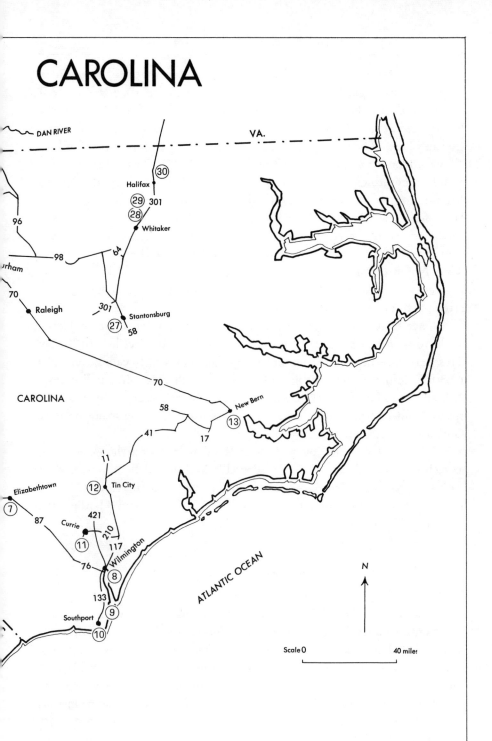

DAN RIVER

VA.

30
Halifax
29 301
28
Whitaker

96

98

urham

70
Raleigh
301
27
Stantonsburg
58
64

70

CAROLINA

58
New Bern
13
41
17

11

Elizabethtown
12 Tin City
7
421
87 Currie 210
11 117
76 Wilmington
8
133
Southport
9
10

ATLANTIC OCEAN

N

Scale 0   40 miles

I have tried to arrange the sites connected with these events in a geographically logical fashion. You will first pick up Cornwallis's trail as he came into North Carolina, hesitated at Charlotte following the British defeat at King's Mountain, and then pursued Greene across Cowan's Ford. The next sequence covers some particularly intense Whig-Tory confrontations at Ramseur's Mill, McPhaul's Mill, Little Raft Swamp, and Elizabethtown. Then you will skip ahead in time by driving to Wilmington where Cornwallis retired after the Battle of Guilford Courthouse for some "R and R" for his men. From Wilmington you will sally forth, refreshed and rested, to visit the dead town of Brunswick and the scene of those Whig-Tory encounters that marked the years 1775–76 when North Carolina, like her sister southern states, was kicking out the royal governor, asserting her independence, and putting down Loyalist attempts to rally around the crown.

Once Greene managed to get across the Dan River ahead of Cornwallis to safety in Virginia, Cornwallis based himself in Hillsboro for six days until Greene, reinforced and ready for another go, came back into North Carolina. After visiting Hillsboro, you will cover sites at Ramsey's Mill and the Haw River (Pyle's Massacre) where Greene and Cornwallis sparred and jabbed at each other as they prepared for the main event at Guilford Courthouse.

In the last section, you will cover the Guilford Courthouse fighting as well as some sideline affairs at Wetzell's Mill and Gillie's Grave, then flash back to when Greene crossed the Dan, then back to North Carolina to cover Cornwallis's march through Peacock Bridge and Halifax, the route he followed from Wilmington to Virginia.

THE CHASE TO THE DAN

Once in North Carolina (on Route 200 going toward Monroe), make a left onto County Road 1117. When it forks, bear left and continue on toward Waxhaw, now two miles away. In Waxhaw 1117 runs into Route 75, which takes you back into South Carolina for a spell and eventually meets Route 521, which you should take north. You are now close to Andrew Jackson's birthplace, a fact you can ascertain by the numerous signs for Andrew Jackson State Park. At the juncture with Route 160, turn left toward Fort Mill. Route 160 will take you back into North Carolina to Route 49. Turn right onto 49 and take it into Charlotte.

CHARLOTTE

Before the news of Ferguson's defeat at King's Mountain in October made him change his mind, Cornwallis had begun his 1780 invasion of North Carolina by occupying Charlotte on September 26. At the time it was a small town of some twenty homes, but it had a spirited militia commanded by Colonel William Davie, which, along with other militia units, put up a lively defense that held up the British army until it could clear them out from behind stone walls and rail fences. The village has become a bustling metropolis since then and has swallowed stone walls, split-rail fences, and the site of the engagement that cost the militia thirty killed and the British fifteen. You will find a *marker* for the site in the heart of Charlotte at one of its busiest intersections, on the right side of Tryon Street just before Third Street. It is a large marker and says in no uncertain terms that two hundred years ago forty-five men fought and died for the possession of a little village.

Cornwallis stayed in Charlotte until October 14 and then returned to Winnsboro, South Carolina. Two months later, on December 2, General Nathanael Greene came to town to take over the command of the Southern Department from General Horatio Gates who had been defeated at Camden. The site where the transfer of command took place has not been marked.

Cornwallis renewed his invasion and pursuit of Morgan and now Greene in January despite Tarleton's defeat at Cowpens. For the next episode you must go north to a dam on the Catawba River.

COWAN'S FORD

Continue through Charlotte on Route 49 to U.S. 21. Take 21 north; approximately nine miles after it crosses Interstate 85, you will see a marker on the left for William Lee Davidson, the Whig general who was killed at Cowan's Ford. A short distance farther, County Road 2145 comes in from the left. Take it to State Route 73. Turn left onto 73 and proceed with Lake Norman, the dammed-up Catawba River, on your right. The lake should tip you off to some drastic changes in terrain and sites. As you skirt Lake Norman, watch the left side of the road for the Davidson memorial about three miles after you turned onto 73. It sits on a rise of ground above the road. You can see the cannon and memorial tablets quite plainly from 73, but be prepared for it, or you may drive right by without noticing.

Take the road leading up to the park and *memorial*, which is set off by a zigzag, split-rail fence. The plaque explains that the exact site on which Davidson was killed is under water at the east end of the dam where he attempted to hold up Cornwallis's crossing of the Catawba.

Some months after his return to Winnsboro from Charlotte, Cornwallis made up his mind to move north again into North Carolina. He and Tarleton tried to pick up Morgan's trail. Cornwallis ordered his troops to burn everything but their essentials at Ramseur's Mill so they could move faster. Aware of this, Greene joined Morgan on the Catawba and together they started a long run across North Carolina to the Dan River in Virginia and safety.

Cornwallis had to cross the Catawba to pursue Greene (it ran north to south and was east of Winnsboro), but the river was swollen with rains. Brigadier General Davidson and about 800 North Carolinians were guarding the four principal fords. Cornwallis intended to make an artillery demonstration at Beattie's Ford, hoping to catch Davidson off guard so he could slip across at Cowan's Ford, which was downstream from Beattie's. The demonstration fizzled out, however, when the soldier carrying the firing match left it behind, but Cornwallis got across nevertheless.

Cowan's Ford was a tricky one: it divided in two at midstream. One branch was a horse ford that turned and crossed a small island before reaching the east bank some distance south of the other ford, a wagon ford that continued straight ahead. Cornwallis's men were guided across by a Tory who left unexplainedly in midstream without warning them about the two fords. While they were crossing, Davidson's men kept them under fire from the east bank. Some of the redcoats were hit and others were swept off their feet by the current but they persisted and got across before Davidson could move reinforcements from the other fords to Cowan's. While Davidson was forming his men along the high bank to delay Cornwallis as long as possible, a Tory with the British took a bead on him from the middle of the stream and dropped him. Davidson, who was only thirty-four, was killed, and his men withdrew, leaving the British securely established on Greene's side of the Catawba.

The tall pillar at the Davidson memorial probably stood on the riverbank before the dam was built. The cannon is marked "G.R. 1767," signifying that it is a British gun and was with the British army during the Revolution. Continue down 73 to the river and the dam, a most impressive structure. Drive over a causeway and visit **Cowan's Ford Hydroelectric Station.** There is a parking area near the administration building which houses a Visitor's Center. Visitors are welcome Monday through Saturday from 9 A.M. to 5 P.M. and on Sunday until 1 P.M. There is a tabletop diorama of the dam and a series of photographs in the downstairs lounge of the construction. One shows the island in the middle of the ford over which the horse trail passed and the nature of the terrain on the banks. Another photograph of the cofferdam in place shows two construction roads built out to the island that seem to follow what may have been the two forks of the ford.

Since the dam squarely straddles the old ford, the banks of the river have been considerably altered. It is a great pity, since the historical documents the administrative office has gathered go into unusually rich detail in describing the British crossing and the militia's resistance. In a letter written at Guilford Courthouse by Earl Cornwallis to Lord George Germain on March 17, 1781, the British commander specifies that his men were under orders not to fire back at the militia until they were across the river, a command they carried out to the letter. He lists his casualties as Lieutenant Colonel Hall and three other men killed and thirty-six wounded.

In the section of *Revolutionary History of North Carolina* dealing with Cornwallis's invasion of 1781, there is an eyewitness account by General Joseph Graham, an American militia officer, of the ford and the crossing.

"That called the wagon ford goes directly across the river. Coming out on the eastern shore the road turns down and winds up the point of a ridge in order to graduate the ascent until it comes to its proper direction. Above the coming out place, a flat piece of ground not much higher than the water grown over with hoar and persimmon bush, stand bamboo briars five and six yards wide [which] extends up the river about thirty-one poles to the mouth of a small branch and deep ravine. Outside of [beyond] this the bank rises thirty or forty feet at an angle of thirty degrees elevation. Then the rise is more gradual. That called the horse ford . . . comes in on the west at the same place as the wagon ford, goes obliquely down the river about two-thirds of the way across to the point of a large island, thence through the island and across the other one-third to the point of a rocky hill. Though longer this way is much shallower and smoother than the wagon ford and comes out about a quarter of a mile below it."

He describes the morning of the crossing as foggy and says the militia sentinels could not see the enemy until the advance units were about one hundred yards out into the river. Graham's cavalry was ordered up to assist the pickets. "By the time they got there and tied their horses and came up in line to the high bank above the ford . . . the British were within fifty yards of the eastern shore. They took steady deliberate aim and fired. The effect was visible, the first being three ranks looked thinned and they halted. Colonel Hall was the first man to appear on horseback behind about one hundred yards. He came pressing up their right flank on the lower side and was distinctly heard giving orders but we could not hear what they were. The column again got in motion. . . . One of the cavalry riflemen reloaded, aimed at Colonel Hall, at the flash of the gun both horse and rider went under the water and rose down the stream. It appeared the horse had gone over the man. Two or three soldiers caught him and raised him on the upper side. The enemy kept steadily on not withstanding our fire was well maintained. As each section reached the shore they dropped their setting poles and brought their muskets and cartridge boxes to their proper places faced to the left and moved up the narrow strip of low ground to make room for the succeeding section which moved on in the same manner. By the time the front rank got twenty or thirty steps up the river they had loaded their pieces and began to fire up the bank."

Davidson arrived and replaced the dismounted cavalry with his infantry. The British continued to advance across the river until their left flank reached the mouth of a small stream and a ravine "thirty poles" upstream. A bugler sounded a cease-fire and all the British troops reloaded. At a second bugle call, the entire line then advanced up the hill of the bank with their arms at trail. The bank was so steep, they had to pull at bushes and trees to get themselves up. Seeing the enemy advancing with all their weapons loaded, Davidson ordered a retreat of one hundred yards and then went back still another fifty feet as the enemy directed a heavy fire from the point of the ridge.

"He then ordered his men take trees and had them arranged to renew the battle. The enemy was advancing slowly in line and only firing scatteringly when General Davidson was pierced by a ball and fell dead from his horse."

He was shot through the left breast by a small rifle ball. According to Graham, it was known that the Tory guide, Frederic Hager, had a rifle that fitted that ball and so it was believed by the general's grieving friends and kinfolk and by his men that Hager had killed him. Most of the other Tories of Mecklenburg County returned to their homes after the war, but Hager moved on to Tennessee where he lived until some of the Davidson family moved into his vicinity. He then moved on with eight or ten others and founded the first American settlement on the Arkansas River near Six Posts, married, raised a family, and died there in 1814.

Davidson's body was recovered that night and buried in the Hopewell Church cemetery by candlelight, for the surrounding countryside was swarming with British patrols. He left a large family and a name that has been remembered in Davidson College, Davidson County, and other memorials in this part of the state.

Robert Henry, a local schoolboy who took part in the battle, says the British suffered many more casualties crossing the river than Davidson's militia have been given credit for. According to Henry, most of the British who were hit fell into the stream and were carried away to watery graves.

The river is still swift of current today. As you walk around the area at the foot of the dam face, you can look across the river and see what is left of the original eastern bank, indeed steep and high, on which the militia made their stand. I could not make out the mouth of the stream and ravine "thirty poles" away from the ford, however, where the British left flank reached the eastern shore.

Once he was across, Cornwallis dispatched Tarleton on a series of raids to keep the militia who had been dispersed at the ford from reforming. From Cowan's Ford Tarleton rode to Torrence's Tavern, pronounced Tarrant by the British.

TORRENCE'S TAVERN

From the dam, go back to the east bank of the Catawba and return along Route 73 around the shore of Lake Norman. Take County Route 2145 back to U.S. 21; turn left on 21 and head north. Eventually 21 joins Interstate 77 and both roads cross the lake on a causeway into Iredell County. About two miles into Iredell, you will see an exit sign for Route 21 north: that is for you. As you come off the exit ramp to a stop sign, turn right in the direction of Mount Mourne; drive slowly, for the road immediately goes into a hairpin turn that takes you east along County Road 1108. In less than a mile of pleasant driving through green fields and past pleasant farmsteads, 1108 T-dead-ends in Route 115 at a stop sign. Turn right onto 115, passing as you proceed south the Mount Mourne Volunteer Fire Department and then a dirt road going off to the right and crossing a railroad spur.

A historical *marker* at that intersection identified this as the site of Torrence's Tavern when we were there. The marker originally stood at the 1108 intersection, however, and was moved here by some zealous road gang who probably mistook one intersection for another. Neither intersection is really the site. The tavern stood somewhere in the vicinity, perhaps along present Route 115 between the two intersections.

Tarleton showed up at the tavern on Thursday, February 1, 1781, merely hours after the battle at Cowan's Ford. Just as Cornwallis had suspected, a large body of local militia, most of them Davidson's men, were reassembling here. Tarleton was outnumbered, but with his customary aggressiveness and his eagerness to make up for Cowpens, he attacked and routed the militia. Later he claimed to have killed about fifty out of 500, but another British officer on the scene estimated the dead at about ten and said that between 100 and 300 men were scattered. From here Tarleton rejoined the main army and Cornwallis for the continued pursuit of Morgan and Greene who were only a few miles away. We'll pick up the chase later.

Backtrack on Interstate 77 into Mecklenburg County; pick up 73 again and head for Cowan's Ford. Take the causeway across the lake past the dam and follow 73 until it ends at a stop sign and merges with Route 27. Continue along 27 toward Lincolnton until you reach an intersection with U.S. 321. Turn right onto 321 and head for the site of one of the bloodiest Whig-Tory encounters of the war and other skirmishes in the continuous civil conflict.

WHIGS AND TORIES

RAMSEUR'S MILL

Route 321 will take you through open land, down a long slope, and up an incline to an intersection and a stop sign. Route 321 turns to the right, but you turn left onto North Aspen Street. As you proceed, check for these landmarks along the road into Lincolnton: a bridge over railroad tracks and a freight area, a National Guard armory on the left, followed by an American Legion Hall and the motor pool for the armory, also on the left. You will then cross a creek. Look to your right front at a range of wooded hills. One of them is the hill on which the battle took place, but at this distance it is impossible to pick out.

When you pass the sign for the Lincolnton city limits, you can see the east slope of the *hill* to your right, its open fields divided into segments. Look for Nest Drive going off to the right. Take it up the hill to a school parking lot just below the summit. A telephone line sweeps up past the school and follows its own cleared path through the woods over the brow of the hill and on to the north. Walk up the slope behind the parking area; over the top of the incline find a *monument* to two Tory brothers who were killed in the battle.

The Battle of Ramseur's Mill takes us back in time to 1780, before King's Mountain and Cowan's Ford. After the surrender of Charleston in May, 1780, to the British, the Tories of North Carolina began to organize and offer active opposition to the rebel Whigs who had had things their own way since the Battle of Moore's Creek in 1776. Secure in the knowledge that the British would eventually invade the state from the south and despite Cornwallis's request that they hold back from an open uprising until he was ready to support them, the impatient Loyalists began to assemble at Ramseur's Mill under the leadership of Colonel John Moore. By the middle of June Moore had assembled about 1,300; the Whigs, well aware of their activities, gathered together about 1,200 men under General Griffith Rutherford and Colonel Francis Locke at Charlotte and Mountain Creek respectively.

Four hundred of them, with Locke commanding, rode and marched to Ramseur's Mill. The Tories were on this hill just north of the present town of Lincolnton which overlooked the mill and its pond. As you stand with your back to the grave site you are facing south, overlooking Lincolnton to your left and front. The telephone line runs along a north-south line. The mill and the pond were at the foot of the opposite side of the hill to your right rear. Ahead of you, hidden by a contemporary sub-development and other buildings, is the Catawba River. The western slope of the hill to your right was cleared ground. There is a wooded area to the east or left as there was then. A main road that ran through the area might be the road you now see at the foot of the hill as you look south. There was a Tory position along that road in the early stages of the battle. Other roads that ran through the battle area are not in evidence and many new roads and streets have appeared. A tannery run by Christian Reinhardt and his home were off to the left at the foot of the hill.

On Tuesday, June 20, 1780, 400 rebels under Colonel Locke came along the main road (on your left)from Dellinger's Ordinary, a tavern in Lincolnton, and attacked the 700 Tories on and around this hill. Many of the Tories were unarmed and fled at once. An early morning fog obscured the scene, but as it lifted and the fighting intensified, the Tories were gradually surrounded by the Whigs who worked their way around the hill on three sides and closed in. None of the combatants, with the possible exception of the officers, were in uniform, making it difficult at times to distinguish friend from foe. Many were neighbors or acquaintances who knew each other as longtime political enemies, and many a long-standing grudge was resolved or intensified during the fighting on this hill. In the close-quarter action friends were sometimes mistaken for foes and heads were broken in by rifle butts by mistake. The Tory position collapsed when one of their commanders, Captain Warlick, was killed. They fled toward the mill and reformed briefly. By that time Locke had lost 110 men dead and wounded; the Tories had lost about the same.

In the Lincolnton Public Library, I found a secondhand account in a locally printed book entitled *Pictorial Walks Through Lincoln County*. It had been written by Wallace M. Reinhardt who was born in 1818 and knew some of the survivors of the battle who were still alive in 1825 when he was seventeen. Reinhardt, who had gone over the site many times, discussed the battle with them and wrote down their accounts. Part of the story is told by a man who joined someone named Adam Reep. Reep led thirty Whigs to join Locke and took an active part in the battle.

The fighting began at the foot of the hill around the Reinhardt homestead and tannery and moved up the hill as those Tories who had weapons and remained to fight were hemmed in on the summit. Captain Warlick seemed to be in command since Moore could not be seen. It was Warlick who persuaded the Tories to hold their ground and rallied them, even as fresh Whig forces arrived. Adam Reep crept around the edge of the action with his thirty men, finally took up a position in a wooded area, and from there tried to shoot down Warlick whom Reep had pointed out to them as the bravest and most dangerous of the Tories.

Eventually the captain was picked off and killed. Then while the sharpshooters on the flanks kept the Tories busy, Locke pulled back his center, had all the men reload, and led them in a charge. During the terrible melee that followed, the Tories lost most of their leaders and fled down the hill and across the milldam, throwing away their weapons as they ran. Some fell into the pond and were drowned. Fifty surrendered while the rest formed on the far side of the creek and, using Ramseur's home as a fort, parleyed with the Whigs. According to the eyewitness account, during the parley Moore and 400 slipped away and across the Catawba. Modern historians, however, say only thirty escaped to join Cornwallis at Camden. By the time Rutherford arrived and he and Locke could organize a pursuit, the fleeing Tories were long since gone.

"The scene upon the battlefield was indescribable, dead men here and there, broken skulls, a few were seen with gunlocks sunken into their heads, disabled men moving about seeking help, men with shattered shoulders, broken arms and legs while others were breathing their last breath. Shortly after the battle many women and children came hunting for their loved ones. Christian Reinhardt's drying house and . . . hot house were crowded with the wounded, dead and dying. . . . The bodies of thirty or more soldiers who were killed in this action were taken to their homes and buried by friends while seventy dead bodies remained on the battlefield and were buried the next day in a long trench which was dug across the hill near where the Tories made their last stand. This trench extended north and south on the top of the hill near the western slope."

I tramped all over the western side of the hilltop, trying to find some evidence of that burial trench, without success. The grading that accompanied the building of the school and the neighboring real-estate development probably wiped out any surface evidence of the grave. The millpond has been filled in, and I was unable to find a marker or anything else to identify the spot on which the mill stood. Parts of the hill that may have been open ground are now wooded. The site of the Reinhardt tannery is unmarked. A map of the area at the time of the battle shows few landmarks that are recognizable today.

Morgan passed by Ramseur's Mill after Cowpens, and Cornwallis paused there soon after to burn the equipment and personal belongings of his men as he lightened his load for his pursuit of Greene and Morgan.

Leaving Ramseur's Mill behind you, continue on North Aspen into Lincolnton and pick up Route 27 for the drive back to Charlotte. In Charlotte take U.S. 74 south to Monroe and then east to Rockingham and beyond to a Tory rendezvous and a raid by a notorious Tory leader.

MC PHAUL'S MILL

At Laurinburg take the U.S. 401 bypass to Raeford twenty-one miles to the northeast. As you travel east, you leave the hilly western country for the flat plains of the seaboard counties. In Raeford on South Main Street make a right onto Route 211 east. Seven miles later, on the outskirts of the town of Antioch opposite a church with a white steeple, stands a marker for McPhaul's Mill 1.7 miles west.

County Road 1105 goes west (or left) at this point. Clock exactly 1.7 miles on it to a little bridge. Just before the bridge, on the right side of the road, are two millstones and a large *stone* into which a piece of old wall has been set. An inscription on the stone identifies it as the site of McPhaul's mill and tavern, a rallying ground for the local Tories. There are some contemporary farm buildings and shacks and the creek itself which powered the mill wheel.

One of the most notorious of the North Carolina Tory leaders was

Colonel David Fanning. He had been a member of a Patriot militia company early in the war and then changed sides. He is supposed to have been trained as a guerilla by "Bloody Bill" Cunningham, an equally famous Tory leader. Fanning was a daring fighter who carried out many a scourging raid on the Whigs. The raid at Little Raft Swamp was in retaliation for a Whig raid on Elizabethtown in August, 1781. Fanning had tried to get to Elizabethtown to aid the Tories, but arrived too late. Hearing that the Whig militia of Colonel Thomas Wade were gathered at Drowning Creek, he moved in that direction to attack them.

THE BATTLE AT LITTLE RAFT SWAMP

Drive back toward Antioch, turn right, and continue on Route 211 out of Hoke County and into Robeson County and the town of Red Springs. On the east side of the town, about a mile and a half along 211, look for the marker for **Little Raft Swamp** at the intersection of County Road 1505.

After being joined by another Tory leader and his men, Fanning and the combined force surprised Wade and his militia in the swamp about noon on Monday, October 15, 1781. Despite their unpreparedness, Wade's men dropped eighteen Tories with their first volley, causing them to dismount and fight on foot. Firing as they came, Fanning's men advanced steadily until the Whigs decided to call it a day and ran into the swamp, leaving twenty-three of their number dead on the field. Fanning's men remounted, pursued, and netted fifty-four prisoners.

This information, which comes from Hugh F. Rankin's *North Carolina in the American Revolution* (published by the North Carolina State Archives), reveals a curious discrepancy. Rankin writes that the Tories "retaliated quickly" for the Elizabethtown defeat which occurred, according to state historical markers, on August 27. Elizabethtown is a little more than forty miles from Little Raft Swamp. According to my calculations, it took Fanning almost two months to march forty miles to exact his "quick" retaliation.

Nevertheless, Fanning carried out a fierce, slashing attack in keeping with his reputation and added another victory to his impresive score. The swamp is still here, but there is nothing besides the marker to remind the passerby of the action which was so typical of the bitter civil war that raged through this part of the state. To continue the story, in a somewhat topsy-turvy manner, drive from here to Elizabethtown to cover the engagement that preceded Fanning's raid. Continue along 211 south. At Lumberton take the bypass and turn left onto Route 41 north.

Elizabethtown is twenty-five miles away. You are in the Cape Fear River region fraught with Revolutionary War history. In this general area many of the first rebellious activities in North Carolina took place, particularly along the Cape Fear River; the region is associated with Governor Josiah Martin who attempted to keep the colony in line for the crown.

ELIZABETHTOWN

Route 87 joins 41 west of Elizabethtown so that you come into town on 87. A historical marker shows up on the left side of Main Street (also 87) in front of a barber shop.

After the Battle of Guilford Courthouse, Cornwallis sent Major James Craig to occupy Wilmington in February, 1781, to provide him with a port through which he could receive supplies to support his invasion of North Carolina. Craig made Wilmington a center of anti-Whig activity and carried out a vigorous campaign of suppressing the Whigs and supporting the Tories in the Cape Fear area. Besides aiding and encouraging Fanning, he conducted punitive expeditions himself and in August burned plantations near New Bern and occupied that town for two days. He was about to proceed farther when he heard that General Anthony Wayne was in North Carolina on his way from Virginia to join Greene in South Carolina. The news sent him scurrying back to Wilmington, denying the Tories of the Cape Fear region his further protection. The Whigs, who had been doing their best to stay out of his way, assembled and launched fresh attacks against the Loyalists.

A Tory officer, Colonel John Slingsby, was holding some Whig prisoners in Elizabethtown. About 150 Whigs crept up on the town during the night of Monday, August 27, 1781; forded the Cape Fear River, which today runs through the town; and attacked just before daybreak. The Tories were taken completely by surprise and rushed about panic-stricken, trying to escape or organize resistance. A large number fell into a ravine now known as "Tory Hole." The Whigs gathered all the munitions, weapons, and supplies they could find, freed the Whig prisoners, and went back across the river. Nineteen Tories were either killed, wounded, or made prisoners. The Whigs had suffered only one man wounded. Slingsby had been wounded, was captured, and eventually died of his injuries. It was this action that led to Fanning's raid at Little Raft Swamp.

Tory Hole is behind the buildings on the left side of Main Street in the vicinity of the marker. Walk around the side of the Bank of

Elizabethtown building and down a gravel driveway to the rear. It will take you to a ravine, a long, deep cleft in the earth some fifty or sixty feet deep which runs diagonally toward Main Street. Today it is overgrown with trees and shrubs and here and there the townspeople use it as a dump. Beyond it the ground falls away to the bank of the Cape Fear River.

As you drive farther along Main Street and look to your left, you can see the ravine as it turns and parallels 87. Road and pedestrian bridges have been thrown across it at intervals and it is a most curious phenomenon. Since we know the Whigs came across the river, we may assume they drove the Tories from the river toward the town and therefore into the ravine.

Continue out of town along Route 87 and take it southeast toward Wilmington. West of Wilmington, 87 meets U.S. 74–76 which takes you into town.

THE ROYAL GOVERNOR AND THE PATRIOTS

WILMINGTON

Wilmington was occupied by the British in February, 1781, as you already know; it was also the base for punitive raids into the interior and north along the coast. Cornwallis marched here from Guilford Courthouse to recuperate, arrived in the city on April 7, and left for Virginia eighteen days later. The town was finally evacuated by the British in November after the surrender at Yorktown.

There is only one site here connected with the British occupation. It is located at the intersection of Market and Third streets, the **Burgin Wright House** built in 1771 and used by Cornwallis as his headquarters. The basement served as a prison. It is a handsome house with an imposing flight of steps leading up to the front door and a Georgian facade which is really an elaborate piazza, despite Georgian pillars. The house is set in a very pretty, eighteenth-century, formal garden, also open to the public. The interior is furnished in period, but nothing is original to the first owners or connected with Earl Cornwallis. It is open on weekdays only for most of the year from 9 A.M. to 4 P.M. and on weekends during the spring. Adults are charged $1.00; children, $0.25. A guide shows visitors through those rooms that are open to the public.

There were fortifications built around the town before and during the occupation, but I was not able to find any evidence of them. Wilmington is a clean, pleasant city with a waterfront along the Cape Fear River. One of its principal attractions for tourists is the U.S.S. *North Carolina*, the World War II battlewagon which is open to the public at its mooring every day. A walking tour of the historic area takes you into the many nineteenth-century houses still extant. They cover the entire century from 1800 through the Federal and Civil War periods and the Gilded Age as well.

From Wilmington, drive south to visit a wonderful dead town site and the scene of some of the earliest anti-British activities in the state.

OLD BRUNSWICK TOWNSHIP

Leave Wilmington on the same road that brought you in, U.S. 74, but take it west. Immediately after coming off the bridge over the Cape Fear River, take a turnoff on your left onto Route 133 south. Driving south from Wilmington takes you through very pretty lowland country with moss-hung trees, flat, green fields, and woodlands on both sides. Watch for a mileage sign: Orton–6, Southport–18. A mile or two beyond, the road forks. Take the left fork onto Route 130. A road mark a mile along 130 is the turnoff for Orton Plantation, which is open to the public; three miles farther is the turnoff for Brunswick. You are now on a winding road lined thickly with trees. Through them you will eventually see a large body of water to your right, Orton Pond. Finally, you will come to a road going off to the left with a sign for Brunswick one mile away. Turn left; a mile down the road you will come to the gate that admits you to **Brunswick.** There is no admission charge.

Founded in 1726 by Maurice Moore, the brother of the builder of Orton Plantation, Brunswick was a prosperous seaport when the Revolution began. Spaniards from Florida captured it in 1748 and lost it back to the townspeople three days later. In 1765, upon the passage of the Stamp Act and attempts to enforce it, Brunswick was the scene of one of the first actions of resistance to the crown. An armed crowd surrounded the home of Governor William Tryon, who lived near the town, and would not allow stamped paper to be unloaded from H.M.S. *Diligence* in the harbor.

Soon after the battle at Moore's Creek in February, 1776, when the Whigs put down a Loyalist attempt to bring back Royal Governor Josiah Martin, Tryon's successor, the British landed 900 sailors and marines at the mouth of the Cape Fear River to carry out a policy of pillage and destruction that included partially burning Brunswick. Under the command of Earl Cornwallis, they paid particular attention to the home of Robert Howe in retaliation for his anti-British activities, which had included forming and training North Carolina militia units. So brutal were they in their treatment of the people on the Howe Plantation, particularly the women, that Cornwallis and Sir Henry Clinton later gave them a financial reimbursement.

As you come through the gate, you will be in a long driveway and parking area leading to a *museum* and Visitor's Center. Audiovisual displays tell the story of the town from its origins and explain the extensive archaeological work being carried out on the site. A very good slide film fills in the background and history not only of Brunswick but of the Cape Fear country in general. Included are drawings of Brunswick houses based on the remains. Do not miss the museum. There is a walk-in reconstructed wharf, displays of the relics found on the site, son-et-lumière maps, and dioramas, all very attractively designed and displayed.

A *walking trail* leads through the ruins of the town, starting at the shell of **St. Philip's**, the Brunswick church. Note the colonial headstones in the old churchyard. The large breastworks that you see almost immediately after leaving the museum are the remains of Fort Anderson, a Confederate fort that was built over a portion of the old town site. The fort was attacked by Union ships, and the effects of the bombardment are still to be seen in partially filled-in shell holes here and there. As you walk along what were the streets of the town, you will come to excavated remains of basements and retaining walls. Twenty-three of the original 160 building sites have been excavated in what was once a town of 250 and more souls. At each house site, a plaque names the owner, gives pertinent information, and in some cases provides a reconstructed view of the building. A nature trail that sometimes coincides with the history trail identifies shrubs and plants that were used by the Indians and colonists. The trail leads down to the old wharf area where some of the original pilings have been located, preserved in the water. The view is over the wide mouth of the Cape Fear River.

There are rest rooms and picnic facilities here as well. The entire site is now covered with a young growth of trees, and with the significance of the spot, its pleasant wooded prospect on the river, and the old breastworks for the young to climb over, it is an excellent place for a picnic lunch and an exploratory walk through colonial history. It is open 9 A.M. to 5 P.M., Tuesday–Saturday and 1–5 P.M. on Sundays. Mondays it is closed.

Return to Route 130; take it north to the turnoff from Route 133, and turning sharp left, head along 133 for Southport thirteen miles away. In Southport continue through the town along Howe Street, passing the park around the town hall, and on down to the end of the street on the mouth of the Cape Fear River where Fort Johnston stood.

FORT JOHNSTON

Turn left onto Bay Street, the road along the river shore, for a short drive to Davis Street where an embankment on the left with a plaque set into a boulder is all that is left of Fort Johnston. A long municipal pier extends into the river nearby; on the site itself a beacon tower stands guard for the benefit of mariners on the river.

There had been a fort on this spot as far back as 1745. The Spaniards who looted Brunswick in 1748 attempted to take the original fort. It was the first in the province and was named for Governor Gabriel Johnston. In 1765 during the Stamp Act crisis the captain of H.M.S. *Diligence* spiked the guns of Fort Johnston lest the Patriots turn them on his ship. Governor Josiah Martin was forced to take refuge in the fort in 1775 as the rising tide of the rebel cause forced him out of the capital city of New Bern. He was protected by the guns of H.M.S. *Cruzier* in the harbor.

Fort Johnston was a center for royalist activities. Loyalist leaders came and went under the watchful eyes of rebel spies. Here, too, came Allan MacDonald in disguise, a veteran of Culloden Moor who was to experience another defeat at Moore's Creek, this time fighting on the side of the British rule he had once opposed so vigorously on his native soil. Eventually Martin moved on board the *Cruzier* and issued a proclamation guaranteeing the end of a long rope to anyone who attacked the fort. Finally he ordered the fort's guns spiked and had all the small arms and powder removed to the *Cruzier*. On Wednesday night, July 19, 1775, a band of Patriots led by Robert Howe entered the fort and razed and burned its building in full view of Martin on the deck of the *Cruzier*. Howe and his followers stayed on the site for a while but made no attempt to rebuild the fort. Cornwallis later placed a detachment here and across the river on Bald Head Island, but for the most part Fort Johnston saw no further action during the Revolution.

Another fort was begun on the site in 1804 under the command of Lieutenant Joseph Gardiner Swift, West Point's first graduate. It was seized by Cape Fear minutemen in 1861 and served the Confederates during the Civil War. The brick building behind the fort site with its two-story center section and one-story wings housed officers in the rebuilt nineteenth-century fort.

From Southport, drive north back to Wilmington and on to the site of the first Revolutionary War engagement in North Carolina.

MOORE'S CREEK

At the Wilmington Bridge, go back toward Wilmington but go off 133 at the exit for 421 north. (It's the same exit as for the U.S.S. *North Carolina*.) Fifteen miles from Wilmington along 421, turn left onto Route 210. Signs for the Moore's Creek battleground will now appear. After two or three miles Route 53 joins 210 from the right and 210 curves to the left. Follow 210, noticing the sign for **Moore's Battle Creek National Park.** You are driving through flat farmlands with clumps of trees here and there and low, boggy ground along the side of the road. The road T-ends at a railroad crossing with 210 to the right and a grocery store on the left. This is the town of Currie.

Turn right onto 210 which curves left in about a hundred yards and brings you to a stop sign and another sign for the battle site. In about a half mile the entrance to the park will appear on the left. You will find the usual flagpole, parking area, and Visitor's Center with rest rooms and museum. The exhibits tell the story of the men involved in the battle and the circumstances that led up to it. There is also an illuminated map explaining the strategy of the action and a diorama showing the Highlanders' charge across the bridge.

By early 1776 Governor Josiah Martin had sold London and General Thomas Gage, the British commander in America, a plan to reestablish British authority in North and South Carolina. He would raise an army of 10,000 composed mostly of the Scottish settlers who were (very strangely I think) royalist and others who wished to remain subjects of the crown. The population of the province was about evenly divided in its sympathy and it did not seem much of a problem to raise that many men. The Loyalists would march to the coast and join a British expeditionary force at Brunswick. From there they would strike out at the rebels wherever they showed themselves.

Gage had already dispatched Lieutenant Colonel Donald MacDonald and Captain Donald McLeod to North Carolina to raise a battalion of loyal Scots. Martin promoted them both and made them officers of the Loyalist militia. All recruits were promised land and extensive tax exemptions as a reward for their service. In February a mixed force of 1,600 Loyalists (Highlanders and Regulators) had gathered at Fayetteville, then called Cross Creek. On February 20 they marched out to the coast. The Regulators were veterans of a movement of Piedmont settlers who in

1771 had defied the government of Governor William Tryon over a matter of currency and had been put down at the Battle of Alamance. They really did not constitute an anticrown movement, but rather expressed local grievances against the vested interests in the provincial government.

Opposing the Loyalists were Colonel Richard Caswell of the New Bern militia and Colonel James Moore. As the Loyalists advanced, they managed to outmaneuver the militia most of the time, but their progress was blocked at vital river crossings. Finally they had to cross Widow Moore's Creek at this spot if they meant to reach the coast. Waiting at the bridge was Colonel Alexander Lillington with 220 militia and Caswell with 800. They also had two guns called "old Mother Covington and her daughter." On February 26 the Loyalists were only six miles away.

An auto road leads from the parking field near the Visitor's Center to another parking field closer to the actual battle site. Along the way you pass the **Heroic Women Monument** erected in memory of Mary Slocum, the wife of a militiaman, who rode sixty-five miles to help the wounded, and the other women of the Cape Fear region. Farther on is a **James Moore Monument** and then the parking field. Close by is a plaque map of the site. Ahead of and around you, you can see the ground leading to the creek, the remains of the *breastworks* behind which the rebel militia took cover, the remains of the old **Stage Road** that led over the bridge, and the **Grady Monument** which marks the grave of Private John Grady, the only Whig to die in the battle.

This is an excellent site for walking out a reconstruction of the events since the whole action took place in three minutes within this comparatively small, self-contained area. A very good audio tape tells the story of the battle from the listener's position and point of view. Two guns off to the left represent Mother Covington, a light fieldpiece on a gun carriage, and her daughter, a small, brass, swivel gun which fired a one-pound ball 750 to 900 yards. The larger gun is a cast-iron British cannon dated 1750. The guns are placed approximately on the spot where the rebel guns were pointing at the creek.

Take the path leading through the breastworks. It takes you along the creek which winds and twists through the swamp. You are walking along an old stage and wagon road. Eventually you will come to the site of the bridge, long since gone, and a monument identifying the site. An iron rail blocks you from going any farther. On the other side of the creek is a wooded area where Caswell was camped before the battle. It belonged to a private hunting and fishing camp when we visited the site.

You may be able to cross the creek over a reconstructed bridge, however, and visit Caswell's camp if the National Park Service is successful in its efforts to buy that land. (The 1776 bridge, according to Professor Hugh F. Rankin of Tulane University, consisted of two logs thrown across the creek with planks nailed across them.)

Early in the morning on Tuesday, February 27, 1776, the Loyalists with Lieutenant Colonel McLeod in command marched to the bridge on the far side of the creek. Aware that part of the rebel command was camped there, they expected to fall in on them unannounced. During the night, however, Caswell withdrew his men across the creek to join Lillington and threw up the breastworks you saw near the parking field. Placing his men behind it, he put his two guns into position covering the bridge and waited.

An advance party of seventy-five claymore-wielding Scots led by Captain John Campbell hit the camp and found it empty with campfires still burning. Regrouping in the woods, the entire force waited for daybreak. Despite the loss of surprise, McLeod decided to attack. To the skirl of bagpipes, the advance guard charged onto the bridge and discovered to their surprise that the planks had been removed and the remaining stringers were greased (or so they later claimed). Thirty yards away, the rebels and their two artillery pieces responded with a hail of lead that cut down McLeod and Campbell and a number of their followers, some of whom fell into the creek and were drowned. The rest turned and fled. Caswell's men rushed forward, replaced the planks, crossed the creek, and hit the confused and demoralized Scots again.

The three-minute engagement cost the Loyalists between fifty and seventy killed and wounded, thirty of whom were hit at the bridge. Eight hundred and fifty were made prisoners and a great deal of booty fell into the hands of the rebel militia, including 350 guns and shot bags, 1,500 muskets, 150 swords and dirks, two medicine chests fresh from England (one worth about 300 pounds sterling), thirteen wagons and their horses, and $75,000 in gold which the Patriots found buried in a stable at Cross Creek. During the following days and weeks, Moore's men spread out across the Cape Fear region, hunting down Highlanders and Regulators who had taken part in the battle and disarming them.

The results were immediate and dramatic. Blown away were British plans to invade North Carolina and any effective Loyalist organization. Supporters for the crown in North Carolina went underground and did not emerge in any strength until 1780. Thwarted in his plan to land at the mouth of the Cape Fear River and meet Loyalist support, Sir Henry Clinton and his fleet and army moved down the coast to Charleston,

South Carolina, where his efforts to establish a foothold were turned back at Sullivan's Island.

Except for the effects of erosion, the breastworks are very much as Caswell's men dug them. Notice they are in the shape of a horseshoe and anchored on the creek which protects the open end. A plaque shows the proportions of the original breastworks, that the parapet was two feet high and a ditch was dug three feet below. The stage road connected Fayetteville and Wilmington and provided access to neighboring plantations and farmers and traders who came here to float supplies downriver to Wilmington; the creek eventually flows into the Cape Fear River. The bridge was the only way over the creek for many miles, which explains why the Loyalists felt they had to force a passage. There are picnic facilities available in a separate part of the park with its own entrance off the road that leads into the Visitor's Center area.

ROCKFISH CREEK

From Moore's Creek National Park, return to Route 210 and take it east. At the intersection with U.S. 421, continue ahead across 421. Watch the signs for 210 carefully, for at one point it meets Route 133 and turns sharply to the left and then curves right again. When 210 intersects U.S. 117, take 117 north to Route 11 which goes off to the right. Take Route 11 a short distance to a bridge over a creek and then a marker on the right side of the road for the Battle of Rockfish Creek.

According to the marker, the action took place 300 yards to the southeast, which puts it to your right rear as you face in the direction you have been traveling. The actual site when we were there was an open area filled with piles of gravel and sand. It was either the highway department's road-repair depot or a sand and gravel company's supply. The creek flows through a low, wooded area below it.

In August, 1781, Major James Craig announced from his headquarters in Wilmington that anyone who refused to come into Wilmington to take an oath of allegiance to the king would forfeit his property and his life as well. Since so few Whigs came to him in response to his appeal, Craig decided to go to them. As he marched north from Wilmington, he was met here by Colonel James Kenan and the Duplin County militia. There was a short, sharp exchange of gunfire which exhausted the militia's ammunition, and they were forced to run for it. No one was killed, but Craig's cavalry scooped up about thirty Whigs and made them prisoners.

Continue along Route 11 into Tin City; pick up Route 41 right (east) and you're on your way to see a fabulous palace in the old capital of the royal province.

NEW BERN

In Jones County, leave 41 for Route 58 east; take it through Trenton and on until it meets U.S. 17. Take 17 north into New Bern. Major Craig arrived here August 19, 1781, on one of his punitive expeditions. A Swiss settlement at the time of its founding in the early eighteenth century, New Bern became the provincial seat of royal government and the site of one of the grandest buildings built in America during the colonial period.

Tryon Palace, as it is known, was begun by Governor William Tryon in 1767 and completed in 1770 for the sum of 15,000 pounds sterling which translates into $75,000 in modern currency. At that price, in terms of what the real-estate dollar buys today, Tryon got a great bargain. Signs in town direct you to its location at the foot of George Street on the Trent River. Admission is $2 for adults and $1 for children and it is open every weekday except Monday from 9:30 A.M. to 4 P.M. and on Sundays from 1:30 to 4 P.M. Visitors are conducted through the mansion by costumed hostesses.

The original main building was destroyed by fire in 1798, the east wing lasted a few years more, and only the west wing is original. All the rest is a restoration. It was restored in much the same manner as Colonial Williamsburg by going back to the original plans and carefully and painstakingly rebuilding (at a cost of a little over three and a half million). The Williamsburg Governor's Palace, though handsome and beautiful, seems pale and colorless compared to the rococo flourish with which Tryon Palace is decorated and furnished. This is partially explained by the fact that the Tryon Palace was built fifty years later. The moldings in Williamsburg, however, are all wood as were the original moldings; many of the moldings in Tryon Palace are made of plaster. How Victorian! None of the furnishings are original to the palace, but all of it is period and priceless.

You should not miss touring Tryon Palace if only to see how the top half could live during the late colonial period. The sitting room on the second floor alone is worth the price of admission. The servants' quarters on the top floor under the roof are eye-openers. The mansion had an undetermined number of servants whose apartments and rooms are almost as numerous as those below. The kitchen is enormous and magnificent, even by modern standards. Note the huge copper kettles, each set into its own oven for cooking for large numbers of people. The gardens behind the palace at one point overlook the Trent River. Josiah Martin, who succeeded Tryon, added the smoke and poultry houses and dovecote. He

also dug up the cabbage patch behind the kitchen and hid cannon, powder, and other munitions there when he left New Bern to take refuge
in Fort Johnston, hoping he would be able to return to dig them up.

Tryon Palace was taken over by the state's first governor, Richard
Caswell (the hero of Moore's Creek), and the first state assembly met in
the council chamber in the palace. The provincial congress which sat in
defiance of Governor Martin met in the old courthouse which is no longer
extant. There are several other eighteenth-century buildings in New Bern,
but none of them, as far as I know, played a role during the Revolution.
A walking tour of the old part of the city takes you to them, and since
New Bern is an interesting old town you might want to spend the rest of
the day here after seeing the palace.

Now take U.S. 70 west to a historic town 150 miles away where
Fanning snatched a governor.

REGULATORS AND REBELS

HILLSBORO

Churton Street, the principal street in Hillsboro, is a veritable midway of historical markers. Daniel Boone set out from Hillsboro to cut
his wilderness trail through Cumberland Gap into Kentucky for the
Transylvania Land Company, and the site is marked on Churton Street.
Most of the other streets are lined with quaint old homes, many from
colonial times. You can spend at least a day walking through the quiet,
shaded streets, up and down interesting little hills, finding your way into
a hundred nooks and crannies, and even spending the night in an old inn.
Cornwallis spent time here on two separate occasions and Fanning raided
the town to capture Governor Thomas Burke.

U.S. 70 takes you right onto Churton Street, which is a good way
to begin a Hillsboro driving tour. Drive up Churton to Tryon Street and
turn left to go to number 118, the **Nash-Hooper House.** A two-story,
frame house set off the street out of line with the other houses on the
block, it was built in 1772 by General Francis Nash and was bought in
1781 by William Hooper, a signer of the Declaration of Independence.
This is the only remaining home of a signer in North Carolina.

Continue along Tryon Street to a stop sign at the intersection with
North Wake Street. Turn right and go one block to make a right onto
Queen Street, which will take you across Churton Street and to number
113, **Heartsease,** a narrow, two-story frame house.

In June, 1781, Thomas Burke, a native of Hillsboro, was elected governor by the general assembly and he went to New Bern, the capital. In September he returned to Hillsboro to organize a campaign aimed at suppressing Loyalist activities. Early on a foggy Wednesday morning, September 12, Fanning and 950 men infiltrated the town and after a brief skirmish captured it and the governor (on the steps of this house, according to tradition), the city council, and a number of Continental officers and soldiers. The victory cost Fanning one man wounded. The defenders lost thirty-five killed and wounded. Fanning left with his prisoners later the same day.

Continue down Queen Street and make a right onto North Cameron Street. Proceed two blocks to East King Street and turn right again. As you walk or drive through this town, notice that many of the homes have placards which give the year the house was built. Many are revolutionary; several are prerevolutionary, and some early nineteenth century.

King Street will take you back across Churton Street. About a half block beyond the intersection on the left is a large, beautiful, old house more than two stories high with a long veranda in front. This is 153 King Street, the Colonial Inn, standing where an inn has stood since earliest colonial times. This is not a colonial building, but the flat *flagstones* in front, according to tradition, were laid down by Cornwallis's soldiers who also paved the entire street for 150 yards in all directions from the intersection of King and Churton streets. The old inn still takes guests and serves meals.

Continue along King Street to South Wake Street at the next intersection; turn right and then right again onto West Tryon Street. Back across Churton Street you go and down to St. Mary's Road. As you turn left onto St. Mary's, notice the Cameron Park Elementary School, one-story high. Immediately beyond that on the right is a hurricane fence surrounding a large plot of ground and a brick entrance way through which a driveway leads up to Montrose, a private house.

It was on this site and in this general area that Cornwallis and his men camped in 1781. He marched in on February 20, looking for food and rest for his tired men after chasing Greene to the Dan River. On February 21, he issued a proclamation inviting the local population to escape "the cruel tyranny" of the rebels by joining him. His reward for anyone who rallied to the cause was ten days' food ration, but he seems to have had few takers. To keep his men from getting bored he put them to work repaving the town streets.

On February 23 Greene crossed the Dan River back into North Carolina. Three days later Cornwallis moved out of Hillsboro and headed toward a collision with Greene at Guilford Courthouse. The house now standing on this site, Montrose, was built in 1898 on the site of two earlier buildings.

Go back along St. Mary's Road to the stop sign where it feeds into Cameron Avenue. King Street makes it a three-way intersection by coming in from the right. Directly opposite King Street is a dirt road, the old Halifax Road, that leads up a hill to a wooded knoll. At the time of my visit, a new county school administration building was being built there just off Cameron Avenue. By the time you visit it will have been completed and I assume the access along the old Halifax Road will still be open to the public. Walk along old Halifax Road up the hill. At the top, look to the right for a bronze *plaque* enclosed by an iron picket fence. Six Regulators were hung on this hill by court order, June 19, 1771, after the Battle of Alamance. Alamance and the Regulators were not actually connected with the Revolution, though some historians, particularly in North Carolina, try to make a case for them as forerunners.

Turn onto King Street; not quite as far as the next intersection (Churton Street), just opposite a little street named Court Street which comes in on the left, look for number 141 on the right. This is William Courtney's **Yellow House.** It is believed to have been built sometime before 1768. Cornwallis is said to have stayed here and at Faddis Tavern which stood next door, moving back and forth from one to the other for security reasons.

Now turn left onto Court Street to Margaret Lane. Turn right onto Margaret Lane and take that past the next intersection, which is Wake Street. As you continue along Margaret Lane, notice to your left how the ground slopes down toward a line of trees that mark the Eno River. Before the Battle of Alamance, at which Tryon put down the Regulators, the governor and his men camped along the river in the area bounded by Wake Street and Occonopchee Street which is two blocks beyond Wake.

At the next intersection, go to the right, then right again on King Street, and right once more at Churton Street. Proceed along Churton Street until you are heading out of town the way you came in. After you cross the Eno River, watch for U.S. 70 east–86 going off to the left. Take 70 and as it climbs a steep incline, notice to the left a big, two-story, frame house standing at the top of a high knoll. That *hill* on the south bank of the river was part of Cornwallis's encampment in 1781. From there he moved toward Guilford Courthouse.

Where Route 86 south leaves U.S. 70, take 86 in the direction of Chapel Hill. In Chapel Hill, pick up the Route 15–501 bypass which takes you into 15–501 proper. Head south for Pittsboro to mix up time sequences and sites to save yourself a lot of back tracking.

CHATHAM COURTHOUSE

Go through the town of Pittsboro. On the other side of town, as you go up a fairly steep grade, notice a historical marker on the left on the site of the old Chatham County courthouse. Fanning staged one of his earliest raids here in July, 1781, capturing a number of local Whig leaders. The courthouse is no longer standing. The site is covered by a wood filled with brambles and thickets.

RAMSEY'S MILL

Continue on to County Road 1012 on the left. Take it nine or ten miles to U.S. 1. Go right onto U.S. 1 south for less than a mile to where it crosses Deep River. Somewhere in this area, on the riverbank, stood Ramsey's Mill. Cornwallis came here about three days after the battle at Guilford Courthouse on his way to Wilmington and spent several days building a bridge about 300 yards along the riverbank to your right as you approach the present bridge. Greene was following Cornwallis and could have attacked him in a very vulnerable position, but lacking the men, he withdrew, and Cornwallis continued along the Cape Fear River down to Wilmington. Lee's Legion may have skirmished with part of Cornwallis's army near here, but there is nothing to mark that site.

Continue south across the Deep River on U.S. 1 until you reach U.S. 15–501. Take 15–501 south toward Carthage. Just outside of town, go off onto Routes 24–22 into Carthage, where 27 joins 22 and 24. As you come out of Carthage, you will drive up a steep incline that begins just after a "Resume Safe Speed" sign. At the top of the hill, look ahead to your right for a historical *marker* for the site where the local Tories met before marching on to the Moore's Creek battle. According to this marker, the house where the rendezvous took place should be behind you to the southwest. We went back and explored the area, looking for either the house or the remains of a house, but though we found a likely site the given distance in the given direction on a low, wooded hill, contemporary homes seem to have been built where the rendezvous house once stood.

Go back along Routes 22–24–27 to 15–501 and pick up the signs for the Alston House also known as . . .

THE HOUSE IN THE HORSESHOE

A sign directs you to the left onto County Road 1644. After driving 9.4 miles, a sign for the house will appear on the left as well as a sign for

Governor Benjamin Williams's tomb. Both indicate a left turn onto
County Road 1624, a dirt road which ends in 0.4 miles at the house.

To your right sits a two-story, white, frame *house* with brick
chimneys at either end and a piazza, or roofed-over porch, along the
front. A split-rail fence zigzags around the property. A caretaker's contemporary house is off to the left. If no one is in evidence, ring his door-
bell and he will be happy to show you around. That's why he is there.
A bronze plaque on a boulder explains that a skirmish occurred here
between Whigs and Fanning's Tories. There is parking space to the left;
admission is $0.50, and the house is open to visitors during daylight hours.
The house gets its names from its location inside a horseshoe bend of Deep
River and from one of its early owners, Colonel Philip Alston.

On Sunday, August 5, 1781, the colonel and some of his Whig
followers were camped here when David Fanning came along with a superior force of Tories. Alston and company barricaded themselves inside
the house for a two-hour battle, during which the Tories tried to set the
house on fire by rolling a cartload of burning straw against it. Eventually
the Whigs surrendered and were paroled. After the Revolution the house
and 3,000 acres passed into the hands of Governor Williams who named
it "Retreat." He died on the plantation in 1814; the house then passed
through a succession of hands and by 1954 it was in a sad state. The
Moore County Historical Association restored it, and the house and five
remaining acres became the property of the state through the Department
of Archives and History. It was administered by the association and
maintained by the state when we were there, but according to the caretaker, the federal government was to take it over in 1972.

The signs of the battle are amply evident. The exterior walls of the
house are marked by numerous bullet holes that look like gouges in the
clapboards. Seventeen in one plank to the left of the first window to the
left of the entrance almost broke the plank and necessitated the metal
plate that now covers them. Bullet holes may also be found inside the
house where the musket balls came right through the clapboards and
inner walls.

There are no original furnishings. The present front door was originally the rear door. The original front door, now at the rear, comes out
onto a flagstone walk and a hill overlooking the surrounding countryside.
The governor is buried close to the house along with other members of
his family. An old photograph in the hallway shows two wings that were
added during the nineteenth century. Both were knocked down by an
earthquake, thus restoring it to its original shape.

Return along the dirt road to where you turned onto it, but instead of going back the way you came, turn left and take County Road 1621 north. When it meets Route 42, turn right onto 42 which will carry you over the Deep River and on to a meeting with U.S. 1–15–501. Turn onto 1, etc. north, which is eventually joined by Route 87. When U.S. 1 goes off to the right, stay on 87–15–501 into Pittsboro to a traffic circle. Pick up 87 north as it leaves the circle and take it to County Road 1005 near the town of Graham.

There is a *marker* at this intersection on the right for Lindley's Mill four miles southwest. The only road going in that direction, County Road 1005, does not take you to the site where the Whigs made an unsuccessful attempt to free Governor Burke from Fanning's clutches. In fact, as of this writing there does not seem to be any way of getting to Lindley's Mill, but take 1005 south (left) anyhow into **Snow Camp,** a crossroads settlement with a filling station at the intersection and a few substantial-looking homes and farms. Cornwallis and his army camped in this area after Guilford Courthouse on their way to the Deep River crossing at Ramsey's Mill. The creek that winds its way through the area suggests they may have been attracted by a readily available water supply.

PYLE'S MASSACRE

Continue along 1005; when it turns sharply right at a stop sign, follow it another 3.5 miles to Route 49. Turn right onto 49 north which takes you into the town of Bellemont where you will see markers for Alamance battleground and Tryon's camp. Just before you enter Bellemont watch for a mileage sign for Graham ("Graham–5"); 2.8 miles from that sign you will find on the left side of the road a historical marker for Pyle's Massacre. A road leads off to the right at a sharp angle to the southwest. Clock three-quarters of a mile down that road to the approximate place where the Americans were responsible for a "massacre." You are at a three-way intersection. There are farmlands all about, woods on the right, and more woods ahead where one of the roads comes to a dead end.

Once he was safely across the Dan River and in Virginia, Greene sent reconnaissance forces back into North Carolina to observe Cornwallis's movements. One of these groups was Harry Lee's Legion. On Friday, February 23, 1781, Lee and his men came across a band of Tories commanded by a Doctor John Pyle on their way to join Cornwallis in Hillsboro. Lee's men were wearing green jackets similar to the ones worn by Tarleton's British Legion. The two groups met on one of these roads in this general area.

Lee was on Tarleton's trail and was hoping to catch him by surprise. Seeing that the Tories had mistaken his unit for friendly troops, he allowed them to go on thinking that so he could get his men past without causing an incident that might alert Tarleton to his presence in the region. He neglected to inform his men, however, of what was in his mind. Pyle's horsemen drew to one side of the road to allow Lee's men to pass. What happened next depends on which account you believe. In his memoirs, Lee says that he meant to disclose his men's identity once they had the upper hand and offer Pyle's men the choice of disbanding or switching sides and joining him. Unfortunately, General Andrew Pickens's militia were with Lee and had been concealed in the woods along the side of the road, but not well enough. Some of Pyle's men saw them and opened fire. Lee's men then turned on the startled Tories.

Professor Rankin's version differs somewhat. He says the two lines of horsemen were abreast of each other for a while and Lee's men were almost past when some member of the legion recognized part of the Tory uniform and sounded the alarm. The legion then turned and attacked. There is no difference of opinion, however, about what happened to Pyle's command. Before they could gather their wits and scatter into the woods, ninety were dead on the road. The rest escaped as best they could; many were wounded and some did not survive for long.

Drive back to Route 49 and take it north to Interstate 85. Take the interstate south for one exit; come off onto Route 62, and follow the signs for the **Alamance battleground** six miles away. Since the link between the Regulators' movement and the Revolution is tenuous at best, you can choose to skip this site. It is interesting, however, with a plaque map and text explaining the Regulators and the battle and with flags marking the exact positions of the opposing forces. If you would rather go on, continue on 85 to Greensboro and the site of an engagement that led up to the big show at Guilford Courthouse.

PRELUDE TO VIRGINIA

WETZEL'S MILL

In Greensboro, leave Interstate 85 for U.S. 220–29 north. When 220 goes off on its own, stay with 29 and find a marker for the mill three to four miles north of Greensboro. This marker presented a problem. It said that the site of the mill is six miles to the east. The 1964 Guide to North Carolina Historical Markers, however, the most recently revised guide at the time I came this way, states that the site is nine miles east. We took the only eastbound road in the area, Hicone Road to the right. After a few miles, Hicone dead-ends in County Road 2770. After going a little north and then straightening out in the right direction, 2770 continues east. We weren't anywhere in particular at the six-mile point. At 7.3 miles we reached Buffalo Creek. We knew that the mill had been on Reedy Fork Creek, however, so we continued on for another three miles. That took us to a dead end into Route 61. Two miles to the left, or north, 61 crosses Reedy Fork Creek at a point exactly nine miles east by a little north of the marker on U.S. 29.

If this crossing is the site of Wetzel's Mill, it was here on Tuesday, March 6, 1781, that Cornwallis attempted to draw Greene into a general engagement nine days before the rebel commander was ready to fight the Battle of Guilford Courthouse. On February 23 Greene had returned to North Carolina from Virginia with his army reinforced and reprovisioned. On February 26 Cornwallis left Hillsboro, his army having eaten the town empty, and moved toward Greene. Greene sent part of his army under General Otho Williams to harass the British and keep between them and the main part of the army until he received additional reinforcements.

Williams was camped east of Wetzel's Mill when Cornwallis began to advance toward him, obviously spoiling for a fight. Williams withdrew to the ford near the mill. Tarleton and a large force of infantry went after him with every intention of attacking with Cornwallis close behind. When he saw he could not make a stand against so large an enemy force, Williams withdrew toward Greene and left a covering force of men under Henry Lee, William Washington, and Colonel William Preston at this ford.

Lee placed most of the men along the creek and his cavalry in the rear to cover the line of retreat. I assume they were on the east bank of the creek, the bank to the left as you face north across the bridge. The British tried to force the ford and at first were driven back. Then with artillery support, the British infantry stormed the east bank as Tarleton's horsemen crossed the ford to cut Lee off; Lee withdrew his infantry while the legion covered them. The British pursued for about five miles until Cornwallis gave up.

The ford could have been anywhere along this stretch of creek, but it is possible the bridge was built at the crossing. Both banks of the creek are now wooded.

The Americans lost approximately twenty killed, the British about twenty-one. By this time Greene was camped on Troublesome Creek near an ironworks, a site we were not able to locate, though we did find the creek.

BATTLE OF GUILFORD COURTHOUSE

Take U.S. 29 back to Greensboro and then U.S. 220 north. A large sign will alert you to the battlefield a mile before you reach it. Between the Greensboro city limits and the site, you will drive through a suburban area which has been built, in part, on ground British and Americans maneuvered and fought over during the battle. **Guilford Courthouse National Military Park** encompasses the main events of the battle, however, and explains them very satisfactorily.

At an intersection with a traffic light, addditional signs direct you right onto County Road 2179, which is New Garden Road. The entrance to the park is 500 yards ahead. Beyond the entrance sign, you are driving with the British troops as they deploy to right and left and advance toward the first American line. Now you come to Battlefield Avenue at right angles to 2179. Proceed with caution, for the avenue curves to the right of the intersection and local, through traffic moves at a good clip. You have already driven right through the center of the first American line. After crossing Battlefield Avenue and then a railroad track, you will approach the second American line which ran through the Visitor's Center area.

The Visitor's Center *museum* is a small building with rest rooms and a parking field. It is open daily from 9 A.M. to 5 P.M. There is no admission charge. A ten-minute slide film covers the events leading up to the battle and the battle itself, orienting you to the various markers and monuments you will find along the way. The museum interprets the battle through maps, dioramas, and relics.

There are two tour roads, one for automobiles that touches the major points, and one for walkers that really involves you in the terrain. There are statues and memorials scattered throughout. The equestrian statue of General Nathanael Greene in the open field on the opposite side of New Garden Road from the Visitor's Center marks the approximate center of the second line. At the time of the battle, this was a heavily wooded area except for a few open fields which were part of a nearby farm. The National Park Service has replanted trees wherever there were trees in 1781 to try to reestablish the terrain as it was. Explanatory plaques along the tour roads interpret each site and individual pamphlets for each of the three American lines are sold for $0.10 each on the honor system: you take a pamphlet from a box and deposit your dime.

The footpath begins next to the Visitor's Center and leads first onto the field opposite and to Greene's statue, then to a large pavilion, then across the railroad tracks and Battlefield Avenue to the American first line. Greene had planned to make a stand on this site at some future date as he passed through during his retreat to the Dan River. Once his army was reinforced in Virginia and resupplied, he moved back into North Carolina looking for a battle at the right moment, confident he could deal Cornwallis a telling blow. Cornwallis thought Greene had about 10,000 men; actually when the battle began Greene had about 4,500. Only 1,600 of them were Continentals, the rest militia. Cornwallis had about 2,000 men, all battle-hardened regulars commanded by experienced, professional officers.

Confident that trained, disciplined troops gave him the advantage, on Thursday, March 15, 1781, Cornwallis advanced against Greene who waited for him at this location. The main attraction was preceded by a skirmish between Tarleton and Lee a few miles east at New Garden Meetinghouse. Tarleton was wounded in the hand and lost two fingers; otherwise the skirmish served only to alert the British to Greene's proximity. Cornwallis then marched his men twelve miles from New Garden early in the morning. They went directly into battle on empty stomachs.

Greene disposed his men along three lines. The first line, along which you are now walking, was composed of two brigades of untrained, inexperienced North Carolina militiamen, 1,000 strong. Greene had planned this battle in a manner that resembled Morgan's strategy at Cowpens. The North Carolinians had been asked to deliver just two volleys from behind a split-rail fence before leaving. The fence is gone, of course, but the area is still wooded and if you can erase the sight of the contemporary homes pressing close upon the site, you can visualize perhaps those green, nervous men as they waited behind the fence for the well-ordered ranks of the enemy to approach. On their left were Lee's Legion and Campbell's riflemen. On their right were William Washington's cavalry, some Delaware Continentals, and a company of riflemen. These flank units were positioned so that they could enfilade the center of the British line.

Cornwallis entered the battle area in complete ignorance of the nature of the terrain; his advance information had been scanty and poor. The battle opened with a brief, ineffectual artillery duel between two British three-pounders, all the artillery they had, and the Americans' four six-pounders. Then the British center, consisting of four regiments, advanced. The North Carolina line flashed flame and the first volley hit them at 150 yards. The British stopped to deliver one volley and then charged. When they got to within 120 feet of the split-rail fence, they stopped. Facing them was a line of muskets and rifles steadied on the top fence rail and aimed right at them. On they came again as the second volley tore into their ranks. The North Carolinians didn't wait to see the effect of their fire; the bayonets were too close. They turned and ran for their lives. They had done what they had been told to do and now it was time to leave. The American units on the flanks held their ground, causing Cornwallis to send in his infantry reserves against them while his center moved on toward the American second line.

The line of the British advance is now built over somewhat by one-family homes; the cleared field over which they advanced is now wooded. Follow them along the foot trail back to the Visitor's Center area and the second American line which stood 300 yards behind the first. The woods were thicker then. This was principally an infantry battle; cavalry action was confined to the New Garden Road. Notice the monument to Gillies, Lee's bugler boy. After the battle, we will find the site where Gillies died (before this battle) under the sabers of Tarleton's dragoons.

The American second line consisted of 1,200 Virginia militiamen who were as inexperienced and untrained as their comrades from North Carolina. Their officers had served with the Continental Army, however, and several had been in battle. The British came against them through a woods so thick they could not use their bayonets. The Virginians fought hard and well while some units from the first line flanks, including Washington's horsemen, fell back to extend the second line to the right and left. Behind the Virginians was a line of sentinels with orders to shoot any man who turned to run. Gradually this line was forced back and most of it pushed to one side.

The British went on toward the third American line which was composed of some of the best units in the army, including the veteran First Maryland, the Second Maryland, and two Virginia regiments. They were stationed on a rise of ground about 500 yards behind the second line. The British formed their line anew two hundred yards in front of them, about one hundred yards past the Visitor's Center building, and charged. They were met by a devastating fire followed up by a counterattack as the First Maryland plunged forward to finish with the bayonet what their rifles had begun. The British pulled back and regrouped. At that point Greene could have ordered a general advance and might have finished off the British center, which was now disorganized and badly hurt. Not wishing to risk his best troops, he held back and let the British come on again.

Follow the trail through the woods along the line where the British reformed noting the markers for the positions of the various units. To the left a row of subdevelopment homes crowds the right flank of the American third line, though most of that position is preserved intact, with markers for the individual American units. At one spot the Americans stopped the British at a distance of only 100 feet. The no-man's-land before you is still a tangle of trees and undergrowth. From here the Marylanders drove forward with their bayonets, advanced, and chopped up the Welsh Fusiliers who were still reeling from the effects of their fire.

The trail skirts the scene of the charge and the left of the American line and comes to a marker for Colonel William Washington's First Virginia Cavalry. You are now on the New Garden Road where it dips into a hollow, the site of one of the best-known incidents of the battle. The British were now focusing their attentions on the third line. As their two guns were brought into play at a site marked on the other side of New Garden Road, the second battalion of the Queen's Guards advanced toward a newly recruited Maryland regiment which broke and ran. The Guards rushed forward into the gap, upon which Washington led his dragoons in an attack that passed through them like a storm of avenging angels.

Close behind him came the First Maryland and a crack Delaware regiment to hit the staggered Guards with rifle butts and bayonets. A fierce hand-to-hand melee raged across the road and through the hollow until Cornwallis ordered his guns to fire grapeshot into the struggling mass of men. "Give them a whiff of grape," he said. The deadly hail scythed both British and Americans, saving the British from wholesale retreat and possible disaster. By this time other British units had made their way through the woods and ravines and were in support. A final assault line was being formed when Greene decided to break off the engagement and withdrew.

As you cross the path of Washington's cavalry charge, bearing to the right, you come upon a marker where Lieutenant Colonel James Stuart, who led the Guards, was killed by Captain John Smith of the First Maryland. The discovery of his sword, which was dug up near here, helped identify the site. Across the road, at the top of a long, grassy slope, is a *monument* to Peter Francisco, a giant young man—six feet eight inches tall, who rode with Colonel Washington, used a five-foot sword, and is credited with killing eleven redcoats during the battle.

Notice the old markers that were probably placed on the field during the 1890s when the site was owned by a private organization devoted to preserving the battlefield. There is also a tall, white marker at the center of the third line. The trail ends where the remains of three Continental soldiers were uncovered in 1888 and reburied. Nearby are the monuments to the Delaware and Maryland regiments.

The walking tour, which actually follows two trails—one covering the first line sites and the other covering the third line, takes about an hour. The auto tour road, much of which is along New Garden Road, takes you to a few sites not covered by the footpath. Tour Stop 4 is where the two British guns were placed during the final phases of the battle. You are up at the top of the slope now, looking down into the hollow where the hand-to-hand fight occurred between the Maryland troops and the Guards. From here Cornwallis's "whiff of grape" was ordered. The auto road also leads to the Francisco monument at Tour Stop 6 and then on to Tour Stop 7 at a traffic circle where two veterans of the battle, Major Winston and Captain Jesse Franklin, were buried years after the battle. A marker on the other side of the circle identifies this as the area where the last shots of the battle were fired. There is a map of the final phase, one of many maps you will find along the auto tour road, each describing one particular phase. Auto Tour Stop 8 is at the site of the first **Guilford Courthouse**. Greene set up his headquarters here during the battle, not a very good spot for a military commander of his day, for he was unable to see most of the battlefield.

Continue on to a stop sign at an intersection. You are now out of the park area. Continue across the intersection onto County Road 2266. On the left just beyond the intersection, hidden by a screen of young pines, is a tremendous oak tree. This is the **Liberty Oak** around which Greene's army camped before the battle. When we were there, it was surrounded in part by refuse which had been dumped there.

The battle ended with Cornwallis remaining on the field and claiming a victory. The reaction to his report of the battle back home in London was that with another such victory the British army would be ruined. Cornwallis had lost almost 600 men, more than a fourth of his command. Greene, who kept his main force intact after inflicting a severe blow on the enemy, lost about half that number. After the battle Cornwallis spent two miserable, rain-soaked days on the field tending to the wounded of both sides and burying his dead. He then left for the march to Wilmington. Greene went down into South Carolina to lose a series of battles that made the British withdraw from their line of forts across the interior.

There are no picnic facilities in the park, but there is a separate park area adjoining this with picnic tables, fireplaces, and some fishing. Ask at the Visitor's Center for directions. Plans at the time of our visit called for an expanded Visitor's Center, a new slide film, and new interpretative displays in the battle areas.

Leave the park the way you entered it along New Garden Road. At the intersection with U.S. 220, turn right and go north to where the bugler boy Gillies met his sad fate.

GILLIES' DEATH

Several miles north, Route 150 comes in from the right and joins 220 for about two miles before it takes off again to the left. Follow 150 and clock almost three miles from that point. In a little less than three miles, the road curves to the left. There is a white, frame house on your right. Just around the curve on the right you will see a tall granite *monument.*

The inscription on it reads: "About twenty-five yards southeast of this spot on February 12, 1780, Gillies, Light Horse Harry Lee's bugler boy, fell under the swords of Tarleton's dragoons. History leaves no record of his given name but his noble sacrifice for his country's freedom will never be forgotten. Erected by Robert Oscar Holt, September 9, 1939."

On the opposite side of the road, almost directly across from the monument, down in the midst of a thicket of the thorniest berry bushes I have ever tangled with, is an older memorial to Gillies, a semicircle of stone with a bronze plaque that was placed there by the local chapter of the D.A.R.

It reads: "On this spot bugler boy Gillies aged 14 lost his life at the hands of British soldiers."

Directly in front of this monument, at its foot, surrounded by a low, fieldstone wall, is a small ground marker with the initial G. It was set here by Judge David Schenck who was responsible for setting up the Guilford Battleground Company that rescued and restored the Guilford battlefield. Actually, this monument marks the path of the *old road* that ran along here parallel to the present Route 150.

On that Saturday in February, 1780, as Greene was marching to the Dan River through this region, he was informed by a local resident that Cornwallis and his men were on a nearby road. Lee was sent with a detachment to investigate. Gillies, who was with this detachment, was ordered to lend his horse to the local resident who went forward with a small party of dragoons. The boy was dismounted on the road when the dragoons reappeared, pursued by Tarleton's men. Lee was in a concealed position and the British did not see the rest of the American detachment. They swept down the road and sabered poor Gillies to death before he could get out of their way. Lee and his men attacked in a rage, killed eighteen of the British, and were on the point of hanging their leader, Captain Thomas Miller, when the advance detachment of the entire British army appeared and Lee was forced to rejoin Greene.

At that time, the old road was clear of trees and bushes. You can find your way down the bank to the monument as I did, carefully avoiding the brambles, and stand where the road once ran and where Gillies was killed. His body was found by some Quaker gentlemen who were following Cornwallis's army, burying the dead, and caring for the sick and wounded. It was taken to the nearby town of Summerfield and buried near the present Summerfield public school. I found the school, but though I was told there was once a cemetery on what are now the school grounds, the cemetery is no longer there and Gillies' grave is lost.

I am indebted to Miss Catherine Hoskins of Summerfield for directing me to the site of Gillies' death. Coincidentally, some of Miss Hoskins' ancestors, who then lived close to Guilford Courthouse, entertained Benson Lossing when he visited the area over one hundred years ago while he was researching Revolutionary War sites for his *Fieldbook of the American Revolution*. Miss Hoskins and I agreed that we were carrying on an old family tradition and were very happy about it.

Go back along Route 150 to U.S. 220; take 220 back to Greensboro; pick up Interstate 85 east to Burlington, and then take 49 north. You are heading for the North Carolina state line for a short foray into Virginia to tidy up the loose ends of the Greene-Cornwallis duel. As you travel north on 49 you will be passing through an increasingly hilly and less settled region. The old, log outhouses on the farms, particularly the tobacco-drying sheds, and the long stretches of open fields and woods between houses put you in mind of an American countryside of another century.

In the town of Roxboro, 49 picks up U.S. 501 north bypass and leaves it north of the town. Stay with U.S. 501 and follow it through the country over which General Greene hurried his army, with Cornwallis not too far behind, as he headed for the Dan River. Greene had prepared for this retreat long before it became necessary. His goals were Irwin's

Ferry and Boyd's Ferry on the Dan where a fleet of small boats had been gathered to take his men across. This countryside was the scene of the last forty or fifty-mile dash. Both armies were almost close enough to see each other's campfires, but Greene's men kept at least a day ahead of the British. Late in the afternoon on February 14, 1781, Greene's rear guard crossed the Dan. Just as they got to the other side, the first of Cornwallis's men appeared on the opposite shore. Cornwallis gave up and turned and marched to Hillsboro.

Just before you reach the state line, you will come to two historical markers. One explains that Cornwallis crossed back into North Carolina a few miles to the west followed shortly thereafter by Greene just before the two met at Guilford Courthouse. The other commemorates Greene's crossing. We crossed, too, and continued into Virginia on Route 501 and on to the town of South Boston thirteen miles north. We could not find a state historical marker for Greene's crossing the Dan River into South Boston where one should be, but we did find the river and the general area in which he crossed.

If you would rather not go through that semi-satisfying exercise, go back to Roxboro and just south of it take U.S. 158 east to where Route 96 joins it north of Oxford. If you went up to South Boston to satisfy your curiosity, turn off 501 onto Route 96 just north of the Virginia–North Carolina line and take it south to U.S. 158. Continue south on 96 through Youngsville and on to the intersection with Route 98. Take 98 east to Route 64 and continue east on 64 toward Rocky Mount to the U.S. 301 bypass south. In Wilson, 58 south joins 301 and then goes to the left shortly after, taking you with it. You are now on 58 south–U.S. 264 east. In less than two miles, 58 will go to the right and you with it toward Stantonsburg eight miles away.

PEACOCK BRIDGE

Go through Stantonsburg, which is smaller than its name, and across a railroad line. Clock 1.1 miles from the railroad to a concrete highway bridge. On the other side of the bridge is a historical marker. You are now on Cornwallis's line of march to Virginia. On Sunday, May 6, 1781, Cornwallis was marching north from Wilmington to the last six months of real fighting in the war. Here, on the shores of Contentnea Creek, 400 militiamen under the command of Colonel James Gorham tried illogically to stop him. They stood their ground for a bit and then scattered into the woods as Tarleton's dragoons came galloping across the bridge. Sensing trouble ahead, Cornwallis sent Tarleton to flush out the other coveys of militia he was sure were waiting for him.

The old log bridge is long since gone, but the woods remain on both banks of the creek. Cornwallis probably approached the creek from your left as you face south; the militia gathered along a line on the opposite bank.

Follow Tarleton and his advance guard by backtracking along 58 to U.S. 301. Continue north on 301 into and beyond Rocky Mount and through the town of Battleboro. Immediately after Battleboro, at the sign to "Resume Normal Speed," start to clock 1.7 miles through the town of Whitaker to a bridge over **Swift Creek**. A marker on the far side of the creek identifies this as the spot where on May 7, the day after the affair at Peacock's Bridge, Tarleton met and scattered another gathering of local militia. There are no houses along this stretch of road other than a motel office up the bank above the marker. Low, swamp ground lies to one side of the creek. A railroad track can be seen to the left. The area is generally wooded though it is quite open on the marker side of the bridge.

Six miles farther along 301 brings you to **Fishing Creek** where a third and similar action took place. The banks of the creek are probably as bushy and wooded as they were when the local militia again did their best to annoy Cornwallis. Whether they were trying to stop him or hurry him on his way is not clear. Had they known what lay ahead for the British, they might have been content to lie low and just let him pass on out of their state and into history. Unfortunately, one last militia stand brought on a most unpleasant business in Halifax, putting a period of death and destruction to Cornwallis's final days in North Carolina.

HALIFAX

As you come into Halifax on U.S. 301, you will come across several markers concerning the town. On April 12, 1776, the famous Halifax Resolves, drawn up and passed here, instructed the colony's delegates to the Continental Congress to second any movement toward independence from the mother country. The resolves did much to push the Congress toward the adoption of the Declaration of Independence.

The town was occupied on Cornwallis's march in May, 1781, after a spirited engagement with the militia which had gathered here in force. Tarleton surprised them by coming not from the south, as they expected, but from a different direction. This militia was also scattered by the charge of Tarleton's dragoons, but this time Tarleton paid for his easy victory with three dragoons dead and a number of horses killed as well. The militia then reassembled and built breastworks on the other side of the Roanoke River from which they fired on British soldiers approaching. A detachment had to be sent across the river to drive them off. As a result, the British soldiery were not kindly disposed to the inhabitants of the town. There was so much looting and insulting of the citizens that Cornwallis had to court-martial and execute two of the worst offenders.

About 0.8 of a mile from the turnoff for the 301 bypass is a marker for Cornwallis and his occupation of the town. On the other side of the road is a small, white cottage with a brick chimney at one end. This is **Constitution House** in which the first state constitution was drafted. It originally stood on another site, was moved here in 1920, and is furnished in period style.

There is a restoration project in Halifax called **Historic Halifax** that can be found by following the signs for it. At the time we were there, much remained to be done. The Visitor's Center was in the old clerk's office built in the early nineteenth century. Close by is the old jail which was built in 1758 and recently restored. There is also a marker on the site of the courthouse in which the Halifax Resolves were adopted. Opposite the clerk's office is the old cemetery in which a number of illustrious North Carolinians are buried. A small museum in the clerk's office exhibits artifacts that have been dug up in the archaeological work that was still going on. As we walked around the area we discovered several recently exposed colonial foundations.

Return to the Cornwallis marker and Constitution House and turn back into town. When you reach an intersection with Route 125 going left over railroad tracks, turn onto it and immediately after the tracks turn left onto a paved road that parallels the tracks and leads to a point opposite the Halifax Railroad Station. The paving gave out at about that point and I had to continue along a rutty dirt road. To the right I found the remains of a brick chimney sticking up out of a thicket of brambles and bushes. In the thicket were foundation walls and the brick rubble of an old house. This was **Grove House** where Cornwallis stayed in Halifax. There are plans to expose the foundations fully and possibly restore the house. You may find the restoration finished when you come. It is also possible that the first skirmish between the militia and Tarleton's troopers took place near Grove House. That site has not been positively identified.

Leave Halifax on 301 north, cross the Roanoke River, and drive on for seventeen miles to the state line. At that point Cornwallis entered Virginia late in May, 1781. He was 140-odd days away from surrender at Yorktown.

IV.

VIRGINIA

If Massachusetts was the head of the snake of rebellion, it was one of two heads, for Virginia was as much a leader in fomenting the Revolution in its own section of the country. It supplied much of the Revolution's military leadership, revolutionary spirit, and political ideology. Count among Virginians prominent in the ranks of rebellion Patrick Henry, Thomas Jefferson, George Washington, Richard Henry Lee, Henry "Light Horse Harry" Lee, and George Mason, to name those who come most readily to mind. Though the prosperous planters of the tidelands were not quite as discontented under royal rule as the merchants of Boston, the fires of independence burned with a flame no less intense in Williamsburg.

Like her sister colonies in the South, Virginia experienced a spate of military activity early in the war as Lord Dunmore, the royal governor, fought the same useless battle other southern governors fought to keep their provinces loyal to the crown. That period ended with the destruction of Norfolk in January, 1776, by Dunmore and was followed by a hiatus of three years, allowing a false sense of security to build up among her people. They were rudely brought back to the realities of the times in 1779 by a British expedition under Admiral Sir George Collier and General Edward Mathew that raided and occupied the port cities of the tidewater. In 1781, Benedict Arnold, newly commissioned in the British army, came down upon them with another expeditionary force to capture Richmond and raid the James River region.

Despite the defeats British and Tory forces had suffered at King's Mountain and Cowpens and the weakening effects of the Battle of Guil-

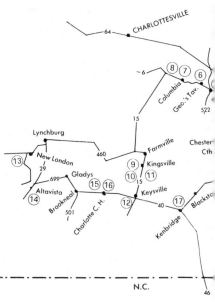

VIRGINIA

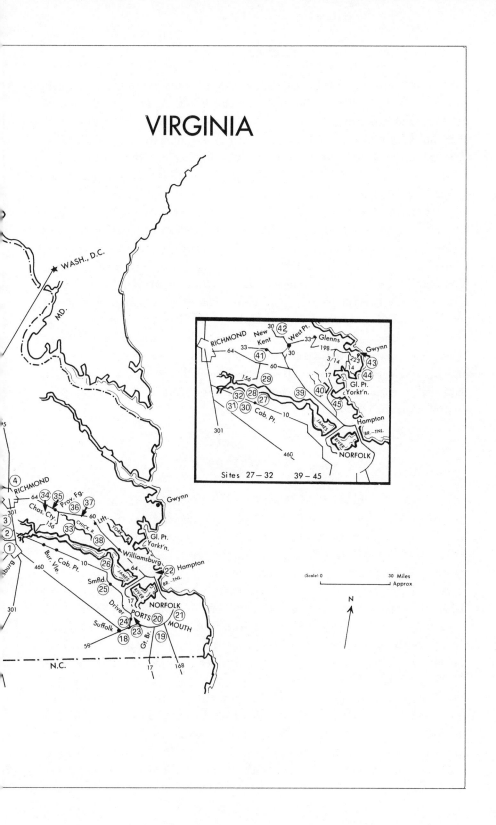

ford Courthouse, Cornwallis continued to press ahead with his own strategy for achieving victory through aggressive action. He joined General Phillips, who had replaced Arnold, in Petersburg in May, 1781, and from then on Virginia was a major theater of war operations as Lafayette, Wayne, Cornwallis, Tarleton, Simcoe, Washington, and the French under Rochambeau marched and fought from the tidelands west to Charlottesville and back again to Yorktown.

As in the Carolinas and Georgia, I have tried to strike a balance between the flow of events and the necessity of getting from site to site in some logical and convenient fashion. We used Petersburg, Richmond, Lynchburg, Portsmouth, and Hampton as bases to cover blocs of sites. You may find other towns or cities more pleasing or convenient, but with some variations, I am passing that plan of action on to you. I did not cover Monticello, Mount Vernon, and the Washington Birthplace National Monument because they are so well known as national shrines. If you have never visited them, however, I advise you to do so. Monticello and Mount Vernon in particular are wonderfully expressive of the men who called them home and seeing them firsthand will complete your mental portraits of both.

THE ARNOLD-PHILLIPS RAID, 1781

In late December, 1780, Benedict Arnold arrived at the mouth of the James River with 1,200 men, including Simcoe's rangers, with orders to destroy supplies the Virginians were preparing to send to General Nathanael Greene in South Carolina. Moving up the James, he took Richmond early in January.

Washington, in New York, organized an army under Lafayette to move south against Arnold. The French fleet undertook to join up with Lafayette, fought a battle with the British fleet near Chesapeake Bay, and then gave the whole thing up. This enabled General Clinton to reinforce Arnold with additional troops. He also sent Major General William Phillips to take over the command.

The Virginians were unprepared to put up more than token resistance. With Lafayette still in Maryland on his way south, it looked as though the British would soon gain control of Virginia. Arnold left Richmond and captured Portsmouth. Then on Wednesday, April 24, 1781, he landed near Petersburg with 2,500 men and advanced toward the city.

PETERSBURG

If you are continuing north from the North Carolina state line where Cornwallis entered Virginia, then all you need do is continue along U.S. 301 to Interstate 95 and take 95 to Petersburg. If you are coming from the north, 95 is also the answer.

In Petersburg get off 95 at the third interchange, if you are coming from the south, the second if you are coming from the north; go east on Washington Street. At the intersection with Crater Road, turn right and drive up to the top of a *hill*. On the left is **Blandford Cemetery** with a brick wall around it, two historical markers on Crater Road, and a granite marker. This is part of the site of the Battle of Petersburg. If you face the way you came up the hill (down into the town), you are facing north.

In 1781 this area was a village called Blandford, which explains the name of the cemetery. Phillips and Arnold and their men came up the James River from Portsmouth to the Appomattox River, landed on the south bank of the Appomattox to the east (your right), and approached the town from that direction. Waiting for them in Blandford on this hill and along the river were about 1,000 militia under the command of Baron von Steuben and General Muhlenberg. The militia put up a good defense for about two hours, but the redcoats advanced up the hill and the Americans stationed here had to retire into the town. They made another stand there until the British drove them across the Appomattox River, which goes through Petersburg at the foot of the hill.

Blandford was eventually absorbed by Petersburg as the city expanded. If you are a Civil War buff, a short distance farther south on Crater Road, which is also U.S. 301, is an entrance to the Petersburg National Military Park which contains the Union siege lines and the famous crater. Civil War sites abound in Virginia and often vie with Revolutionary War sites for attention. In this case, the British are supposed to have stopped for a break in the Battery Five area, now in the park, before the battle.

Drive back down the hill to East Bank Street and turn left; after passing under Interstate 95, you will come to Fifth Street. This is about where the militia regrouped and turned to fight again after they were pushed off Blandford Hill. A block farther, at the intersection of East Bank and Fourth streets, a marker identifies **Bollingbrook** where Phillips, Arnold, and later Cornwallis stayed. The house is no longer standing, but it was in the line of fire when Lafayette bombarded the British in Petersburg the following month. Phillips became ill shortly after taking Petersburg, died, and was buried, according to tradition, in Blandford Cemetery, but the grave site has been lost.

In general, the battle was fought in this section of the city, from its eastern edge (the direction from which the British came) as far west as the Pocahontas Bridge. When the Americans retreated across the river, they took up the planks behind them. The bridge site is close to the present bridge which takes U.S. 301 and 1 over the river, the bridge you will use to continue north toward Richmond.

Follow the signs for 301 north, cross the Appomattox River, and head north out of Petersburg on U.S. 301 Alternate and U.S. 1A. Stay with U.S. 1 into Colonial Heights, a suburb of Petersburg where 1 is called Boulevard. At the intersection of Boulevard and Marvin Avenue, which goes to the right, is a small area shaped like a triangle with a Revolutionary War *marker* directly opposite a marker for Robert E. Lee's headquarters.

After the capture of Petersburg, Arnold and Phillips raided the countryside between Petersburg and Richmond and then attempted to retake Richmond. When they reached the south bank of the James opposite Richmond, however, they discovered Lafayette had beaten them to it. He had finally come south from Maryland with his army and the picture for Virginia had improved somewhat. Arnold returned to New York and Phillips returned to Petersburg via Jamestown to await Cornwallis, who was marching north from North Carolina. Lafayette moved south, reached this point, and on May 10 set up his artillery and treated the British to a pretty effective bombardment. Notice the high boxwood hedge near one of the two, big, old houses just beyond the marker along Marvin Avenue. There is a local legend that Lafayette's guns were positioned behind that hedge and fired through it, accounting for the gaps. One of the American cannonballs is supposed to have hit Bollingbrook, the house in which Phillips was staying.

Cornwallis reached Petersburg on May 20, having left the Carolinas against Clinton's orders. From here he moved north across the James River, with Lafayette withdrawing before him, and then west toward Charlottesville. Lafayette kept his men out of Cornwallis's reach, retreating north to a point on the Rapidan River north of Fredericksburg. We shall pick up Cornwallis's trail again when we cover the sites west of Richmond.

Continue north on 301 to Route 10 and turn left, or west, for a five-mile drive to **Chesterfield Courthouse**. Route 10 takes you first through the town of Chester and then five miles farther widens into a four-lane highway just long enough to take itself by Chesterfield Court-house. The little town is actually spread out for about a quarter of a mile along a side road parallel to 10. Two of three side streets on the right lead to a post office, a courthouse, a school, a fairground, a new town hall, and so on.

Baron von Steuben maintained a supply depot here, and there was also a barracks for the militia. Simcoe and his rangers, raiding up from Petersburg, forced the militia out and burned the buildings. There is no marker or identifying sign to pinpoint the site of the barracks and depot buildings, but the town's oldest inhabitant, ex-Sheriff Gates, remembered hearing about such a site and thought it might now be occupied by the fairground.

Return along 10 to U.S. 1–301 and take it north into Richmond to cover sites connected with Arnold's raid and occupation.

RICHMOND

In Richmond U.S. 1–301 takes you over the James River via the Robert E. Lee Bridge and into the downtown area. Traffic patterns per-mitting, turn right after the bridge onto U.S. 60–Second Street and take it to Broad Street. Otherwise, proceed to Belvidere Street, which makes a right turn at Monroe Park and goes onto Broad Street. In either case, turn right onto Broad Street and take it past the State Capitol, over some railroad lines, and on about another half mile to **St. John's Church.** You will see it on the right with its white, clapboard steeple and enclosed churchyard and cemetery between 24th and 25th streets. Since this is a residential area, parking is no problem. Admission on weekdays is from 10 A.M. to 4 P.M., Sundays, 12 to 4 P.M.

During the Revolution, Richmond was a town of less than 2,000 souls, most of whom were slaves. It has been the state capital since 1779. When Arnold marched on the town on Friday, January 5, 1781, Gover-nor Thomas Jefferson did what he could to defend it with the small num-ber of militiamen available. At the time, the town was concentrated along the James River on the north bank, the side you are now on. Today most of the town north of the downtown area is built on what was then known as **Richmond Hill.** In 1781, that was all open country and on that hill the militia made its ineffectual stand.

St. John's was built in 1741. The churchyard is filled with colonial tombstones, including that of George Wythe next to the entrance. Wythe, whose home has been restored in Colonial Williamsburg, was the first professor of law in the United States, a signer of the Declaration of Independence, and the teacher of John Marshall, Chief Justice of the

Supreme Court. He died in 1806 of arsenic poisoning at the hands of his principal heir, a grandnephew who got away scot-free since the only witness was a slave whose evidence was not admissable in Virginia court. Arsenic takes a long time to kill, however, and Wythe lived long enough to change his will.

It was in this church that the Virginia State Assembly met in March, 1775, after being dissolved by Governor the Earl of Dunmore. St. John's was chosen as its meeting place because it was the largest public building outside of Williamsburg, the governor's seat. Within these walls on Saturday, March 25, 1775, Patrick Henry made his rousing choice between liberty and death. The pews originally faced the two windows with the chapter from Exodus between them. The pulpit was also on that side. The pew Henry stood in when he made his speech is marked. You can find it by walking to the second aisle from the entrance, turning left, and counting four pews. Notice to your right as you enter the church a small baptismal font on a pedestal which was used to baptize Pocahontas. Originally it stood in a church no longer existing.

Drive back into midtown along Broad Street and continue on past the State Capitol. After you pass Lombardy Street, make a left turn on the first available street and go to Grove Street. Turn right on Grove and drive to the intersection of Grove and Mulberry streets. Look for 2618 Mulberry Street, the West End Medical Building, and an old granite marker in front of it which is indecipherable. It is set off in a little brick corner on the lawn on a pedestal. A more recent bronze *plaque* explains that Arnold's picket was driven in here by Colonel Jay Nicholas on January 4, 1781.

Revolutionary War sites are really at a minimum in Richmond and with these two you have covered what there is to see, the Civil War and urbanization having eclipsed the rest.

Now you must decide either to cover the sites to the west and southwest of Richmond next or those to the east and southeast. I suggest you go west first to the lightest concentration of sites. You will be able to follow a roughly circular route back to Petersburg and then east to Portsmouth. You can then follow the Yorktown campaign and finish your tour of Revolutionary War sites at the scene of Cornwallis's surrender.

THE RAVAGING OF VIRGINIA

After occupying Petersburg in May, 1781, Cornwallis decided to let Lafayette sit on the Rapidan for the time being and concentrate on destroying rebel supplies. He sent Simcoe and Tarleton west on raids to Point of Fork, site of an important arsenal and supply depot, and to Charlottesville where Tarleton tried to capture the Virginia legislature and Governor Thomas Jefferson. Cornwallis followed as far west as Jefferson's farm on Elk Hill in Goochland County.

In the meantime, General Anthony Wayne reached Lafayette with reinforcements from the north, strengthening the marquis and allowing him to move far enough south to prevent any further British raiding in the western part of the state. Cornwallis then turned around and marched east to Richmond. Before turning east yourself, you will follow Cornwallis and the raider Tarleton, and along the way visit Red Hill, Patrick Henry's last home and final resting place.

Take Interstate 64 west from Richmond toward Charlottesville and leave it at the exit for Goochland Courthouse—522. Follow the signs for **Goochland Courthouse** and come into town on Route 6, which joins 522. As you come in, look for the post office on the right. Directly opposite is the old brick courthouse and jail on a knoll overlooking the town's main street. Cornwallis and his army marched west along this road and passed the courthouse and jail.

Turn around, drive back to where Route 6 met 522, and head west on 6 until you come to a blinker light at an intersection with County Road 600, also called Rock Castle Road. You are near the site of another of Banastre Tarleton's exploits, this time at the home of a relative.

ROCK CASTLE

Rock Castle is off the foot of Route 600, seven or eight miles from Route 6, at the end of a private driveway which leads up a hill through woods and pastures to a gateway in a long, brick wall. Immediately beyond is a brick Norman manorhouse that was built recently. To the left, on the near side of the wall, is a story-and-a-half, white, frame cottage which is referred to as the **Queen Anne Cottage.** It was built sometime before 1732.

The land it stands on, a high bluff overlooking the James River, was part of a royal grant of 1,430 acres given to Charles Fleming in 1718. The land and the house was passed down by will to his son, Tarleton Fleming, who built the house and in turn passed the property on to his son, Tarleton. The second Tarleton Fleming was a lieutenant in the American army when Banastre Tarleton visited the house in June, 1781, after his unsuccessful attempt to capture Governor Thomas Jefferson at Monticello. The two families must have been related, for when

Tarleton entered the house he found the Tarleton coat of arms on the paneling above the parlor fireplace. Outraged, he cut it down, set fire to the house, and rode off, having rescued his family's escutcheon from his "traitorous" cousin. Luckily Tarleton Fleming was not at home, or he too might have been carried off.

The servants were able to put out the fire and so saved the house. The property stayed in the family until 1798 and then passed into other hands down through the years. In 1865 General Sheridan's men destroyed its furnishings but left it intact. In the midnineteenth century an Italianate front was added after the cottage's owner returned from a European tour during which he had been much taken with the Italian villas he visited. In 1935 it was bought by an author, James Osborne. It stood then where the Norman manorhouse now stands. During the dismantling of what appeared to be an imitation of an Italian villa, the original cottage was revealed. It was carefully taken apart and rebuilt where it stands today, facing the same direction it faced when first built.

The house has been modernized, but the plumbing, heating, and lighting are concealed and the original, hand-carved staircase and old, paneled wainscoting and mantles are still there. On the other side of the brick wall are the famous Rock Castle Gardens which were laid out by John Coles Rutherford, the lover of Italian villas. At the far end of the Norman manorhouse, you look out over grassed or wooded slopes leading down to the James River and a good stretch of the river itself winding off toward the west.

Though the cottage was empty when I visited, it has been lived in recently and may be still occupied, though not by anyone of flesh. Footsteps were frequently heard by its recent occupants and a psychical researcher who conducted a table-rapping session one night came up with the name "Pierson," a former owner. A Massachusetts man who spoke with a slightly British accent, Pierson was killed one night in 1922 in an automobile crash along Route 600. A similar accident took the life of James Osborne, though not at the same place. His widow remarried and now lives with her husband in the manorhouse facing the old Queen Anne Cottage.

I have not given you exact directions for getting to Rock Castle because this site and the one that follows are on private property. The Goochland County Historical Society conducts yearly garden and house tours of some of the historic homes of the county and you may be able to get in on one. If you want to visit the site, get in touch with the historical society and be advised by them.

Continue west on Route 6 to the westernmost point in Virginia reached by Cornwallis before he turned east.

ELK HILL

As you drive west on Route 6 you will eventually come to George's Tavern at the intersection of 6 and State Route 45, a crossroads hamlet consisting of a filling station, a general store, a church, and a few houses. A mile west of that is an intersection with County Road 608. Turn left on 608, noting a historical marker for Elk Hill. This is a bituminous road exactly 1.7 miles long. It leads down a gradual slope to a railroad crossing and an old ramshackle building that might once have been a hotel. On the other side of the tracks, a dirt road continues over a rickety iron girder bridge and onto Elk Island, once an Indian camping ground on the James River, now a cow pasture. A short distance before the railroad tracks, however, you will see a high, grassy *bluff* just off the road to your right. The original Elk Hill stood on that bluff and it was here Cornwallis came in June, 1781, for a destructive ten days.

The property had been purchased by Thomas Jefferson in September, 1778, and included 307 acres and probably a house which had been built before 1766 by the previous owners. To it Jefferson added outbuildings and possibly a wooden shed attached to the rear. There was a separate kitchen house as was the custom to protect the main house from fire should anything go amiss in the kitchen. The Spring 1971 issue of the *Goochland County Historical Society Magazine* published an article about the house by Elie Weeks, the society's president, and a conjectural drawing, based on remains and two fire insurance policies taken out in 1806 and 1815. The drawing was the work of Calder Loth, architectural historian of the Virginia Historic Landmarks Commission. It shows a story-and-a-half cottage, somewhat like the Queen Anne Cottage at Rock Castle, measuring thirty-two by eighteen feet with brick chimneys and fireplaces at either end, a single entrance flanked by a window on either side, a sloping roof, three dormers, and a rear shed about thirty-two by ten feet inside and one story high. Though not a pretentious house by modern standards, and certainly nothing like Monticello, it was substantially built and furnished and represented the kind of home built by people of some means in what was then still a frontier settlement.

Cornwallis was following his advance units led by Tarleton and Simcoe. In June, 1781, Tarleton raided Charlottesville to the west trying to capture Jefferson and the Virginia legislature. He managed to net some of the members of the state assembly, but his men missed Jefferson at Monticello by about ten minutes. Simcoe went on to raid the Point of Fork arsenal. Tarleton raided Rock Castle Cottage and other sites, and Cornwallis went into camp in this area along the James River, making Elk Hill his headquarters. He was about to order Tarleton out on another raid to the west when he heard that Wayne had joined forces with Lafayette and that both were advancing on Elk Hill. He decided to turn back toward Richmond.

Jefferson complained in a letter, quoted by Weeks, of the damage Cornwallis permitted his men to wreak at Elk Hill. They destroyed the barns and took all the corn and livestock and every horse that could be ridden or hitched to a wagon. The young colts that were not yet broken to either saddle or shaft were killed, the servants were turned out, and the slaves were marched off with the livestock. Cornwallis made a habit in his southern campaigns of collecting slaves as he went along and shipping them to the West Indies for safekeeping. According to Jefferson's letter, the account of the damage was based not merely on second-hand reports, but also from his own eyes; he visited the site soon after the British left.

The bluff is seemingly quite empty now of anything that pertains to the house or the British occupation, though part of the brick chimney and some of the foundation bricks were still to be seen in 1969 and 1970. They have since been removed, and the depression marking the basement has been filled in. The land now belongs to a cattle farmer who lives close by in an old house that incorporates part of a mill located on Boyd Creek during the Revolution. He and his wife are fully aware and highly appreciative of the historic quality of their property, but there are no plans to research the site or attempt reconstruction or interpretation.

There are plans to develop a map for the bicentennial, based on a map drawn by Lafayette's engineers, that would trace the routes followed by Cornwallis and the marquis in Virginia. The routes would be laid out to follow contemporary roads, where possible, with dotted lines to show where they cut across what are now pastures and woodlands. The campsites of both armies would be marked and new markers set up, and there may be audio tapes at specified points along the trail to fill in the historical background. This map should be available at the courthouse in Goochland or from the historical society and the state bicentennial commission.

Return to Route 6 and pick up the trail west, following it into Fluvanna County and the site of Simcoe's raid on an arsenal and depot.

POINT OF FORK

As you drive through Fluvanna County, notice the James River to your left. It it less than half the width it attains as it flows through the Tidelands to its mouth. You are very near to its source, the meeting of the Fluvanna and Rivanna rivers, the "point of fork" where the arsenal stood. Exactly 0.8 of a mile west of the little town of Columbia, you will find two historical markers on the left side of the road, one of which relates to the arsenal and Simcoe's raid. The site of the arsenal is on the high ground behind the marker, on the wooded ridge on the other side of the Rivanna River, which you will cross shortly.

Immediately after the bridge, watch for County Road 656 to your left. Take that left and look for two brick gateposts and a white fence on the left. A private road leads from the gateposts to a farm cottage and a garage. A cow pasture takes up the rise of ground beyond the garage with trees fringing it to left and right. Beyond that cow pasture, though you cannot see it from the road, the ground drops down to the Rivanna River at a point opposite where you saw the arsenal marker on Route 6. That cow pasture is the site of Point of Fork arsenal.

Though there was an arsenal from at least 1781 until 1801, according to the *Fluvanna County Historical Society Bulletin* of March, 1967, there is no written record indicating the number of buildings or when the first was built. Nevertheless, the Point of Fork arsenal was a principal military supply depot in Virginia during the Revolution. It stood on land then owned by David Ross who was a quartermaster in the Virginia militia. Simcoe attacked the arsenal on Tuesday, June 5, 1781. At the time, Baron von Steuben was there training 500 recruits destined to join Greene's army.

Word had come of Simcoe's approach some days before and there was ample time to move the arms and munitions out. According to the historical society, von Steuben moved "many of the supplies" across the James, but abandoned a "great many of them." Simcoe, who had about 400 men, entered the arsenal, destroyed the buildings, and, as he wrote in his journals, "two thousand five hundred stand of arms, a large quantity of gunpowder case shot, etc., several casks of saltpeter, sulphur and brimstone, and upwards of sixty hogsheads of rum and brandy [fancy that being stored in an arsenal!], several chests of carpenter's tools and upwards of four hundred intrenching tools . . ."

Simcoe also wrote that he could not pursue von Steuben because of a lack of boats with which to ford the river. Resorting to cunning, Simcoe lighted enough campfires to make von Steuben think the entire

British army had arrived with him. Von Steuben abandoned the rest of the supplies and retreated. Some of Simcoe's men then crossed the river in canoes and destroyed the supplies at their leisure.

I came across another version of what happened to those supplies at the Virginia State Library in Richmond. According to recent research on Point of Fork, von Steuben removed most of the arsenal's supplies and concealed the gunpowder in local tobacco barns. When Simcoe marched in, he threw much of what he found into the river and burned the rest. After he left, David Ross fished out most of what Simcoe's men had consigned to the Fluvanna. He also found 200 horses Simcoe had left behind, sold them for his own profit, and then charged the state for the forage. As for the gunpowder, local people discovered where von Steuben had hidden it, but instead of returning it to the state and the militia, kept it for themselves.

Once Simcoe had left, the arsenal was rebuilt and expanded after the war. It continued as an arms manufactory and depot until 1801 when its remaining supplies were removed to a manufactory in Richmond and the buildings were presumably allowed to deteriorate. Before my visit, a state archaeologist had carried out a preliminary survey and discovered the remains of a brick powder magazine built in 1788, a long foundation, and an unusual amount of debris from military material that was probably destroyed in a violent and deliberate manner. With the permission of the owners I explored the site myself, but found only the remains the archaeologist had already identified. The far end of the pasture overlooks the slope that goes down steeply to the riverbank. Route 6 runs close by around the shoulder of the hill.

TARLETON'S RAIDS

A little distance farther along Route 6 take U.S. 15 south, following the route of Tarleton's raids into this part of Virginia. Along the way you will pass markers that identify this region as the area of the final actions of the Civil War. Appomattox Courthouse is not very far west. Soon after entering Prince Edward County, you will pass through the county seat, Farmville. Continue south for another 4.5 miles to the intersection with State Route 133 and the hamlet of Kingsville. **King's Tavern** once stood at this site, attracting Tarleton who camped nearby. According to the marker, a number of sick and wounded French soldiers were brought here after the siege of Yorktown and seventy were buried somewhere in the area. We tried to find the site of the old church that stood near here, but discovered its site is on private property and that the graveyard, where we assumed the Frenchmen would be buried, is now a flower garden.

About 1.1 miles farther are three markers on the left, again identifying the path of Tarleton's raid and indicating a site to the east where Tarleton burned a glebe house, later called **Providence House** because a providential rain put out the fire. These markers are just beyond County Road 665 which goes east. Accordingly, we took it, clocked two miles, and found on the left an old frame house badly in need of repair with a central chimney. It is a matched house: that is, it has two entrances and the same number of rooms and windows on each side. Houses like these were built during colonial times to accommodate two families under one roof, but to keep them separate in their own private quarters.

Two miles from the Kingsville marker on the right is a wayside picnic table with open fields beyond. A mile to the west stood **Slate Hill**, the home of Nathaniel Venable, a member of the county committee of safety. Tarleton visited the house hoping to capture Venable, but since he was not at home Tarleton had to content himself with plundering the military stores he found there and burning the place. There is a road leading to the west, but it was posted and we could not investigate the actual site.

Continue south on U.S. 15 into Keysville in Charlotte County. Do not take the bypass, but do take the business route into Keysville. On the southern edge of town on the right side of U.S. 15 is another *marker* for Tarleton's progress, this one for his return from a raid on the town of Bedford. As you go along, it becomes increasingly obvious that Tarleton and company cut a wide swath through Virginia.

Backtrack to the north along 15 into Farmville and pick up U.S. 460 to Lynchburg. Take U.S. 29–460 south from Lynchburg and when 460 leaves 29, follow it to an intersection with Route 623. Turn left onto 623 for about a quarter of a mile to a T-dead end with Route 858. Turn left onto what is the main and only street for the hamlet of **New London**. A marker on the left side of the road proves, however, that this tiny spot is loaded with historical significance. Once the county seat of Bedford County, it was also raided by Tarleton in 1781, the same year two steers owned by a local Tory were confiscated for the American army. The Tory, John Hook, sued for the value of the steers. Patrick Henry stood up in the county courthouse in New London and succeeded in having Hook's suit laughed out of court, according to the marker.

Tarleton obviously had good cause to raid New London, for there was an arsenal here that probably supplied the local militia with its arms. We explored the short stretch of road, trying to find at least the site of the courthouse in which Henry made his famous defense. The road leads only from 460 to 460 in a semicircle, and though we asked local people for information regarding possible sites, we were unable to come up with any leads.

Back on 460, a short distance west of New London, we discovered an old *cemetery* in a cow pasture high on a hill overlooking the road from behind a couple of billboards on the right. The pasture gate was locked, but over the fence I went and up to the cemetery. The old broken wall encloses a number of tumbled tombstones, including one marking the grave of a Revolutionary War veteran named James Callaway. Remember that name.

Go north on 460 back toward Lynchburg as far as the intersection with County Road 622. Turn right onto 622 and take it east to an intersection with U.S. 29. Turn right onto 29 and drive south toward Altavista. Just before you come into Altavista, notice the railroad line that comes in from the east to parallel the road closely on the left. You are driving through an industrial area with freight yards and grain elevators in the immediate area. As you approach the town, keep a weather eye out for a marker on the right side of the road. The marker identifies the **Lynch tree** 100 yards west under which Colonel Charles Lynch, William Preston, and James Callaway administered vigilante justice in the form of floggings to Tories in 1780: hence the term, "lynch law." Lynch led a company of Virginia militiamen who fought at Guilford Courthouse and then stayed with Greene's army until Yorktown.

As you look to the west (your right), you can see an old house with a grove of trees in front, but at this distance it is impossible to pick out the tree referred to on the marker. If you walk back a few feet, however, you will find a dirt lane just before the marker leading between two gateposts up toward the house. When you get to the head of the lane, you will find that the house is separated from it by a picket fence. On your side of the fence is an old walnut tree. Most of the trunk has been filled in with tree cement, but a sign identifies it. It looks big and wide enough to be two hundred years old, and on the ground we found walnuts.

Go back along U.S. 29, but only for a short distance. When you get to the top of a hill about two miles or so north of the Lynch tree, you will come to an intersection with County Road 699. Take it to the right and head for the town of Gladys and the last home of Virginia's most famous orator.

RED HILL

When you get to Gladys, take U.S. 501 south to the town of Brook-neal and then Route 40 east. Coming out of town, you will cross a bridge over a creek followed by a sign on the right for the Patrick Henry Shrine and Boys' Home. To the right is County Road 600; take it for over two miles through woodlands and farm lots. At one point 600 goes off to the left, but another sign for Patrick Henry's home tells you to bear right onto 619 south again. In less than a mile you will see a tall, tabard-style sign for Red Hill at the intersection with County Road 677. Follow 677 to the right past a collection of low, brick buildings on the right (the Patrick Henry Boys' Plantation) until the road dead-ends in a grassy parking area at a fence. Beyond that is what looks like a small, white, frame cottage with two wings, several smaller outbuildings nearby, and a large, contemporary, frame house to the left. The contemporary building is the home of the caretaker and curator of Red Hill.

Red Hill is the home to which Patrick Henry retired to spend the last three years of his life from 1796 to 1799. The little clapboard house to the left, an original building on its original site, was his *office*. The house with the big chimney, directly to the left of the large, central cottage, was the kitchen. Beyond that are two, small "necessary houses" and beyond that a slave cabin moved here from an outlying part of the plantation to represent the home of Henry's servants. The path to the left from the main house as you face it takes you to the family cemetery in which Patrick Henry, his wife, his youngest son, his son's wife, and one of his grandchildren are buried.

A hostess will take you through the main house, which is actually a reconstruction built on the original foundations of only the right wing. The porch to the left was actually a breezeway connecting the right wing with the main or central section, which was destroyed by fire in 1919. A framed photograph of the old house with its magnificent boxwood hedges may be seen on the wall of the entrance hall.

Small as this house is in comparison to others you have visited, few of the others exhibit as many personal furnishings and belongings of the original owners. In the bedroom to the right, on the ground floor, is Henry's granddaughter's bed and a washstand he used himself. In that room notice the odd deacon's bench on rockers. A removable wooden rail identifies this piece as a mammy bench on which a nurse could sit and rock a baby. The baby rested on the part protected by the rail. In one of the upstairs rooms is a cradle used by Henry's grandchildren.

The showcase in the ground-floor room opposite the downstairs bedroom has a wonderful collection of items that belonged to Henry. Among them are six finger bowls, his violin, his wife's lute, and a mourning brooch holding a lock of Henry's brilliant red hair. In that same case is a ring that belonged to Patrick Henry's mother. It was bequeathed to him in her will and contains a lock of her hair; the other side is inscribed with her name and the date of her death. Also in the room is a drop-leaf table that belonged to John Randolph.

Notice the paintings, both of which you will probably recognize. One is a copy of Sully's portrait of Henry; the other is the original of the painting by Peter Frederick Rothermel showing Henry delivering the famous address in the Virginia House of Burgesses in 1765 that ended with "Caesar had his Brutus, Charles the First, his Cromwell, and George the Third may profit by their example . . . if this be treason, make the most of it." Many of the figures of the delegates in this picture are actually portraits of men who were in the House of Burgesses at the time of Henry's address. The seated figure in the red cloak with his left hand on the table is Richard Henry Lee; the figure leaning over Lee with his right hand extended forward and his back showing is Edmund Pendleton; over Pendleton's outstretched hand is the face of George Wythe of Williamsburg.

You may enter the law office to see the big wing chair with the writing arm and the filing cabinet Henry used. You can also enter the slave cabin to see how favored plantation slaves lived. Do not miss a visit to the huge, osage orange tree that covers with its branches and leaves most of the ground between the office and the main house. This tree was a hundred years old when Patrick Henry came here to live. Tradition has it that Henry delighted in sitting under the tree and playing his flute for his children. He had seventeen children, six by his first wife and eleven by his second. He died at the age of sixty-three when his youngest was three.

Red Hill is on top of a hill overlooking the surrounding countryside in one of the most charming settings of a colonial home I have visited. Isolated as it is, surrounded by open woodlands, and adorned with trees, it is a delightful place to visit at any time of the year. Future plans call for a separate museum building and the acquisition of furniture and other articles that belonged to the Henry family and are scattered around the state.

From Red Hill, return to Route 40 and take it east to Charlotte Courthouse. You will find the *courthouse* itself, after you have gone through a good part of the town, on the left side of the street opposite the Old Dominion Telephone Company Building. The courthouse is an old, red, brick building with Georgian pillars and portico and is still in use. If you are there after court is over for the day, however, walk inside the old chamber. It was here Patrick Henry delivered the last speech of his life. In January, 1799, at Washington's behest, Henry ran as a Federalist against John Randolph for a seat in the Virginia House of Delegates. The central issue in that election was whether a state had the right to nullify acts of the federal government.

On March 10, Henry left a sickbed in Red Hill, rode the twenty miles to Charlotte Courthouse, and addressing the assembled listeners in a debate with young Randolph, declared that "No state has the right to pass upon the validity of federal laws. No part can be greater than the whole." He won the election, but died before he could take his seat.

The portraits of those debaters of long ago adorn the walls on either side of the judge's bench. The other portraits are of illustrious sons of the Old Dominion. The furnishings I am sure do not date to the early days of the Republic, but the walls still echo the voices.

Continue east on Route 40 into Lunenburg County and to yet another site connected with Tarleton and his British Legion.

CRAIG'S MILL

Route 40 will eventually take you into the town of Kenbridge. At a blinker light in town where 40 goes to the left and north, turn right onto County Road 637 and clock two miles. You are then at the Kenbridge Filtration Plant on the right. Beyond it is a large pond, part of the plant. The stream that feeds into that pond is Flat Rock Creek. A quarter of a mile up the creek from the plant the remains of Craig's Mill can still be seen if you care to hike in to see them. By great good fortune, I found the owner of the property on which the mill remains stand in the filtration plant, which he ran at the time for the town. He has visited the site many times and vouches for the mill or what is left of it.

Tarleton burned the mill in July, 1781, and forced the owner, the Reverend James Craig, to slaughter his hogs so that Tarleton's troopers' bellies might be filled. The big house with the tall chimneys on the hill off to the right as you go a little farther on 637, is said to be the mill owner's house, though we subsequently discovered it was a Presbyterian glebe house then.

Return to Kenbridge and go straight ahead onto Route 40 north at the blinker. Take it to Route 46. Turn left onto 46 and take that into

Blackstone to U.S. 460 east. That will connect you with Interstate 85 just west of Petersburg. Take 85 into Petersburg and leave it at the exit just before the interchange with Interstate 95. The exit should be marked either Montebello Road or Crater Road. The exit ramp becomes a service road paralleling the southbound lane of Interstate 95 and intersects Crater Road. Proceed across Crater Road, noting that a road curves in from the right to meet the service road which also curves to the right. About midway around that curve a road goes off to the left under the interstate. Take that road and follow it to a juncture with Winfield Avenue which is also U.S. 460. Take 460 south and head for a sequence of actions that marked the last days of the Earl of Dunmore as the royal governor of Virginia and three cities that were raided by Collier and Mathew in 1779.

INVASIONS ALONG THE COAST

SUFFOLK

U.S. 460 will take you into the town of Suffolk, which was occupied by Colonel Robert Howe in February, 1776, with a mixed force of Virginia and North Carolina militia. General Edward Mathew raided it on Thursday, May 13, 1779, after occupying Portsmouth two days before. Unfortunately, the town was destroyed by fire in 1837 and had to be rebuilt. Little if anything remains of its colonial heritage to remind us it played a role in the Revolution.

U.S. 460 comes into Suffolk from the north and meets U.S. 58. The two roads combine and go east toward Portsmouth. Take them east as they cross the north end of the Dismal Swamp. On the other side of the swamp in the town of Bowers Hill, Alternate 460 goes ahead into Portsmouth. Instead, make a right turn onto 460–Business 13. You will cross the Norfolk and Western Railroad, then go under Interstate 64 and cross a long bridge over the southern branch of the Elizabeth River. Soon after that bridge, 460 goes off to the left via an exit ramp and into Portsmouth. Stay on Business 13 as it passes the interchanges for Interstate 464 and finally intersects State Route 168. Turn right onto 168, which is also called Battlefield Avenue, and proceed south into Great Bridge.

GREAT BRIDGE

The main street of Great Bridge is Route 168 with some streets and roads going off to the right or west. It is the site of one of the locks of the Intracoastal Waterway and also of the first battle of the Revolution fought in Virginia. A drawbridge in the middle of town carries 168 over the waterway. Just before you cross the bridge as you are going south, a historical marker stuck in between two other markers, one for the waterway and the other for the Virginia Game Commission, says a British fort built to guard the causeway stood a little to the east.

Lord Dunmore, who had just done his best to destroy Hampton and was raising a force of Loyalists, built that fort to prevent a force of militia under Colonel William Woodford from crossing the bridge on their way to Norfolk. When Woodford arrived, he had his men build their own fortification on the other side of the bridge and they camped behind it. On Saturday, December 9, 1775, having been informed the rebels were only a few hundred strong, Dunmore ordered an attack against their position. To reach the other end of the bridge, his men had to cross not only the bridge, which was over 100 feet long, but also a causeway over the swamp area around the bridge. Dunmore had over 400 men with him, among them a black company called Dunmore's Ethiopians. Woodward had about 300, including future Justice John Marshall, then a young lieutenant.

The attack began soon after daybreak and was driven back. With two cannon supporting them, the British advanced across the causeway again. The Americans held their fire until the attackers rushed forward, believing the redoubt deserted, right into a volley that drove them back again. The rebels then left their redoubt, advanced, and captured both guns and a number of prisoners. The British suffered sixty-two casualties, including thirteen killed; the rebels had only one man wounded and none killed. The entire business lasted less than a half hour.

This was the first military action of any size after Bunker Hill. There should be two *markers* in the town, one for the north end of the causeway where the British built their redoubt (you just found that one) and another for the southern end where the Americans built theirs and where the actual fighting took place. We were unable to find the second. Perhaps by the bicentennial it will have been replaced, and you will be able to view the site from the perspective of both sides.

Great Bridge is a busy, little town with a fair tourist trade; its location on the waterway makes it a yachting and boating center. There are hamburger stands and restaurants galore along 168 as well as other culinary possibilities. A very good new library in town has a section that contains early maps of the area. I found one curious map which purports to show a star fort built by Simcoe after he is supposed to have taken the town. Since the date given on the map for the fort is 1782, however, a year Simcoe was in England invalided out of the army, the authenticity of the map is understandably in doubt.

Return to the north along 168 on your way to the tideland port cities of Portsmouth, Norfolk, and Hampton to fill in further details of Lord Dunmore's story and to pick up sites connected with both the Mathew and Arnold raids.

PORTSMOUTH

When Route 168 intersects Business 13 again, turn left and take 13 to U.S. 17. Turn right onto 17 and take it north into Portsmouth proper, where it is also called the George Washington Highway. When Washington Highway ends at Frederick Boulevard (where 17 turns to the left), continue straight ahead on Route 141, which skirts the U.S. Naval Shipyard. At Seventh Street, which comes in from the left, turn onto Seventh to Wythe Street. Jog right there and make an immediate left onto Court Street. As you drive along Court, the Elizabeth River and the town of Norfolk on the opposite bank are on your right. The old city of Portsmouth was built along the river in a strip only a few blocks wide; to be exact it ended a block to your left. Where Court Street meets Crawford Parkway on the river, you have reached the first of the Arnold sites in Portsmouth.

Arnold sailed up the Elizabeth River and landed with his raiding force in January, 1781. Cornwallis came here in July that same year and went from here to Yorktown. The intersection you are now at marks the northern end of a line of redoubts Arnold had built in March, 1781, to protect the town from American attack from the west. If you turn left onto Crawford Parkway and go one block to Washington Street you have traversed the depth of the line of redoubts. Now turn left again and go along Washington Street to Brighton Street. Those sixteen or so blocks you have just covered mark the length of Arnold's defenses. The redoubts stretched down what is now Washington Street to Brighton and extended in depth a block east toward the river to Court Street. Washington Street marks the western limits of old Portsmouth. Arnold's *defense line* was anchored on Gosport Creek on the south about where Brighton Street now runs.

Return along Washington Street to Crawford Parkway; turn left onto the parkway, and take it to Effingham Street where you will see a sign for the U.S. Naval Hospital stop on the Portsmouth tour. Turn right and drive along the approach to the hospital which takes up most of the area on which **Fort Nelson** stood.

On Sunday, May 9, 1779, the Collier-Mathew expedition captured the rebel fort that stood on this site north of the town. From here the raiders moved into Portsmouth and Norfolk, then into the town of Gosport, and then into Suffolk. They seized a lot of supplies and weapons and captured or destroyed 130-odd vessels, including several privateers, all without the loss of a man. The militia garrison in Fort Nelson offered no resistance at all. In fact, they were nowhere to be seen when the British landed to invest the fort.

Drive back along Crawford Parkway to a little *park* and paved area at the edge of the U.S. Naval Shipyard opposite the entrance to the Portsmouth Shipyard Museum. It was here on the old Portsmouth waterfront that Cornwallis embarked his troops for Yorktown. The museum is interesting, but exhibits nothing of Revolutionary War significance. The guns that line the walkway leading to the entrance, however, deserve your attention. Among them are a British twelve-pounder, circa 1777, the first on the right as you walk toward the building; and an American twelve-pounder, vintage revolutionary era, directly opposite the British gun.

NORFOLK

Take the Downtown Norfolk-Portsmouth Tunnel under the Elizabeth River and into Chesapeake. The tunnel exit comes out directly onto a road to a bridge that crosses another branch of the river into Norfolk. You are now in the old part of the city which in revolutionary times occupied a stretch along the river, as did Portsmouth, and extended inland for only a short distance. The revolutionary town was destroyed by Governor the Earl of Dunmore in 1776, and the only building left standing is **St. Paul's Church** on St. Paul's Boulevard.

As you come off the bridge, you will come to a cloverleaf at the new Civic Center. Go off onto City Hall Avenue, and turn right onto St. Paul's Boulevard. The church is set off from the street by a high brick wall with a historical marker. Next to it is a long parking area divided into sections. Around it are the skyscrapers of a downtown renewal project that has just about rebuilt this section of Norfolk.

On Monday, January 1, 1776, Governor Dunmore killed whatever chance he may have had to make a comeback in his province. The month before he had been frustrated at Great Bridge, as you know, by a Patriot unit under Colonel Woodford who continued to Norfolk where he was joined by Colonel Robert Howe and his North Carolina militia. Dunmore and his Tory supporters were on British ships in the Elizabeth River suffering from a lack of supplies. When the rebels refused to allow them to come ashore to forage, Dunmore had the ships line up along the Elizabeth River from one end of Main Street to the other and start a bombardment. In retaliation, the rebels set fire to Loyalist homes and the entire town burned as a result. Norfolk was Virginia's biggest town at the time and its destruction was laid at the governor's door. Though he attempted to establish a beachhead amid the ruins, he finally had to withdraw to Gwynn's Island in the Chesapeake Bay.

St. Paul's Episcopal, built in 1739, was the only building to survive the fire. A marker set into the brick wall commemorates the burning of the city. Standing with your back to the marker and the wall, you can see the river stretching from left to right beyond and between the new buildings on the other side of the boulevard. Directly above the marker, in the wall of the church, a cannonball is embedded. The plaque beneath it identifies it as a cannonball fired by Dunmore.

Most of the graves in the churchyard are eighteenth century and a number predate the Revolution, including one dated 1673. Note the raised catafalque toward the parking area. In it lies Miles King, a Revolutionary War soldier who served from 1775 to 1783. There are other veterans of the Revolution buried in this churchyard, including Thomas Mathews who commanded the militia garrison at Fort Nelson.

We tried to mark the line of Dunmore's ships by locating the two ends of Main Street. Unfortunately, Main Street is no longer one continuous street, but is broken up into two widely separated sections. The western section comes down to the river, but the other section now butts up against a railroad track terminal.

From Norfolk your way leads north to Hampton, where a British naval captain attempted to enforce the royal authority, and beyond that to sites connected with Arnold's advance on Richmond.

The easiest and fastest way to get to Hampton from Norfolk lies through Portsmouth, unless Interstate 64 within Norfolk is completed as far as the Hampton Roads Bridge Tunnel. If it is, take Monticello Avenue into U.S. 460 north, also called Granby Avenue, to Interstate 64 and on into Hampton. An alternate route to 64 from downtown Norfolk is State Route 168. Exxon Service Stations have a very good map for the Hampton Roads area showing the Tideland port cities in specific detail and clearly outlining all the alternate routes in and out of each city.

If 64 is not completed, take Brambleton Avenue, also 460, to the entrance ramp to the Midtown Tunnel to Portsmouth. At the Portsmouth end, you will come out onto U.S. 58. At a fork where 58 goes to the right, stay with 58 until it meets High Street. Turn right onto High Street and you are on U.S. 17. Take 17 first west then north to where it meets U.S. 258 and swings east to cross the James River via the James River Bridge into Newport News. At the traffic circle, 17 turns left to go north. Stay on 258 which will take you into Hampton along Mercury Boulevard.

HAMPTON

This charming, contemporary town occupies an ancient site of human life. Before Europeans came to Virginia, a village of Kecoughtan Indians lived here, fishing the waters and growing corn. White settlers drove them out and began the settlement that eventually took the name Hampton. Edward Teach, the pirate known as Blackbeard, terrorized the waters and capes around Hampton until he was finally killed by a British naval expedition. His head was displayed from the end of a yardarm in Hampton Harbor. Hampton was the scene of much rebellious activity during 1775 and 1776 and of one attempt by Loyalist and British forces to land. It was occupied by the British during the War of 1812 and in the Civil War enjoyed the dubious honor of being burned by Confederate forces to deny it to the Union for rather obscure strategic reasons.

The fire destroyed whatever was extant of the revolutionary town with the exception of a church, but Hampton's early days have been kept in memory. Five of the original streets are still known by their old names, including King and Queen streets, two of the city's main thoroughfares, and Wine Street. You can find the only eighteenth-century building in Hampton by going west on Queen Street to **St. John's Church** on the right. St. John's serves the oldest English parish in continuous existence in the country. It was damaged during the Revolution and again during the War of 1812 and was gutted during the great fire of 1861. The walls of the church date back to 1728 when it was built. During revolutionary times, St. John's was at the edge of town. There was a town gate here on Queen Street close by.

It was in Hampton that the first armed confrontations occurred between crown and rebels in Virginia. On September 2, 1775, a British sloop, the *Otter*, under the command of Captain Mathew Squires, was forced by the weather to shelter in the James River near the town. The more adventurous local Whigs took advantage of the opportunity to relieve the sloop of her guns and burn one of her small boats as a bonus.

Squires was entertained at the home of a local Patriot that same night, but that didn't smooth the matter over as far as the captain and the royal governor were concerned.

Drive down to the foot of King Street on Hampton River and walk out on the fishing **wharf.** On Tuesday, October 24, 1775, acting under Dunmore's orders, Squires returned and sailed six tenders into Hampton Creek, today marked on the maps as Hampton River. Fully expecting his return, the county committee of safety had sunk five sloops across the entrance to the creek and had sent a message to Williamsburg asking for reinforcements.

Unable to sail his sloop into the creek, Squires sent in the tenders and began to fire on the town. At the same time, he sent in a landing party with orders to burn the town. The landing party never reached the shore. Even without the Williamsburg reinforcements, the townsfolk were waiting for them, sheltered behind the brick homes and willow trees that then lined the waterfront, according to Marion L. Starkey's history of the town. Unable to get his men ashore, Squires waited out the night.

By daybreak 100 Williamsburg militiamen had arrived after riding all night and were in position to give his men and ships an example of Virginia squirrel-hunting marksmanship. Squires resumed the bombardment, for he managed to move his ships into positions from which he could enfilade the town. The musket fire from the shore was so effective, however, that the captain had to order his fleet to slip its cables and withdraw. Minimal damage had been done to the town, though St. John's Church and one other building had been set afire. Squires himself lost two men killed and two wounded and the Virginians reported no casualties.

At present, the waterfront area on the old creek is the scene of commercial fishing activities. The present wharf, which replaced the old one on which Squire's men hoped to land, is a terminal for fishing boats that bring in their catches to be processed in the nearby seafood plant. The brick homes and willow trees where the embattled Virginians took cover have been replaced by more recent and less attractive structures.

There is another site in Hampton of particular interest because it represents a side of colonial life not often touched on. Food in colonial times, particularly meat and fish, had to be preserved as well as flavored. One of the principal preserving agents was salt, which was rarely found in its pure form and was hard to come by. Much of it was obtained through the evaporation of seawater. In coastal areas like the Virginia tidelands, salt flats or pans were operated to produce the precious commodity. Hampton was a center for salt production in both the Revolution and the Civil War.

To get to the **Hampton Salt Pans**, go back up King Street across Queen Street and turn right onto Pembroke Avenue, which will take you across the Hampton River to Buckroe Beach. Chesapeake Bay is known for its oysters and crabs and bathing beaches, and Hampton abounds in all three. Buckroe Beach is a resort area with cottages for rent and sale, along sandy beaches backed up by grassy sand dunes and bathhouses. It is a great place to spend a day or two or a week if you fancy breaking up the history trail with a seashore idyll. Hampton's beaches are popular and crowded during the summer, however, and if you plan a respite for anything longer than a day or two, it is best to make reservations ahead of time.

Pembroke Avenue will take you to First Street. Turn left onto First and follow it out with the bay and the beaches on your right and summer bungalows on both sides. Continue as far as you can until the road turns into a sandy track over the dunes. Unless you are driving a dune buggy, park and walk the rest of the way on the dunes with the bay to the right and salt marshes off on your left. To your left front in the midst of the marshes, notice a body of open water, a salt pond, and others beyond it. From them the colonists scooped up saltwater, poured it into broad shallow pans which were then buried in the sand, and let the hot sun do the rest, a technique the white settlers probably learned from the Indians.

You can walk out over the hard-packed sand until you are as close to the pond as the marshy ground around it will permit. Keep in mind that some hurricanes have been severe enough to change the character of the coast. The region is basically as it was two hundred years ago, however, and it was here the town of Hampton and the county of Elizabeth City produced its salt. In fact, these saltworks were so vital that a detachment of militia was stationed here during the Revolution to guard them.

Take a walk along the waterfront in Hampton, particularly on the streets that parallel Queen Street at the edge of Hampton River. Much of the land the streets are laid out on is fill and covers part of the colonial town. An archaeological program of excavations, part of Hampton's plans for the bicentennial, is expected to uncover many houses and wharf sites from the revolutionary period. A Heritage Park will probably have been built along the waterfront by the time you visit the town.

Beautifully located in an attractive water area, Hampton offers a number of other attractions. Charter boats for deep-sea fishing are available and so are a number of restaurants that serve up the finned and shelled delights of the sea. The Syme-Eaton Museum Park on East Mercury Boulevard has a unique fold-in map of Hampton at its Visitor's Center. Other spots can be reached along a self-guided motor tour which is laid out in a folder you can pick up at the Hampton Information Center at 413 West Mercury Boulevard.

ARNOLD'S RAID AND OTHER SKIRMISHES

Take Mercury Boulevard west back to the traffic circle in Newport News; pick up U.S. 17 west, and take it back across the river for some distance to the intersection with County Road 626. Turn left onto 626 and take it south to a dead end with State Route 337. Turn right onto 337 and drive toward the town of Driver.

As you approach Driver from the east, look for three very tall radio towers ahead of you and to the left. Eventually you will pass them as well as the low, brick building which houses Radio Station WEVC. About 0.3 of a mile farther, you will cross railroad tracks and 0.8 of a mile beyond that you will see a ramshackle, clapboard building set well off the road to the left. Opposite that building, on the right side of the road in an open field, is the approximate site on which **Hargrove's Tavern,** also known as Halfway House, stood.

Here in May, 1779, the local militia under Captains King and Davis were surprised by General Mathew's raiders who were advancing on the town of Suffolk a few miles to the south. Both Davis and King were killed and presumably the militia was dispersed, for Mathew did occupy Suffolk, destroying the supplies he found there.

A short distance west, 337 takes a wide curve to the left and heads south. Right in the curve, two other roads, County Roads 125 and 629, fork off 337 to the west and north, respectively. Two markers have been placed in the apex of the triangle at the fork. One is a marker for the **Sleepy Hole Ferry** and states that Arnold used the ferry on his return from Richmond January 16, 1781, and that Cornwallis crossed it on his way to Portsmouth in July the same year. The marker says the ferry was three miles east, which would put it out in the middle of nowhere and a good three miles from the nearest water, the west branch of the Elizabeth River. On the other hand, three miles to the west is the Nansemond River and near the Nansemond River on 629 is a town called Sleepy Hole. We investigated 629 and other roads in the area, trying to see how close we could get to the Nansemond, but though I feel certain the marker is wrong, we could never get down to the river. As we drove farther west from Drivers along 125, however, in a little less than three miles we came to a drawbridge crossing the Nansemond, and on the other side of the river, a short distance from the bridge, we came upon Ferry Point Farm. Since modern highway bridges sometimes replaced colonial ferries, we will vote for that bridge as the approximate site where Arnold and Cornwallis ferried their way to Portsmouth.

Several miles to the west of the river, you will come to the town of **Chuckatuck** and an intersection with State Routes 10–32. The town was the site of a Civil War skirmish and was also a point along Tarleton's route in July, 1781. Turn right on Routes 10–32 and take them into Isle of Wight County and the town of Benn's Church. Seven miles north of the intersection where 32 leaves 10 and goes off to the right stood **Macclesfield,** the home of Colonel Josiah Parker, an officer in the Virginia militia. Tarleton also raided Macclesfield in an unsuccessful attempt to capture the colonel.

Continue west on 10 into **Smithfield,** which was occupied by Benedict Arnold on January 15, 1781, on his way back from Richmond. Beyond Smithfield, Route 10 takes you through very lovely, Virginia Tidelands farm country, flat and lush with green fields and pine woods, into Surry County. It will then take you through the town of Surry and on to a crossroads hamlet called Spring Grove and then to another hamlet called **Cabin Point.** Here Baron von Steuben gathered together a company of militia to oppose Arnold's raid up the James. Here, too, General Muhlenberg headquartered while he kept an eye on Arnold after he had gone back down the river and south to Portsmouth. At the present time, there is a general store and six or seven homes, some of which look old enough to have housed Muhlenberg.

Route 10 now takes you into Prince George County and shortly after the county line into the little town of Burrowsville. Four miles north of there is a cape sticking out into the James River. On that point, the local militia had positioned a gun that became known as **Hood's Battery.** On Wednesday, January 3, 1781, the gun opened up on Arnold's ships as they lay at anchor off Jamestown, which is just downriver. Simcoe came ashore with a detail of rangers, but found the locals had left. Two days later, Arnold occupied Richmond.

We spent the better part of an afternoon trying to get out to Hood's Point. We knew the militia probably floated the gun to the river along Ward's Creek, which we found. Unfortunately, or perhaps fortunately as it turned out, the county roads that go out in that direction miss

Hood's Point completely. In fact, the name Hood's Point does not show up on contemporary county maps. We tried all the possible roads and finally had to give up. By that time it was getting dark. There wasn't a soul to be seen or a farmhouse in sight, just a flat, threatening sky and the flat land in the rapidly fading light. The few lights showing in Burrowsville brought us back into the world.

We later discovered that there is a trail leading out to Hood's Point, but that it is not wise to follow it. A Confederate fort was built on the site on the remains of an 1813 fort and a big supply of ammunition, including black powder, was stored there. Most of it was abandoned after Appomattox and forgotten, but the few hunters and fishermen who have followed the trail report that it is still there and highly dangerous. Black powder decomposes when exposed to the elements and time and becomes extremely unstable. The site of Hood's Battery is better left to time and the history buff's imagination.

The search was not entirely fruitless, however. One road we tried, County Road 611, led us north by east to Route 653 going left and then onto 602, which is just a short stick of road that leads to **Brandon** on the James. In Brandon we found a handsome house, possibly an old plantation house, at the end of a long private driveway. It stood at the site where General Phillips landed when he was sent by Clinton to assist Arnold.

According to the marker in Burrowsville, Arnold came back down the ridge on January 10 and landed some men on Hood's Point who were ambushed by George Rogers Clark, but to my knowledge Clark was occupied at the time with trying to organize an expedition to capture Detroit in the Northwest Territory.

Continue west on 10 for another 5.3 miles to markers for a Revolutionary War mill, **Bland's Mill**, along the route used by General Phillips in May, 1781. Six miles to the north, at the site of **Maycock's Plantation**, Cornwallis crossed the James River on May 24, 1781, and so did Anthony Wayne, August 30, 1781. Four miles north is **Coggin's Point**, still so named today. From there von Steuben kept his eye on Arnold's fleet as it sailed back down the James from Richmond.

Several miles farther west, Route 10 meets Route 156 coming in from the right. Turn onto 156 and take it across the James River to cover the sites on the north bank of the James as you travel east toward Williamsburg.

Route 156 will meet State Route 5 at a T-intersection. Turn right onto 5 and take it to **Charles City Courthouse** where you will find another Simcoe site at a historical marker. At that spot Simcoe, part of Arnold's raiding expedition, surprised a detachment of Virginia militia on January 8, 1781.

Take Route 155 north out of Charles City until it meets County Road 602. Take 602 as it goes off to the left. It will eventually come to a dead end in County Road 609. Turn right onto 609; follow it past an intersection with County Road 631, then around a long curve to the left, around another long curve to the right, and finally to a bridge over the Chickahominy River.

This is **Long Bridge**, a position to which Arnold sent Simcoe during his raid on Richmond. The bridge has long since been replaced, but Simcoe was stationed here as Arnold advanced on the city. Continue along 609 until it joins U.S. 60, which in 1781 was the main road between Richmond and Williamsburg. Today it is a four-lane highway with a wide divider. On it you will pass through small settlements and the fringe areas of larger towns; filling stations are in good supply. Turn right onto 60 and head east for another five or so miles until you see a sign for Providence Forge. Just before you come to a traffic light, you will be at the intersection of County Road 608 north. A marker on the right identifies this as a **Lafayette campsite** during July and August of 1781. The exact spot where he pitched his tent is not marked.

About eleven miles farther east, you will come first to markers for the Chickahominy Indians and Fort James and then immediately after the intersection of County Road 622, to a group of three markers; two concern you. One is for the **Tyree Plantation** where Layfayette had his headquarters for a week during the summer of 1781. The plantation was somewhere north of the road and is not extant. The other marker is for the **Diascund Bridge** where a supply depot, for the "Virginia navy" according to the marker, was destroyed by the British during the Arnold raid.

A little farther east, County Road 603 goes off to the right. Follow it for about two and a half miles to the modern bridge over Diascund Creek. Less than a mile farther, 603 meets County Road 610. Turn right onto 610 and follow it down to the Chickahominy River and a little fishing park run by the Norfolk Naval Shipyard. There are some picnic facilities there, and if you have a state license, you can drop a hook into the Chickahominy. A mile or two south along the river is Shipyard Creek and at its mouth, according to the county map, is Shipyard Landing. This general area from the bridge to this point on the river and the area south is probably the approximate site of the Virginia naval depot referred to on the marker.

SHADOWBOXING WITH
CORNWALLIS AND LAFAYETTE

In June, 1781, Cornwallis marched west as far as Elk Hill, then moved slowly east to the peninsula through Richmond with Lafayette following. The marquis was careful not to get too close so that Cornwallis would become aware of him. As he went along Lafayette gathered as many reinforcements as were available; eventually he was joined by von Steuben and newly trained Virginia troops and Wayne and his Pennsylvanians until he had about 4,500 men, mostly untrained militia.

Finally aware that the young Frenchman was shadowing him and getting stronger all the time, Cornwallis continued to move out onto the peninsula and came to Williamsburg. He had been having a disagreement with Sir Henry Clinton, his superior officer, who had ordered him not to leave the Carolinas for Virginia. When he did, Clinton ordered him to take up a position on the coast where he could be reinforced. He also asked Cornwallis to send a good part of his army to New York, since Washington and the French army seemed to be preparing to attack him. Cornwallis, however, maintained that he needed every man he had, and since the matter was left to his discretion, turned the request aside.

East on 60 will take you into York County and to the town of Toano. Four and a third miles beyond that are three historical markers in a little hamlet called Lightfoot, recognizable by County Road 646 which meets 60 on the left. In the immediate neighborhood when we visited were two filling stations and an S and J Home Center. Two of these markers are for Spencer's Ordinary and Green Springs, the third for the Six Mile Ordinary, the scene of a Tarleton skirmish.

A short distance east of the markers, County Road 614 (Centerville Road) goes roughly south to the right. Turn onto it and clock four miles to a small brick church, the **James River Baptist Church**, at the right on a rise of ground at an intersection with County Road 633, which goes off to the right. Stop here. About five and a half miles along 633 is the Chickahominy River.

SPENCER'S ORDINARY

. While Cornwallis was in Williamsburg, he sent Simcoe out with his rangers and some Hessians to raid a rebel supply depot on the Chickahominy River. When Lafayette heard of the raid, he dispatched Colonel Richard Butler with a mixed detachment of infantry and cavalry to hit

Simcoe as he made his way back to Williamsburg. Route 633 was the Chickahominy Road Simcoe used, probably from this point to the river, and present 614 was part of Jamestown Road, the main road between Williamsburg and Jamestown.

After an all-night march, an advance unit of Butler's men caught up with Simcoe here at Spencer's Ordinary on June 26, 1781, and engaged Simcoe's men immediately. When the main body of Americans came upon the scene, probably along the road you followed to get here, a fierce action took place. Simcoe was getting the better of his opponents when he became concerned that Lafayette's main forces might be close by, broke off the engagement, and withdrew to Williamsburg. In the meantime, Cornwallis began moving toward Simcoe with reinforcements and Butler withdrew, not anxious himself to get involved with the main enemy force.

Simcoe lost thirty-three men; Butler suffered nine dead, fourteen wounded, and fourteen missing. Simcoe gives a detailed description of this affair, crediting it with an importance it does not deserve. According to his description of the area, there were no woods to the right as you face the church, but an open field. There was an open field, however, on the opposite side of the Jamestown Road, as there is now opposite the church, and there was high ground as there is now behind the church. The Chickahominy Road climbs that hill just as it did then. The American forces were drawn up roughly across the Chickahominy Road on the high ground. Simcoe's men were along the Jamestown Road facing the Chickahominy Road.

The Hessians moved to the right up through what are now woods, but were then ploughed fields; then pivoted to their left and moved in a flanking movement back down toward the present church against the American left. Simcoe placed a three-pounder about where the church stands. There were fences along the road which Simcoe had thrown down, permitting his dragoons to ride into the open fields on the right. According to his journal, many of his men were "collecting" cattle from the nearby Lee farm, which is no longer in existence. Butler's advance unit surprised them at the farm and it was the sound of that preliminary engagement that alerted Simcoe to the enemy's approach.

Most of the fight took place along the Chickahominy Road on the high ground behind the church. As you walk up that road, you are advancing with Simcoe who led his men in a column through the woods paralleling the road to your right. Simcoe deployed across the American front and charged as the Hessians pressed home their flank attack. He claimed a victory, but so did Butler. The outcome was probably a draw.

All of these details come from Simcoe's own account and from a map he drew of the scene. The map corresponds with this site in every detail covering the roads, the high ground, the small hills in the area, and so on. The map also shows where two farms were located close to this fork in the road. Either one of them could have been the "ordinary" where travelers stopped to purchase refreshments from the farmer. According to Simcoe, the **Six Mile Ordinary** was along the Chickahominy Road up behind the church where the road curves around to the right before turning left to go down to the river. Six Mile was the scene of a fight between Captain Thomas Mathews and his militia and Tarleton in August, 1781. We explored the Chickahominy Road, but could not find the site.

Continue along 614 in the direction of Jamestown. Along the way you will stop off at a plantation site and then a field of battle that was almost the scene of an American disaster.

THE BATTLE OF GREEN SPRING

Several miles along 614, you will drive past a lumberyard on the left and a large mobile home park on the right surrounded by a hurricane fence, then through woodlands followed by open fields on the right. Look for a fence on the right side of the road partially hidden by a high hedgerow or mound of dirt and a short dirt road leading into a small squarish plot of ground. A barrier across the dirt road is flanked by a large sign which reads "Green Spring Plantation," followed by a long legend that describes the plantation and its history. Beyond are the broad fields of the plantation and its *remains.*

Originally the home of Governor Sir William Berkeley during the seventeenth century, Green Spring was a showplace. It was known for its agricultural innovations, its greenhouses and horses, and its pottery.

The main house was about 300 feet beyond where you are parked on a rise of ground. It faced in the direction you were traveling. As you explore the site, to the right of the house remains you will find what is left of an *old jail;* down at the foot of the slope of the hill on which the house sat, in low marshy ground, you will find a *springhouse* covering a spring, still flowing, from which the plantation drew its water.

By the summer of 1781, Cornwallis had decided that his situation on the Virginia peninsula was becoming difficult. Clinton had been urging him to get into a defensive position, either at Williamsburg or Yorktown. Clinton, afraid of an attack on New York by the combined American-French armies of Washington and Rochambeau, had also been ordering him to dispatch several thousand men to New York as reinforcements. Cornwallis decided to send the men and to cross the James River from the peninsula to establish a base in Old Point Comfort opposite Norfolk. As you will see, he subsequently changed his mind and dug in at Yorktown.

Early in July, 1781, Cornwallis left Williamsburg and marched to Jamestown on the James River, en route to Portsmouth following Clinton's plan. Lafayette followed with Anthony Wayne and 500 men out in front keeping contact with Cornwallis's rear guard. At Jamestown, Cornwallis attempted to draw Lafayette into a trap. Realizing how vulnerable he would be while crossing the river and knowing Lafayette would be aware of it, Cornwallis hid most of his army along Powhatan Creek near Jamestown and along a swamp which lies to the left of 614 a mile or two east of Green Spring Plantation. Wayne's men skirmished with the British rear guard all Friday afternoon, July 6, 1781, as Cornwallis tempted the Pennsylvanian and, he hoped, Lafayette deeper into the trap. Not entirely convinced his opponent was really leaving the Peninsula without one last try at a general engagement, Lafayette ordered the main body of his army to catch up with Wayne at Green Spring Plantation.

This site is under the administration of the National Park Service which has conducted some archaeological work on the foundations of the main house, the jail, and at other selected spots. When we were there, the results of the dig had been filled in awaiting further and fuller development. When you visit the site, there may be much more to see. There was humpy ground where the plantation house had been located to indicate where the archaeologists had dug; three of the jail's brick walls were standing; and there was the springhouse displaying a sign that warned against drinking the water. There are also a number of big, old, black walnut trees on the site and in November, the ground was covered with the nuts.

Continue along 614 and clock a mile to approximately the spot where Cornwallis tried to close the trap. Lafayette, who had carried out a personal reconnaissance along the river, realized what Cornwallis was up to and hastened to warn Wayne. It was too late. Wayne suddenly found himself facing not Cornwallis's rear guard, but his entire army.

Drive on toward Jamestown Plantation, looking for the marker for the battle. It is very close to the entrance to the parking area at the plantation Visitor's Center and should appear after you pass the intersection of State Route 5, but before Route 31. Near the turnoff for the present Jamestown Beach Campsite, Wayne's men saw the British army deploying before them in preparation for an attack. The marker directs your attention to the *field* in front of you, which is now private ground. Move a little farther along the road to get a better view. As you face the field, the James River is very close. Cornwallis's point of embarkation was where the present Jamestown restoration stands. If you face toward Green Spring Plantation in the direction from which you came, the river will be to your left.

Wayne did not hesitate when he realized what was happening. Aware that the British line extended in both directions beyond his flanks, he charged, taking the enemy by surprise. Though they raked his lines with grapeshot and musket fire, his men stopped the British advance cold. Lafayette appeared on the field, and as the Pennsylvanians withdrew in good order, he helped hold them together. During the action Lafayette had two horses shot from under him. The Americans lost about 130 killed and wounded, the British seventy-five. Wayne and his men moved back to the Green Spring Plantation; Cornwallis, having lost daylight and the chance to pursue the retreating rebels, resumed his crossing of the James.

The field on which the main action took place is still there and so is Powhatan Creek, now part of the Jamestown restoration area. You can see the trees beyond the field marking the swamp in which the British hid while they waited for Wayne to take the bait.

Before you go on to Williamsburg, you should visit the **Jamestown restoration,** site of the first permanent English settlement in the New World. The *museum* at the Visitor's Center is probably one of the most unusual you will visit in this country. There are demonstrations of glass blowing, a reconstruction of James Fort, an Indian encampment, three full-scale ships which can be boarded, and an automobile tour road along a wilderness trail. There are also picnic facilities, rest rooms, refreshments, and a restaurant called the Mermaid Tavern. The park is open every day except Christmas and New Year's from 9 A.M. to 5 P.M. Admission is $1.00 for adults; $0.50 for children aged twelve to seventeen; $0.25 for children seven to eleven. It's at least a half-day excursion, so allow for it.

COLONIAL WILLIAMSBURG

To get to Williamsburg from Green Spring battlefield, you can take Route 31, which is direct and fast, or the Colonial National Monument Parkway from the Jamestown restoration. The parkway is a slow road and covers more ground, making for twice as long a drive, but for a long stretch it hugs the north bank of the James River through beautiful estuary country, which we thought more than compensated for the extra time.

Colonial Williamsburg is probably the best work of historical restoration and reconstruction ever attempted in this country, and it is doubtful it will ever be matched. If you have never before visited Colonial Williamsburg, prepare to stay for at least a day. Actually it takes two or three days to see everything and to really savor the atmosphere. Within those few blocks is an eighteenth-century town revived down to the smallest detail—homes, shops, streets, inns, gardens, and so on. You can stay at the Market Square Tavern, which is a reconstruction of the original, or at the contemporary Williamsburg Lodge or Inn. Meals are served regularly at Chownings, the Kings Arms, and Christina Campbell's, and the menus consist almost entirely of eighteenth-century dishes served by costumed waiters. There is also a Visitor's Center a mile or so from the restored area which has a very good motor inn and an excellent cafeteria. The cafeteria is good and cheap and the varieties of foods and the amounts served are well worth the money. Prices at the lodge and inn are high for rooms, but restaurant prices are reasonable and the food is excellent. Reservations are necessary for any meal at the restaurants.

There are also dozens of places to stay in Williamsburg outside the restored area. Every large motel chain has built at least one and sometimes two motels in the immediate Williamsburg area; 60 and Richmond Road are veritable Motel Rows.

Be forewarned that Williamsburg is usually crowded. Schoolchildren come by the busload and tourists by the carload and tour-busload. There are few times of the year, however, when the throng thins out and you can stroll the streets free of crowds, pausing to watch the cabinetmaker or printer or shoemaker at work or the blacksmith making the sparks fly at the forge. But before you do any of that, sit through the orientation films in the auditorium at the Visitor's Center. If you can, see all the Williamsburg films. They are the best films ever made on American colonial life.

Williamsburg was a mustering place for Virginia militia from the beginning of the Revolution and the scene of stirring actions against the royal governor. Late on Thursday night, April 20, 1775, and into the wee hours of April 21, Dunmore had the powder removed from the town's *magazine* on Market Square. Patrick Henry had just made his "give me Liberty or give me death" speech, and Dunmore was understandably nervous. His nerves were not steadied by what followed—a march of armed volunteers led by Henry, who demanded that the powder be returned or the town be paid for it. The town was paid and the volunteers went home.

The **Governor's Palace,** a complete restoration, was broken into in June, 1775, by a band of Patriots who made off with 300 stands of arms. During early 1776 General Charles Lee was quartered in the palace and the grounds were used as quarters for cavalry horses. It was later a hospital for American sick and wounded. During its restoration the graves of 156 Revolutionary War soldiers who died there during the war were uncovered. The site is marked by a weeping willow and a stone. When the palace was destroyed by fire in 1781, it was still a hospital for many of the sick and wounded from the Yorktown siege.

A number of American generals established headquarters in Williamsburg, including Lafayette, Weedon, von Steuben, and Washington. Cornwallis was here from June 24 to July 4, 1781, before he went to Portsmouth. He lived in the **President's House** at College of William and Mary, which is at the end of the Duke of Gloucester Street where the college's campus begins.

Several buildings were burned during the war through the carelessness of American troops, but though none were damaged during the British occupation, the British and Hessian soldiers made free with the inhabitants' furnishings. They were only emulating their commander in a small way. When Cornwallis marched out, following his custom, he took with him every able-bodied slave he could find in the town and surrounding area. A French officer who came to Williamsburg with Rochambeau's army soon after Cornwallis left described it as "almost completely deserted."

The **George Wythe House** on the west side of the Palace Green was the scene of much coming and going before and after Yorktown. Lafayette may have stayed there until Washington and Rochambeau arrived, at which time Washington took it over. Rochambeau stayed at the **Peyton Randolph House** at the intersections of Botetourt, Colonial, and Queen streets. Washington left for the allied siege lines at Yorktown on September 28, 1781, and with him went all the rest of the French and American soldiery as the scene of action moved to the final curtain.

Now for a little back tracking. Take U.S. 60 west out of Williamsburg, beyond Toano to where State Route 168Y meets it from the right and 60 makes a sharp turn to the left. Continue straight ahead on a short spur of unnamed road past County Road 645 which goes off to the left, to an intersection with 168–30. Turn left onto 168–30 and take it into New Kent County. When it T-dead-ends in State Route 33, turn left and go east into the town of **New Kent,** through which Cornwallis's army marched on June 22 on its way to the Jamestown embarkation wharves and the Battle of Green Spring. Three days later Lafayette's troops came through trailing the British. Washington and Rochambeau and their combined forces passed through on September 14 on their way to Yorktown and victory.

Reverse your direction and go east on 33 into the town of West Point. Take a left onto State Route 30 and follow it into King William County to a point 3.4 miles north of West Point. A mile due east, Lafayette and his army made *camp* on August 13, 1781. They had just crossed the Pamunkey River. Here Lafayette waited, watching Cornwallis who had moved into Yorktown, ready to block any move he might make to leave.

Return south to West Point; turning left, head east to tie up the loose threads of Lord Dunmore's sad story.

GWYNN'S ISLAND AND CRICKET HILL

In the town of Glenns, continue east on State Route 198 into Mathews County to State Route 223. Follow 223 and the signs for Gwynn's Island to a Coast Guard station and a bridge with a drawspan to an island. You are on Chesapeake Bay at the mouth of the Rappahannock River. The island is Gwynn's Island, the last bit of Virginia soil on which Lord Dunmore set foot.

It was a lovely place to visit in 1776 when Dunmore and his 500 Loyalist supporters arrived here after his attempts to reassert his royal power had failed at Norfolk. On the island he established a fortified camp and built breastworks. His plan was to use it as a base from which to launch punitive expeditions against the mainland.

On Monday, July 8, 1776, General Andrew Lewis and a large force of Virginia militia came to this shore, about where you are now, and set up a battery of guns, including two eighteen-pounders. The next morning he opened fire on the governor's ships, which were anchored in the channel between the island and the mainland. Dunmore was wounded on his flag ship. The ships and the batteries on the island answered the fire, but Lewis's guns had their range and the ships were finally forced to slip their cables while the fire from the island died away. The rebels shelled it for the rest of the day, but the Tory guns were strangely silent. The next day, Lewis sent a storming party who discovered that a smallpox epidemic had turned the island into a charnel house. Most of the Loyalists were either dead or dying. Few had been able to stand to their guns.

Those who could had gone aboard the ships and left with the exgovernor.

There is no vestige of the earthworks on Cricket Hill that Lewis and his men must have thrown up to protect their guns. The Coast Guard station and private homes along the shore have probably covered all evidence of them. The island is now a picturesque series of small communities and private homes, some summer homes, and farms. You can drive around it in a few minutes, but there is nothing left, as far as I could determine of Dunmore's camp, not even a marker. There are camping and picnic facilities on the island, and Cricket Hill State Park on the mainland offers similar facilities within a half mile of the bridge on 223.

Return along 223 to 198, but instead of turning right to take 198 west, continue ahead along 198 south. When it meets State Route 14, turn right onto 14 and take it west to where it is joined by State Route 3. Take the combined road 3–14 to U.S. 17, then U.S. 17 south. You are on your way to the scene of Tarleton's last battle.

THE YORKTOWN CAMPAIGN

While Cornwallis and Clinton were disagreeing on strategy and where a major attack against them might come, Washington had learned that a French fleet under de Grasse was sailing from the West Indies for North America. Convinced that he should give up his plan to attack Clinton in New York, Washington launched the Yorktown campaign. While Lafayette held his forces poised north of Yorktown should Cornwallis see the trap he was in and decide to make a run for New York, the American-French army marched from Westchester County in New York to Virginia, through Williamsburg east along the peninsula and into siege lines around Yorktown.

TARLETON'S LAST FIGHT

U.S. 17 leads to the George P. Coleman Memorial Bridge at Gloucester Point. Across the York River is Yorktown. Before you become involved with the main action there, stop on the north side of the York to cover the side actions at **Gloucester Point.**

As soon as the British troops began arriving on August 1 in Yorktown from Portsmouth, they were put to work building defensive positions around the town, and by August 2 on Gloucester Point. Clinton had ordered Cornwallis to occupy Old Point Comfort, establish a naval base there, and occupy Yorktown as well if that suited his purposes. When his engineers advised him against Old Point Comfort, Cornwallis moved into Yorktown. Gloucester Point was his back door. There he could station troops to raid the surrounding countryside for food and fodder and at the same time build the naval depot Clinton wanted so badly.

By the time the combined American-French forces arrived, 1,500 Virginia militia under General George Weedon were in position facing the British force on Gloucester Point, which was commanded by Lieutenant Colonel Thomas Dundas. Weedon's men were joined by a French cavalry troop of 600 and then by 800 French marines; Tarleton joined Dundas, raising the strength of his command to 1,000.

According to a French map of the Yorktown campaign which shows the disposition of the troops and the fortifications, the British fort on Gloucester Point was a semicircular structure with its broad, open end on the southeast shore of the point. If the map is even roughly drawn to scale, the fort extended across most of the point with the rim closest to the present bridge beginning some distance to the north. U.S. 17 cuts right through the area it encompassed. The National Park Service booklet on the siege says the fortifications enclosed the village of Gloucester Point and consisted of a single line of entrenchments with four redoubts and three batteries. We explored all the roads in the immediate area, but could find nothing that suggested breastworks. You may have better luck.

Most of the French troops were in positions to the left of U.S. 17 as you face the bridge and extending several miles to the northwest. A line of American and French troops was drawn in a rough arc across the interior of the point, probably a little north of the site of Tarleton's last fight about two miles back along 17. Behind that line, toward the York River and to the right of U.S. 17, a four-sided redoubt with bastions at each corner was built.

In a way, Gloucester Point was a scaled-down version of Yorktown. The British were contained behind their works by an allied force of Frenchmen and Americans. On at least one occasion the British tried to break out; skirmishes were fought at other times; and when the British army in Yorktown marched down to surrender, a similar ceremony was held simultaneously in Gloucester Point. There is a *marker* for that site along U.S. 17 on the right side as you drive north from the Gloucester Point bridge.

Drive north from that marker, clocking a little less than two miles to a marker for the site of an exciting engagement between Tarleton's Legion and the French cavalry. On Wednesday, October 3, 1781, Dundas and most of his men were returning to the point fortifications from a search and seize operation for food when the French forces under the Marquis de Choisy began a movement toward the position. Tarleton, who was bringing up the rear, became involved in a skirmish with Lauzun's Legion that might have been his last.

According to Lauzun, Tarleton had been tarrying with a young woman who informed Lauzun that Tarleton wanted to "shake hands with the French duke." Lauzun wrote that the woman "seemed very sorry for me, judging from experience, I suppose, that Tarleton was irresistible." Shortly after, the French hussars and British dragoons clashed and Lauzun joined the fray. He and Tarleton were rushing to a personal meeting at pistol point when Tarleton's horse went down, pinning him underneath. Before Lauzun could capture him, Tarleton's dragoons intervened and rescued their commander. According to Tarleton's account, when the report of his misadventure reached his camp the rest of his men came charging out to have their revenge on the French and drove the hussars back. In Henry Lee's account, Tarleton's men took shelter behind an infantry company, and while they reformed, the infantry made the French retire. The Virginia militia then formed a line that halted the British advance and held them. Tarleton called his men back and the entire British force retired to its lines.

Shortly thereafter, the combined French-Virginia detachment closed the siege lines around the Gloucester Point fort and Tarleton's fighting days were just about over. He surrendered with the rest of his compatriots and was paroled in 1782, upon which he returned to England and was never seen again in America.

Lee wrote that the skirmish occurred along a road with fenced or hedgerowed fields on either side about four miles from Gloucester Point. Lauzun's hussars entered the action with a woods on their left and an open field on their right. A half mile along the road was a small redoubt. If the marker has been correctly located, the scene has changed drastically, for 17 at this point is flanked by pine woods on one side and small homes, drive-in restaurants, and filling stations on the other. The marker (which was not there at the time of my visit) was located only 2.1 miles from Gloucester Point, though accounts of the fight place it four miles from the Point. A curious point about the marker is that it refers to the skirmish site as "the Hook," suggesting a site closer to the river. The best I can say is that the action took place in the general area to which I have directed you.

Before you follow 17 south across the York River to Yorktown, note that on the night of Tuesday–Wednesday, October 16–17, Cornwallis tried to break out of the Yorktown siege by ferrying his men across the river to Gloucester Point. Under cover of a severe storm, he managed to get half of the army over, but winds and waves drove the rest back. Those who made it to the fort attempted to break through the French-American lines around it, but were not strong enough and had to return to the Yorktown trenches.

YORKTOWN—THE WORLD TURNED UPSIDE DOWN

U.S. 17 will take you across the York River to and a little beyond the town to Ballard Road, which goes off to the left. Take Ballard to the Colonial Parkway, watching for the signs for the Visitor's Center of **Yorktown National Park.** A left turn onto the parkway takes you to the parking field at the center where you will find a museum, slide film, rest rooms, and the beginning of the tour road. The breastworks in the immediate vicinity are Confederate breastworks built on the remains of the British works; Yorktown was besieged by Union troops as well as by Continental and French, and evidences and remains of both events are commingled at several sites.

The *museum* has some unique exhibits, including a sketch of Yorktown made by a British naval officer in 1754, one of the few sketches of a colonial town in existence; the artist neglected, however, to sketch in the wharves that lined the town's bustling riverfront. Check an exhibit case opposite which displays some copper, gunpowder-barrel hoops. Archaeologists came upon them while excavating Civil War works. At the bottom was a filled-in ditch with the hoops. They were made of copper to prevent accidental explosions, for copper will not produce sparks. What seems to have happened is that when the British surrendered, the troops at this gun position decided not to turn in their powder, but instead buried it in its barrels. The wood disintegrated over the years, but the copper hoops survived. Powder barrels were oddly made with leather tops that were closed by draw strings as a safeguard against flying sparks. Other exhibits include several excellent dioramas which will give you an idea in perspective of the distance between the allied siege lines and the British defense positions.

One of the best exhibits is on the lower floor, a reconstruction of a gun deck and captain's cabin on the British forty-four-gun frigate *Charon,* which was destroyed in the York River during the siege. Many of the items in the reconstruction, including three guns, were brought to the surface from the wreck. As you walk through, you hear the shipboard sounds of creaking rigging and gear coming from an audio tape. Other exhibit cases nearby display a wealth of artifacts brought up from the town's harbor, many from sunken British vessels. The top of the Visitor's Center building is an *observation deck* with a wonderful view of the battlefield area, including Redoubts 9 and 10, the town and the river, and headlands beyond. Signs along the rail orient you to key features, making this an excellent place to start the tour. A topographical model of the battlefield, similar to the one at Saratoga, shows all the salient points and the restorations.

The greater part of the siege lines and the battlefield area are contained within this park, though a few fringe sites are still on private lands. The park takes in some 4,500 acres and the automobile tour road is fifteen miles long. There are also shorter five- and ten-mile tours. You can obtain a map of the tours at the Visitor's Center.

The one feature about the Yorktown campaign that is so amazing to us two hundred years later is how, during an age of such poor communications and bad roads, Washington, Rochambeau, de Grasse, and Lafayette were able to coordinate their armies and ships so well and get them to where they had to be on time and in readiness.

By 1781 the rebel cause was in a sad state. The French alliance had not yet produced victory; the Continental Army was as badly off as ever, and the spirit that had inspired the Patriots during the early years had all but vanished. Washington himself, the man who had sustained the Revolution singlehandedly on the Delaware and during six years of war, wrote despairingly in his diary in May, 1781: "Instead of having everything in readiness to take the field, we have nothing; and instead of having the prospect of a glorious offensive campaign before us, we have a bewildered and gloomy defensive one . . ."

Military supplies were at an all-time low; there was little transportation available and no money to buy more; none of the states had come up with their promised quotas of men, and morale among the troops and the general public was dangerously low. On the other hand, the British were not much better off, at least not in retrospect. They had only tenuous toeholds in New York, Charleston, Savannah, and Wilmington. The South was still unconquered, and for all his maneuvers and countermarches, Cornwallis had not taken undisputed possession of Virginia. He came to Yorktown with 4,500 men, about a third of the British army, which included some of the best-trained and most experienced units. Lafayette, with almost an equal number, took up positions to the north at the campsite you visited near Providence Forge.

Clinton was in New York with 10,000 men. A French expeditionary force was in Newport with their commander, Jean Baptiste Donatien de

Vimeur, Comte de Rochambeau. They had been there since May, 1780. A French fleet under Admiral de Grasse was in the West Indies. The British were threatening an invasion of northern New York from Canada. Washington had met with Rochambeau to map a strategy which at first was aimed at relieving the British pressure against Greene in the South, but was changed when Cornwallis moved into Virginia and Lafayette was threatened.

At first Washington's plan was to move against Clinton in New York and possibly begin siege operations. The French army marched from Newport and joined his Continentals at Peekskill during the first week in July. Operations began in lower Westchester County and Clinton called for reinforcements from Cornwallis, an order he was later to rescind. Clinton was concerned at this time with fighting a defensive war. The main objective of his plan was to hold onto South Carolina at all costs. Cornwallis, however, was not the man to command holding actions. Rewarded with an independent command by Lord Germain after defeating Gates at Camden, Cornwallis took the bit between his teeth and went ahead with his invasion of North Carolina and then Virginia where he was unable to bring Lafayette to decisive battle, and so to Yorktown he went where he was reasonably assured of naval support. Lafayette informed Washington of Cornwallis's moves on the Peninsula and sat in place watching Cornwallis and awaiting developments.

In the middle of August, Washington learned that de Grasse had set sail for Chesapeake Bay with twenty-nine ships and over 3,000 troops and decided to switch his strategy. Another French fleet under Admiral de Barras was at Newport and was available to sail to meet de Grasse with siege artillery and provisions. Abandoning his New York campaign, Washington, with Rochambeau, began to move the combined armies south on August 20. By keeping his plans secret from the entire army, so that no word would get through to Clinton from deserters or prisoners, Washington feinted and maneuvered his way through Jersey, keeping Clinton guessing, now threatening to attack Staten Island, now disappearing from sight completely. On September 2, he was in Philadelphia; on September 6 at Head of Elk, and on the fourteenth in Williamsburg with Lafayette.

By that time, de Grasse had arrived at Chesapeake Bay where on September 5 the French and British fleets fought an indecisive battle; the British fleet decided to call it quits and sailed for New York, leaving de Grasse a free hand to bottle up Cornwallis in Yorktown. On the tenth, Barras joined him. By the twenty-second, units of the allied armies had begun to land along the James River from ships provided by de Grasse.

By September 27 the French and American armies were at Williamsburg in full strength: about 8,200 Americans, including Continentals and militia, and about 7,500 French. The American army was divided into three divisions commanded by Lafayette, von Steuben, and Lincoln. The artillery was under the command of General Henry Knox. The French were commanded by the Comte de Rochambeau. The American militia was commanded by General Thomas Nelson, Jr., whose home was in Yorktown. On Friday morning, September 28 the allied army began its march to Yorktown. At midday they made contact with the British pickets, and the encirclement of the town took place during the following two days.

By this time Cornwallis's army was being seriously affected by the French naval blockade. Clinton wrote to tell him that a reinforced British fleet was to set sail with reinforcements on about October 5. On September 29, Cornwallis decided to shorten his lines; withdrawing within the British inner defenses, he settled down to sweat out the week or so before his relief would arrive.

On October 6, 1781, just at dusk of a Saturday evening, the allied troops began digging the first siege line. On October 9, the first French battery went into action from a position west of Yorktown, and within hours the first American gun was fired by Washington. By the tenth, a ring of artillery was hammering at the British defenses and the town. The British suffered heavily. The Nelson House, in which Cornwallis was headquartered, was hit repeatedly until Cornwallis had to find shelter below the bluff on which the town was built. The first shot fired at the house was directed by General Nelson who had suggested that his own home was the best target because the British general probably had his headquarters there. The British ships caught in the harbor by the French blockade were the targets of red-hot shot fired by the gunners on de Grasse's ships; several were set afire.

James Thacher, an American army surgeon, recorded his impressions of the bombardment in a journal.

"The bombshells from the besiegers and the besieged are incessantly crossing each other's path in the air. They are clearly visible in the form of a black ball in the day, but in the night they appear like fiery meteors with blazing tails, most beautifully brilliant, ascending majestically from the mortar to a certain altitude and gradually descending to the spot where they are destined to execute their work of destruction. It is astonishing with what accuracy an experienced gunner will make his calculations, that a shell shall fall within a few feet of a given point and burst at the precise time, though at a great distance. When a shell falls, it whirls round, burrows and excavates the earth to a considerable extent, and bursting, makes dreadful havoc around. I have more than once witnessed fragments of the mangled bodies and limbs of the British soldiers thrown into the air by the bursting of our shells, and by one from the enemy, Captain White, of the seventh Massachusetts regiment, and one soldier were killed, and another wounded near where I was standing. About twelve or fourteen men have been killed or wounded within twenty-four hours; I attended at the hospital, amputated a man's arm and assisted in dressing a number of wounds."

By the night of October 11–12, a second siege line was begun halfway between the first and the British positions. The tour begins at the *second siege line* and **Redoubts 9 and 10,** which blocked the construction of the second line. Parallels had to be dug from the first line toward the redoubt to bring attacking troops as close as possible. If you think digging these positions was just a matter of wielding picks and shovels, remember that, as in most sieges, the work had to be carried out at night under the guns of the enemy and with the everpresent danger of an attack in force that would call for the diggers to drop their tools and seize their weapons.

The two redoubts were captured by French and American assault forces on a Sunday night, October 14. Lieutenant Colonel Alexander Hamilton led a group of 400 Americans carrying unloaded muskets tipped with bayonets against Redoubt 10, while a party of 400 French soldiers moved against Redoubt 9. Each party was preceded by a unit of "forlorn hopes" to cut through the abatis. The men left the parallels under cover of darkness and made their way to the ditches at the foot of the redoubts as quietly as possible. The Americans did not bother waiting for the abatis on 10 to be chopped through and as a result lost less men. The French held back until the logs were chopped away and suffered fifteen killed and seventy-seven wounded. Redoubt 9, however, was also the stronger of the two and was defended by 120 of the enemy, including a number of Hessians. Redoubt 10 was defended by only forty-five. Hamilton's unit lost nine killed and twenty-five wounded.

The two redoubts are quite close to each other and have been partially reconstructed with logs made of indestructible concrete sticking out at the appropriate angle. They are situated near the edge of the bluff overlooking the York River on which most of the town is built. Over the years erosion has eaten away the bluff, until by the time we were there, most of Redoubt 10 had been lost, only a corner remaining. This is a double loss, for in this redoubt Washington waited in darkness lit only by faint candles for his commissioners to bring him the completed surrender document, to which he added a line before he signed: "Done in the trenches before Yorktown in Virginia October 19, 1781."

What had happened to bring Cornwallis to this extremity? The completion of the second siege line would have meant the end for him; sickness, casualties, and the gradual destruction of his entrenchments and batteries further forced his hand. On the night of October 15–16, Cornwallis launched an attack against the second line which accomplished nothing. The next night he attempted to evacuate his troops across the York River to Gloucester Point, hoping he would be able to force a breakthrough and march to New York. The boats began to ferry the troops over, but a severe storm made the crossing impossible. On the morning of October 17, the drums beat for a parley. Cornwallis requested a twenty-four hour cease-fire to settle surrender terms. Washington gave him two hours; Cornwallis complied, and Washington found the terms satisfactory in part. On the eighteenth, representatives of both sides met to iron out their differences and to draw up Articles of Capitulation. The articles were signed the next day, and the siege was over.

As you drive from site to site, you will find parking, identifying plaques, and interpretative maps and paintings. The road will cover campsites, hospitals, storage areas, routes of march, and so on. The paintings are particularly effective. Keep in mind that the terrain and the woods, fields, and ponds are almost exactly as they were two hundred years ago.

Along the way you will come to the **Moore House**, the home of Augustine Moore, a local merchant, where the surrender terms were drawn up on Thursday, October 18. The house, a partial reconstruction, is open to the public every day from April to November. A small admission charge applies only to adults. The furnishings are period and not original to the house. Much of its original woodwork was used for firewood by Union soldiers during the second siege of Yorktown. Additions made by a tenant after the centennial of the Revolution were removed during the final reconstruction and the present structure is the house as it was in 1781.

There is a small *cemetery* on the property surrounded by a white picket fence. On the ground in it is a tombstone that was found in the basement of the house. It once marked the grave of John Turner, a York merchant who went outside to watch the bombardment and was struck and killed. As you drive on past Wormley Creek, note the explanatory plaque for Wormley Pond, which has been reconstructed through an earth dam that represents the dam for a mill once operated by Moore.

The sites of the encampments of the various units have been identified and marked, as have the headquarter tents of their commanders, including those of Lincoln, Lafayette, and Washington. There are a few private homes, many of which the park department expects to acquire.

Stop at **Surrender Field** where an overlook gives you a view of the field. To the right is a piece of the original York-Hampton Road the British army marched along to lay down their colors and arms on October 20, 1781. An audio tape enhances the scene for you. Thinking of Jan Blarenburghe's famous painting of the surrender, which was based on a sketch made by Captain Louis Berthier of Rochambeau's army, does not help at all. The artist's wide landscape may correspond to the Virginia peninsula, but the feeling is definitely Flemish and bears no resemblance to the scene before you. Most interesting is the fact that Washington and Rochambeau had their troops level their siege works and fill in the trenches before the British army marched out of theirs, expecting to move quickly behind the British lines in case they in turn were besieged by a British retaliatory force. In fact, the British fleet did finally set sail from New York to relieve Cornwallis, but did not arrive off Virginia until October 27, a full week after the surrender.

The British band played an appropriate tune called "The World Turned Upside Down." Cornwallis himself was not there. His place was taken by General Charles O'Hara who told Washington his commander was too ill to appear. O'Hara at first attempted to surrender to Rochambeau, but the French commander passed him on to Washington whom Rochambeau acknowledged as his superior officer and the general in command. Washington, who could recognize a double snub when he saw one or two, passed O'Hara, Cornwallis's second-in-command, on to his second-in-command, General Lincoln, who accepted O'Hara's sword and handed it back to him.

The British soldiery marched to the field between lines of French and American soldiers. At the surrender field they laid down their flags and arms inside a circle of Lauzun's French hussars. There wasn't a sound from the watching allied troops and civilians, but the British marched badly that day, according to eyewitness reports. British officers cried and bit their lips in vexation. Some of the men in ranks appeared to have been drinking. A number of them threw their surrendered arms onto the growing pile in an obvious fit of temper until General Lincoln, who was supervising the proceedings, intervened. Hessians cried in their ranks as the final commands were given to lay down their arms. A similar ceremony was carried out on the other side of the river at Gloucester Point.

That night British and American officers dined together at Washington's headquarters, though Cornwallis still did not put in an appearance. In Yorktown itself, many of the redcoats drank heavily and were disorderly. According to one of Wayne's men, Ensign Ebenezer Denny who was on guard duty that night and kept a journal, one British soldier killed an American sentinel with a bayonet. Two days later the defeated men marched off to prison camps in Virginia and Maryland. The senior officers remained to attend a series of camp dinners. The American units marched back to the Hudson, and the French stayed on the Peninsula until the following spring when they returned to Rhode Island.

The tour road leads on from here through a number of other campsites and then to the area in which the French army was encamped. **Washington's headquarters** site is interesting for its painting of the tent he slept in, pitched near a plantation house that no longer exists, and for the nearby spring at which he and his headquarters detachment drank. The *spring* can be reached by a footpath that leads down from the parking area to where the water trickles out of the rocks, just as it did in 1781. The tents Washington slept in are on display in the Visitor's Center museum.

The **French cemetery** is notable for a large, white cross marking the grave of fifty unidentified French soldiers killed during the siege. The **French artillery park** is marked by reconstructed earthworks and a battery of French guns. The tour road along the siege sites ends at a **British redoubt,** part of the first line that Cornwallis abandoned early in the siege. The works close at hand, where the road loops and heads back, are reconstructed. The road then leads to a parking area near the original works which you can walk into and examine.

From that point the road T-dead-ends. Though there may be no sign to direct you, turn left and come to another T-dead end at what looks like a major road, but is actually Surrender Road. Turn right and in a short distance turn left into the **Grand French Battery,** one of the best siege sites along the tour. You are on the first allied siege line. The breastworks here are both original and reconstructed and along them are French mortars on wooden mounts. Some of these guns were in use during the siege. You can get a gunner's view of the town from the top of the breastworks.

The road now leads into town and the site of the home of Secretary Thomas Nelson, the general's father. The house was destroyed during the bombardment and the former secretary of the colony of Virginia was permitted to leave and pass into the American lines, where he told Washington and his officers of the extensive damage their artillery was causing.

The British inner breastworks went right through the town. Much of the damage was caused as the British cleared away houses and trees wherever they were in the way of the works. Some of the works are still to be seen in backyards and gardens where they look like golf-course bunkers. The principal feature of the British defenses, a hornwork, actually incorporated the area now around the Visitor's Center and extended along the old York-Hampton Road which runs by it. As you drive along that road to the Visitor's Center you can see the remains of the *hornwork* just off the road on the river or north side.

The **Nelson House**, the general's house where Cornwallis had his headquarters until the American guns forced him out, the Ballard House behind it, and the Wisteria House across the street are all owned by the park service and will be open eventually to the public. The Nelson House was severely damaged during the siege. A sketch made by Benjamin Latrobe in 1796 shows it with one corner broken off and a number of holes in the roof and walls. The building was razed and then reconstructed with cannonballs embedded in the wall facing Nelson Street as mementos.

The town itself is worth half a day or more. The old part, founded in 1691, is as filled with atmosphere and colonial charm as any street in Williamsburg. The streets are lined with homes and shops, many with plaques giving the vital statistics. The gardens down the side streets are quaint and lovely, and the view from the top of the bluff is breathtaking.

Comte de Grasse Street leads you down to Water Street along the river where you will find a cave cut into the marl bluff, called **Cornwallis's Cave**, in which the general is supposed to have taken shelter. The entrance is barred, but an audio tape fills you in on its history.

Cornwallis's Cave was formed by sea action aided and abetted by human hands. It was probably used for storage of various commodities which need a cool, dry place—like potatoes—and during the war by the British for powder and munitions. It is called Cornwallis's Cave because it is known the general was forced to meet his war council in a "grotto" under the bluff beyond the reach of the French and American guns, and this grotto seems to be the only one. During the Civil War, the Confederate army in Yorktown put it to a similar use, storing ammunition for a battery of guns stationed nearby. When it was in use, its entrance was protected by a curtain wall of earth and wooden beams. The square holes in the marl near the entrance were where the ends of the beams fitted.

Actually this stretch of road along the river was the busiest part of Yorktown. This area along the York River and for some distance inland had been subjected to white settlement from 1630 on. As the town grew, the importance of the river wharf area grew with it. The better homes were situated up on the bluff, the lower part of the town along the waterfront contained warehouses, shops, taverns, and victualing sites where the ships of the royal fleet could put in for supplies. At the height of its prosperity in 1750, Yorktown had a population of about 3,000. Farm crops and tobacco were its main commodities which it exchanged for clothing, furniture, luxury items of all sorts, and slaves. By 1760, however, the farms on the peninsula had worn out the soil through overplanting and the center of tobacco growing moved south. As a result, Yorktown began to decline and to this day remains only a village.

If you continue along Water Street past Read Street (leading to your left up the hill to the town and the Visitor's Center) onto State Route 238, you will see to the right **Fusiliers Redoubt**, which covered the road to Williamsburg on the right of the British line. It was manned by the Welsh Fusiliers, hence its name, and is a reconstruction. A little farther along 238 you will come to a *trench* marking the western end of the allied siege lines. From this position the French fired on British ships in the York River and on the redoubt you just visited. The distance between these two positions is at best a few hundred feet, which means the French and British shot at each other at almost point-blank range. Another breastwork shows up on the left just at the entrance to Colonial Parkway.

You can now follow 238 back toward Williamsburg to see a house that was used as a hospital for French soldiers. Clock three miles along 238 from the Fusiliers Redoubt to the Lebanon Church on the right. A short distance beyond the church, on the left, a private driveway leads to a two-story, white, clapboard *house* with two white chimneys. The house has been in the same family for more than two hundred years. The residents showed me a copy of an old map of the area with several houses marked as hospitals. This house may have been one, since all the houses in the area were put to that use. Tradition has it that Washington and some of his troops stopped off to water their horses at a spring behind it. There is a *spring* behind the house which feeds a creek that washes down artifacts from time to time. The owners of the property have found bits of delft pottery and clay pipes that predate the Revolution and Indian relics that may predate the first settlers.

Part of 238 skirts a U.S. Naval Weapons Station in which are four miles of the old Williamsburg Road and the site of a tavern called the **Halfway House,** probably because it was halfway between Williamsburg and Yorktown. As the allied armies marched from Williamsburg they separated at the Halfway House, the French continuing on directly to Yorktown, the Americans going off to link up with the Virginia militia.

There is probably no more fitting place to wind up your tour of the Yorktown campaign and of all the Revolutionary War sites you have visited than at the **Victory Monument** in Yorktown. It stands on a rise of ground overlooking the York River a block and a half from the Nelson House as you go toward the Visitor's Center. Though authorized by Congress in 1781, it was not begun for another hundred years and was completed in 1884 during the Yorktown centennial celebration. The figure at the top represents Liberty. The original statue lost its head when it was struck by lightning in 1942 and was replaced by a new figure in 1956. Around the base on bronze tablets are the names of French and American soldiers who died at Yorktown. Part of the monument has the vital statistics of the siege carved onto it, from the number of troops of each army involved to the number of ships. The view up and down the York River and across to the north bank is magnificent.

Total allied casualties were not quite 400. The British lost 600 dead and wounded and 8,000 captured. The French lost sixty dead and 197 wounded. American losses were twenty-three killed and sixty-five wounded. Though the British still held New York City and the main port cities of the South, Yorktown was the last major battle of the war and signaled the end of the conflict. By this time, Congress had agreed on the general terms of the peace settlement; peace commissioners had been chosen; and negotiations had actually begun in 1780, but were not completed until 1783. The British declared an end to hostilities in February, 1783, and Congress did the same in April. The Peace Treaty of Paris was signed on September 3. Britain recognized United States independence; the boundaries of the new nation were defined; and arrangements were made for fishing rights, the payment of debts, the treatment of Loyalists, and the evacuation of British forces. The treaty was ratified by Congress in January, 1784.

I give you one last site, that portion of the present United States that constituted the original thirteen colonies and states. We have traveled it from the Canadian border to the northern Florida state line, along every conceivable kind of road in all types of weather and into regions both lonely and populous. Despite the ugliness of congested areas along heavily traveled roads and despite the despoilation of the natural scene here and there, we found it filled with beautiful green and blue spaces, city streets of grace and charm, and people who were kind and friendly. We listened to the story of the American Revolution told by voices speaking in a dozen different regional variations of the same language, filled our eyes with clouds and skies, caught glimpses of the American past in the midst of the present, and came away with new horizons.

BIBLIOGRAPHY

GENERAL

ADAMS, JAMES TRUSLOW, ed. *Atlas of American History.* 2d rev. ed. New York, 1943.
——— ed. *Dictionary of American History.* 5 vols. 2d ed., rev. New York, 1942.
The American Heritage Book of the Revolution. The Editors of American Heritage. New York, 1958.
American Heritage Pictorial Atlas of United States History. The Editors of American Heritage. New York, 1966.
BEARD, CHARLES A. and MARY R. *A Basic History of the United States.* New York, 1944.
BOATNER, MARK M., III. *Encyclopedia of the American Revolution.* New York, 1966.
CARRINGTON, HENRY B. *Battles of the American Revolution.* New York, 1877.
CHASTELLUX, MARQUIS DE. *Travels in North America . . .* Translated and Edited by Howard C. Rice, Jr. 2 vols. Chapel Hill, N.C., 1963.
COMMAGER, HENRY STEELE and MORRIS, RICHARD B., eds. *The Spirit of 'Seventy-Six . . .* 2 vols. Indianapolis and New York, 1958.
DUPUY, R. ERNEST and TREVOR N. *The Compact History of the Revolutionary War.* New York, 1963.
FLEXNER, JAMES T. *George Washington: The Forge of Experience (1732–1775).* Boston, 1965.
———. *George Washington in the American Revolution (1775–1783).* Boston, 1967.
FORD, COREY. *A Peculiar Service.* Boston, 1965.
FREEMAN, DOUGLAS S., et al. *George Washington: A Biography.* 7 vols. New York, 1948–57.
GREENE, EVARTS B. *The Revolutionary Generation 1763–1790.* New York, 1943.
HICKS, JOHN D. *The Federal Union.* Boston and New York, 1937.
HIGGINBOTHAM, DON. *The War of American Independence.* New York, 1971.
HUNT, GAILLARD. *Fragments of Revolutionary History.* Brooklyn, N.Y., 1892.
LANCASTER, BRUCE. *From Lexington to Liberty.* Garden City, N.Y., 1955.
LOSSING, BENSON J. *The Pictorial Field Book of the American Revolution.* 2 vols. New York, 1850–52.

MILLER, JOHN C. *Origins of the American Revolution.* Boston, 1943.

MONTROSS, LYNN. *Rag, Tag and Bobtail* . . . New York, 1952.

NATIONAL PARK SERVICE. *National Register of Historic Places.* Washington, D.C., 1969.

SARLES, FRANK B., JR. and SHEDD, CHARLES E. *Colonials and Patriots.* Vol. 6. National Survey of Historic Sites and Buildings. Washington, D.C., 1964.

SCHEER, GEORGE F. and RANKIN, HUGH F. *Rebels and Redcoats.* Cleveland and New York, 1957.

TALLMADGE, BENJAMIN. *Memoir of* . . . Boston, 1876.

TREVELYAN, GEORGE M. *History of England.* New York, 1953.

TUNIS, EDWIN. *Colonial Living.* New York, 1957.

VAN DOREN, CARL. *Secret History of the American Revolution.* New York, 1941.

WARD, CHRISTOPHER. *The War of the Revolution.* Edited by John R. Alden. 2 vols. New York, 1952.

WASHINGTON, GEORGE. *Affectionately Yours, George Washington.* Edited by Thomas J. Fleming. New York, 1967.

THE WAR IN THE SOUTH

DAVIS, BURKE. *The Campaign that Won America: the Story of Yorktown.* New York, 1970.

FELTMAN, WILLIAM. *Journal* . . . *of the First Pennsylvania Regiment 1781–82.* Philadelphia, 1853.

GILMAN, CAROLINE, ed. *Letters of Eliza Wilkinson* . . . New York, 1839.

HATCH, CHARLES E., JR. *Yorktown and the Siege of 1781.* National Park Service Publication. rev. ed. Washington, D.C., 1957.

HATCH, CHARLES E. and PITKIN, THOMAS M., eds. *Yorktown: Climax of the Revolution.* National Park Service Publication. Washington, D.C., 1941.

HUDSON, J. PAUL. *George Washington Birthplace National Monument Virginia.* National Park Service Publication. Washington, D.C., 1956.

JONES, CHARLES C., JR., ed. *The Siege of Savannah by the Fleet of Count d'Estaing.* Albany, N.Y., 1874.

LAWRENCE, ALEXANDER A. *Storm Over Savannah* . . . Athens, Ga., 1951.

LEE, HENRY. *Memoirs of the War in the Southern Department.* New York, 1869.

MC ILVAINE, PAUL. *The Dead Town of Sunbury, Georgia.* Asheville, N.C., 1971.

MACKENZIE, GEORGE C. *King's Mountain National Military Park.* National Park Service Publication. Washington, D.C., 1955.

MOULTRIE, WILLIAM. *Memoirs of the American Revolution* . . . 2 vols. New York, 1802.

PETIT, J. PERCIVAL. *Freedom's Four Square Miles.* Columbia, S.C., 1964.

REID, COURTLAND T. *Guilford Courthouse National Military Park.* National Park Service Publication. Washington, D.C., 1959.

ROBERTS, KENNETH. *The Battle of Cowpens: the Great Morale Builder.* New York, 1958.

SIMCOE, J. G. *A History of the Operations of a Partisan Corps.* London, 1844.

SYDNOR, CHARLES S. *Gentlemen Freeholders: Political Practices in Washington's Virginia.* Chapel Hill, N.C., 1952.

TARLETON, BANASTRE. *A History of the Campaigns of 1780 and 1781* . . . Dublin, 1787.

TRIDELL, CLYDE F. *Colonial Yorktown.* Riverside, Conn., 1971.

UHLENDORF, BERNARD A. *The Siege of Charleston: With an Account of the Province of South Carolina: Diaries and Letters of Hessian Officers from the Von Jungkenn Papers in the William L. Clements Library.* Arno Press Eyewitness of the American Revolution Series. New York, 1938.

WELLS, LOUISE SAVANNAH. *The American Revolution by a Daughter of an Eminent American Loyalist . . . 1778.* New York, 1906.

INDEX